All you need to survive
Three Black Skirts

Written and Illustrated by **Anna Johnson**

WORKMAN PUBLISHING · NEW YORK

for Jasmine Johnson

Library of Congress Cataloging-in-Publication Data

Johnson, Anna, 1966–
Three black skirts : all you need to survive / by Anna Johnson.
p. cm.
Includes index.
0-7611-2236-2 (hc)—ISBN 0-7611-1939-6 (pb)
1. Women—Life skills guides. 2. Women—Conduct of life. 3. Women—
Psychology. 4. Self-esteem in women. 5. Body image in women. I. Title.

HQ 1221 .J53 2000
646.7'0082—dc21   00-042626

Workman books are available at special discounts when purchased in bulk for premiums and sales
promotions as well as for fund-raising or educational use. Special editions or book excerpts can also
be created to specification. For details, contact the Special Sales Director at the address below.

Workman Publishing Company, Inc.

708 Broadway

New York, NY 10003-9555

Printed in the United States of America

First printing October 2000

10 9 8 7 6 5 4 3 2 1

Acknowledgments

Many hands brought this book together. Special thanks is due to the dominant women in my life: My Mum, Margot Farelly Johnson, for putting up with a lot of whining long distance with both humor and common sense. My agent, Sally Wofford Girand, who believed in this book from the second she clapped eyes on it and who has remained an unflappable ally ever since. My editor, Ruth Sullivan, whose patience, diligence and inspired work meant a great deal to this project and whose red pencil should be bronzed and donated to the Met. My comrade, Rosie Schaap, for assisting in the chapters Political Responsibility and Eco Girl. My hardware expert, Ralph Titus, for getting into the nuts, bolts, and dark recesses of the Handywoman chapter. My designers, Paul Hanson and Morris Taub, for keeping it groovy. My publisher, Workman, for its enthusiasm and high standards. The Hamptons support team—hot dinners: Gus and Rosemary; grocery runs and good counsel: Michael Shnayerson; red wine/savoir faire: Mario and Natasha; philosophy and lunch: Mary, Lisa, Celia, and Helen. The New York support team—strawberry ice cream and fireworks: Karlo Pastrovic; diva alert: George Epaminondas; style counsel: Alicia Richardson; poetry: Julie Patton; duende: Barney McAll; recipes and dirty jokes: Wendy Frost; spiritual backbone: Kevin Doyle.

The following people (in nonpartial order) provided inspiration, information, help, and divine spark for this book: Jessica Adams, Rona Berg, Anitra Blackford, Carlos Bolado, Robin Bowden, Mary Angela Buffo, Canio's Bookstore (Sag Harbor), Karin Catt, Elizabeth Clementson, Leonard Cohen, Julia Dickinson, Gregory Duncan Powell, Sue Fairlie Cuninghame, Julie Gibbs, Josh Gilbert, Lulu Guinness, Sophie Hamley, Thich Nhat Hanh, Margot Herrera, Kristyna Higgins, Julia Hill Butterfly, Emmylou Harris, Michael Hutak, Marion Hume, Carmen Indovino, Patrick Knowles, Zorka Kovacevich, Michael, Margot, Matthew, Helga and Remy Johnson, Laura Marmer, Stephen Leeder, Eskimo Design (Sydney), Penguin Australia, Katie Purvis, Tina Matthews, Peg McColl, Ellen Morgenstern, R. B. Morris, Anne Murray and Richard "The Quiff" Goodwin, Provisions (Sag Harbor), Meghan Rowe, Jay Sawyer, Margaret Thorsborne, Marion von Adlerstein, Sharyn Storrier Lynham, Kate Robertson, Patricia Suhardiman, Tom Waits, Di Yee, and Kenny Vaughan.

Contents

Introduction

Self-help books tell you how to live. I can't do that. I've got a diet built on raw watercress, strawberry ice cream, oolong tea, and Chinese noodle-bar soups of ambiguous stock. I don't own three black skirts, only two. I can't drive a car. By the time this book is published, I will buy an ironing board, stop using a blue straw beach bag as an attaché case, and finally cut my credit card in two. Let me be the first to admit that we teach what we need to learn. I wrote this book not because I'm spiffingly together and pregnant with worldly wisdom, but because I want to be more relaxed, organized, and socially useful. Actually, I just want to get to yoga once a week and remember to floss.

The nagging feeling of always being a little behind becomes a life state. It's often the petty details that clog the wheels of your chariot: a broken sandal strap, an old debt you can't shift, a receipt you can't find the night before filing your taxes, the belief that you look hideous in jeans, or a forgotten birthday. Gradually little glitches start to sculpt your world and, more insidiously still, your delicate sense of self.

When your life is messy it's easy to feel that the hand of destiny is shuffling you to the back of the class, doomed to the dunce's corner with the pencil suckers and the self-tattooed delinquents. And the frenzied pace of the way we live does nothing to allay our own (perceived) inadequacies. How does any woman get ahead when the stakes are so high? Beating beneath the skin of our lives is an unwritten, but very blatant, timetable. It is a timetable for study, for work, for shopping, for saving and planning and love and babies and gym and e-mails and housework and loans and eye-wrinkle creams and relatives and divorce and patching up and affairs and vitamin supplements and car registration and Christmas dinners and all the damn rest. Given what's expected of us, life starts to feel like a succession of high jumps with new aspirations slapped down in front of us before we've cleared the first.

As a result, most of us are just coping, barely scraping by with enough time to commune with ourselves let alone make a deep connection with other people. No wonder we "forget" to have kids or learn a language or join an organization we admire; we also "forget" to take pride in small victories or take proper stock of our milestones or even just to breathe. Hopefully this book can help you regain a sense of balance and give you the strength and spark to repair and replenish the parts of your life that are so often overlooked—your spirit, your self-esteem, your secret life and hidden talents, your dreams, your financial independence, your creative soul.

Given a limited time frame and very limited experience in some areas (I'm not a mother, a runner, or much of a saver), I've done my best to address some basic life skills and employed several "experts" on the subjects I wasn't fit to tackle. My role models were girlfriends with guts. Kristyna, who would rather hand-cement a driveway than watch daytime TV. Emma, who taught herself how to replace a car engine, in heels. Kate, who drove across the United States alone (without a radio!). Karen, who commutes two hours a day to teach the kids of immigrant families. Tina, who sings her sons to sleep with a ukelele. Jessica, who donated the royalties from her bestseller to a charity she loves. Margaret, who thinks nothing of organizing major environmental rallies at age seventy plus. I'm moved by women who approach life with that rare mix of independent thought, constructive action, common sense, and madness. The spirit that animates this outlook is more a matter of discipline than magic. It takes a lot of willpower to make changes to your life, to stick to a goal and be true to your ideals. Sometimes it even feels a little boring. I know, because I'm a lazy dreamer. This book was born, essentially, out

of sloth. Inertia drove me to act. An inability to stick to a relaxation program, manage money, or even keep simple promises led to incredible frustration. To escape from the valley of the flakes I found simple answers to complex life problems. I stopped saying yes when I meant no, I tried to get up earlier, I established routines, and, even if I broke them, I attempted to make every day count—be it shifting debt or shaking my rump.

Living with a flaming sense of purpose doesn't apply to everything, of course. Hair, bosses, and love remain unpredictable. Especially love. Applying a five-year plan to relationships or trying to force romance like a bulb out of hard earth is a waste of precious energy. And there's so much misinformation out there when it comes to relationships. Most of it is thinly disguised propaganda urging women to be decorative, toe the line, and marry (rich). Most of it tells us to put our passion and sacred fire into looking happier, younger, and dumber than we are to attract the love who will make us whole. Sheesh! That's precisely the reason why marriage and weddings have been omitted from this book. I hate to burst the bubble, but the aim of getting order into your life isn't to snare a husband. The aim is to be fulfilled and focused, to be enough in your own right, and to learn when to get out of your own way in order to get on with it. If this book can rouse you to sew on a loose button, paint your kitchen violet, open a savings account, call up a long-lost friend, help start a community garden, or even just clean your room—I'll be happy.

I've got a fake fur collar and velveteen shoes,
I've got the freedom to shop and the freedom to choose,
I wake up each day to the sanitized news.
Is that why they call it the mass-culture blues?

I drink Diet Coke and watch Friends at eight.
I don't waste my time on heated debate,
I wanted to vote but I got there too late.
Does that mean I'm losing my rights?

Bouncing flesh at the gym that volleys for favor,
Sun-dried tomatoes that lost all their flavor,
A dream that's recurring where I marry my neighbor,
And he spends all day washing his car.

Honestly, life ought to be better at twenty
With condoms and Lycra and a city of plenty.
Instead I feel sorrow as deep as a lake,
Brooding for hours over sheer or opaque.

On Fridays I drink and Sundays repent,
Plastic gets burnt when the cash is all spent.
I've got a cousin who lives up the coast in a tent.
She says she's a paganferalwhitewitchbitchQueen or something.

Some days in bed or lugging dry cleaning,
I wonder if life is meant to have meaning.
I read the right mags to be chic and empowered,
But my boss is oblivious and our leaders are cowards.

I guess there is strength in learning to cruise.
Why press on those thoughts that feel like a bruise?
No point in fighting a battle you'll lose,
While I'm drowning in perfume and the mass-culture blues.

Rebel Song

BALANCE

The Whole Shebang

Strict dieting without exercise, exercise without rest, worry without sleep, sex without love, love without work, duty without fantasy, a slice of cheddar cheese without a Granny Smith apple—there's just no point in striving for well-being without balance. And balance is hard to find when the information on how to become healthy is so overwhelming, life moves so fast, and natural instincts are blunted by stress.

Because we expect so much of ourselves on so many levels, getting healthy is often a fraught affair. A day spent drinking the requisite two quarts of water, exercising for forty minutes, eating okra and sesame seed stew, and chewing each mouthful thirty-five times before swallowing is enough to make us sick with tension. Why? Because trying too hard is a strenuous bore. Anything that feels like homework usually works in reverse. To make an inroad into our general bounce and immunity, we need to start with baby steps that close the gap between the ideal and reality.

Little things add up. The more exercise you get, the more your body needs it. The better the food you eat, the more hideous junk food tastes. The more quiet time you take, the less appealing TV becomes. The incidental wholesome treats that you give yourself have a way of becoming good habits. Something as simple as detoxing one night a week—banning coffee, junk food, the phone, alcohol, and compulsive worry—can be enough to bring you back to balance. Of course this remains the ideal. Making even the tiniest changes to established routines takes a lot of willpower.

For some of us it means changing the habits (and the mind-set) of a lifetime. I dream about being Katharine Hepburn in *Philadelphia Story,* the sort of character who leaps into the lemony air of early morning and then plunges into an icy-cold pool of water screaming "Yaahhh!" at the top of her hearty lungs. Fat chance. But the dream remains, and sometimes I use Saint Kate as a mentor. Kate's discipline (be it real or fictional) is an aspirational force, a coach for the days when I can't listen to my body, and a firm friend on the days when I can, but don't want to hear what it has to say.

To get an immediate handle on wellness, try spot-cleaning the areas in your life that feel sludgy. To keep your sense of balance lively, change your routine week to week. Splatter some linseed on your oatmeal along with your usual drizzle of honey, go ice skating instead of running, use everyday situations (a train strike, a broken elevator, an urgent errand) as exercise opportunities.

Forgive yourself along the way, and when you hit a glitch be honest about it. If you're eating pasta three nights a week, do not pass go; go directly to the Nutrition chapter. If your thighs feel like refrigerated tagliatelle, start shakin' 'em. If you feel slothful and shrunken and abjectly stagnant, jump up right now, stretch your spine heavenward like a beanstalk, wave your arms around like a gorilla in springtime, and breathe in and out with an almighty passion. It's easier than you think. Get well soon.

BARE BONES BASICS FOR WELL-BEING

Drink a lot of water (at least two quarts a day), eat something raw and something green at every meal (even in winter), don't fear garlic, sleep eight hours, exercise once a day, and try to worry less. Those are my absolute basics of body survival. The key to well-being is not just stopping the body from getting fat or breaking down; rather, it's to fully enjoy the body for the subtle and miraculous organism it is. Don't wait till you're sick to get well—build on your existing strength.

ATTITUDE

Melted cheese is not going to kill you; anxiety might. It's easy to believe that toxins are assaulting us on all fronts, but the worst toxins are often within. Worry is a toxin, envy is a toxin, self-loathing and fear and free-floating anxiety are all poisonous to our health. The body absorbs all our tides of emotion (both negative and positive) and stores them. Thoughts become cells. Don't let this fact worry you more; instead draw inspiration. Outlook conditions everything, so it's worth pouring every ounce of your passion into improving it. How you look at the world *is* your world. Quit kvetching and be blessed.

✿ Budget your worries. If you worry about everything with the same level of intensity, from a burnt slice of toast to a disconnected phone, you exhaust the energy you need for a real crisis. Look hard at a problem or a situation and ask coldly, "How bad is this on a scale of one to ten?" Then spend your worries wisely. Set aside a specific time, fifteen minutes or half an hour each day, as your official worry time. If an anxious thought pops up, jot it down and promise yourself you'll deal with it during your "worry hour."

✿ Enter and leave the day on a positive note. Before your legs swing over the edge of your bed and your toes hit the floor, declare, "Be happy, be free," and then face your morning. As you drift off to sleep, count three blessings and declare, "I am blessed." Do this for a week and observe any resistance that arises. Nasty little voices in your head might say, "How ridiculous!" or, "Who are you fooling?" Ignore them and persist.

✿ How well you feel depends on the spirit in which you do things, and the best way is calmly. Calmly also means slowly. Despite the fact that everyone has no time, the slower and more deliberately you do things, the better you'll do them and the more relaxed you'll feel. What's the point of working like a fiend in order to pay for one decent vacation a year when just one of those overtime hours could be spent meditating or gardening?

✿ Positive thinking is like good posture. Every time you drag yourself up and out of a circular anxious thought or hurtful mental image, sit up straight and strong, shoulders back, head held with dignity. Worry makes you stoop.

✿ Don't forget to cry. If you feel sad, give yourself permission to crack open and cry yourself a river. Demanding jobs don't leave a lot of space for expressing emotion. If you don't want the indignity of using the office rest rooms to bawl your eyes out, make a date with a friend to go see a really weepy movie. Accepting and expressing bad feelings—anguish, fear, anxiety, and unmanageable stress—help dissipate their force. Who knows, maybe that's why nature created PMS—to gather up the storm clouds of a whole month and then release them all in a wash of tears and blood.

❀   Beware of spinning your wheels on too many "head miles." Head miles involve covering uncharted ground in your mind: anticipating every step of a three-week vacation, rehearsing an argument over and over, planning a speech weeks before you have to give it. Head miles create exhaustion because you are effectively living two lives—one real and one projected. Put aside a fixed few hours to deal with planning and structuring future events, and then return to the present. The only life really worth living is in this minute.

ROADBLOCKS TO BALANCE

Few people have a life that is blossoming in all arenas. If work is empowering, your fridge will be a junkyard of empty juice bottles and take-out boxes. Love will come knocking and your bills and tax returns will accumulate in a filthy heap. The day you learn to meditate your mother calls and announces a three-week visit, starting tomorrow. Most of us have at least one area of life that is blocked or easily obscured by our established routines. I know a woman who meditates, writes poetry, sings beautifully, and does yoga; she is also three months behind on her rent. Many more women are good at the

practicalities but have a flimsy inner life.

To strike a balance, first make a list of the six main areas of your life that represent your personal needs—for example, the physical, spiritual, practical, financial, emotional, aspirational. This list should be annotated in a way that is entirely personal to you. It could be as simple as the following to-do list:

PURSE - Bank Savings
HOUSE - Get Room-mate
HEART - Visit Grandma
BODY - Start swimming
BRAIN - Collect library card
FEELINGS - Walk the beach,
Sing at the top of my
lungs, Breathe in & out!

Then construct a weekly table with life areas listed vertically and the days of the week spread across. When you fill in this table, you can see how time gets spent and whether you're getting the balance you need. For example, if you exercise only once a week and work twelve-hour days, there will be a lot of empty boxes in the emotional and spiritual departments. Reviewing your table at the end of seven days may give you the urge to find small ways to even up the score: a visit to the bookstore, a new gym subscription, or even a silly poem you recite to yourself can do the trick. Do this for a month, trying to balance yourself out in all departments. If one box goes empty for too long, you've got a block. Don't panic, just work on it.

DIET

Improving your diet has less to do with what you take away and much more to do with what you add. The best way to get good food into your fridge is to focus on nutritional rather than caloric content. Yes, whole-milk yogurt is high in calories, but it's also one of the best and most easily absorbed sources of calcium. Standing firm about nourishing your body rather than starving it or clogging it involves avoiding "diets." The notion that food is the enemy ruins diets, and diets in turn become the body's enemy: messing with metabolism, creating food neuroses, and—worse still—triggering reactive bingeing. You can cut down on sugar, fried foods, and salt without going on a diet. All it involves is learning to cook a little differently (steam and grill), shop a little carefully (*don't* walk down the cookie and candy aisles), and satisfy cravings in healthier ways. Okay, there is *no* substitute for chocolate, but there are plenty of ways to enjoy sweet, starchy, indulgent flavors without resorting to foods stuffed full of sugar, fat, and additives. Toasted walnut bread, fat-free cream cheese, and a drizzle of organic honey has an aura of sin but gives your body more benefits than a slab of tiramisu.

Often your body will tell you what you need, but you have to get in touch with it enough to hear it. Good food makes you feel good. Junk food makes you feel good but heavy. Because you're only human, you have to balance the two. Choosing foods by their nutritional content rather than their calories is also very liberating. Labels reading "sugar-free" or "fat-free" dupe consumers into thinking they are eating healthfully. If you let fresh (rather than processed) food dominate your diet, then you can enjoy the occasional luscious foray into chocolate, cookies, and crème brûlée with a lot less guilt.

DRUGS AND ALCOHOL

A friend who works at a large city magazine noticed some subtle changes in two coworkers who shared her cubicle. They were always coping and just a little too chirpy. Out of curiosity she conducted an anonymous survey among her peers about prescription drugs. She was shocked to discover that nearly 20 percent were taking a popular antidepressant, "just to get through." The Orwellian nightmare of an office full of pacified workers hasn't arrived yet, but the sort of world that makes those conditions possible (heavy stress, popular and accessible drugs) is already here.

Drugs to make us happy, drugs to make us sleep, drugs to make us virile, and drugs to counter stress are available legally, but they are still drugs—chemical substances designed to alter the state and symptoms of the body. People get worked up about the nature of the substance (be it illegal, toxic, or numbing), but few discuss the pain that inspires drug use. Tobacco, heroin, and Prozac are all substances that are used, in differing degrees, to block out pain. Because every substance we put into our bodies exacts a side effect, it makes sense to weigh our level of pain against the physical, emotional, and spiritual price that the substance makes us pay.

✿   Certain social contexts can make highly illegal drugs seem cool or chic. It's easy to have double standards for yourself when it comes to drugs—failing, for instance, to see beyond a smart dinner party to the sordid web that supports your momentary pleasure. Movies, music, celebrities, and the myth of the beautiful people can give drugs like coke and Ecstasy a false cachet. Strip away the hype and think about the chain of suffering that narcotic drugs create.

✿   Find your natural high. Exercise vigorously and your body will release endorphins, a feel-good chemical that combats pain. Fall in love and you will literally float through a hostile world suspended by a state they call limerance. Hold a baby (preferably dozing) in your arms and feel the warmth of affection spread through every fiber of your being. These natural bursts of joy are transient. Learn to savor them and life becomes inestimably richer.

Alcohol   To maintain good health, doctors recommend three alcohol-free days a week to cleanse and replenish your system, and then never more than two standard drinks a day. Yet even this quota can be too high for some women. Also, the effects of alcohol before a period are accentuated because of the altered fluid retention levels in your body. My personal moderation maxim is four glasses of wine a week—and that can mean one a day or three on a big Friday night and another at Saturday lunch. The less I drink, the more focused I become on quality over quantity. For some people there is no middle ground, but most of us have a choice. Remember, you don't have to drink anyone under the table—ever.

EXERCISE

Life begets life, energy creates energy. It is by spending oneself that one becomes rich.
—Sarah Bernhardt

The math for exercise is simple: The less you do the less you want to do, the more you move the more you want to move. Exercise lets you feel and express your whole body, evens out your moods, strengthens your bones, improves your balance, oxygenates your blood, shakes out emotional knots, and makes you feel alive in the fullest sense of the word.

To find your own joy in exercise, you need to skip the trimmings and keep it simple. Play with a jump rope in your backyard, touch your toes every morning, deliberately join an aerobics class full of seniors in sweats.

Noncompetitive sports, activities that let you go at your own pace and even dream a little, are a good way to get exercise into your life, but so are organized classes. Drag yourself to a stretch or aerobics class and it's likely you'll be so busy concentrating on each move that time will fly by. That level of involvement isn't always possible at home.

What motivates us to exercise is a very personal affair. For some women it's a fat issue, for others it's a good habit from childhood, for many it's a form of stress relief. Whatever your bent, the body needs to move. Most women begin to lose bone and muscle mass after age forty and to put on about one to one and a half pounds of fat every year. Lack of exercise lets fat sit there, but movement turns it into muscle. A regular routine of weight-bearing exercise has the power to retard and sometimes to reverse bone loss, and that is very good news. Maintaining a healthy skeleton is even more vital than the cosmetic benefits of push-ups, handstands, and lifting weights.

No matter what state you're in now, no matter how old, clumsy, fat, or introverted you are, you can get exercise into your life. There is one crucial point to remember when you are summoning the motivation to begin: No one starts perfect, but everyone who moves her body gets results.

✿ Don't panic—there is a bare minimum for movement and this is it: thirty minutes of light activity every day. That means anything that allows you to move and speak normally without running out of breath. You can get it with three ten-minute bursts of different household chores or one long, brisk walk before dinner.

✿ If you're sedentary (deskbound, housebound, magnetized to your couch), do some stretching throughout the day. Do everything you can to remember you have a body: Rotate your ankles, roll your head gently clockwise, clench your bottom, and, hey, do a few Kegel contractions while you're at it. You can strengthen your pelvic floor any old time.

✿ Check out the chair you use at work, the level of lighting, the angle of the computer screen, and the height of the keyboard. If your chair is too high or set back too far from the desk, it's impossible to keep your back from scrunching into a human wonton.

✿ Pin this fantastic quote from the buxom Belle Epoque good-time girl Lola Montez to the shelf where you keep your running shoes: "Exercise, not philosophically and with religious gravity undertaken, but with the wild romping activities of a spirited girl who runs up and down as if her veins were full of wine."

EIGHT WAYS TO GET TO SLEEP

Planning for sleep the way you'd plan for a special diet is not as fuddy-duddy as it sounds. Sometimes on a Friday night when the rest of the world is out drinking cocktails and listening to boorish anecdotes, it's a smug little treat to go to bed at nine. I call it desert-island snoozing, a bed holiday for the righteous *and* the wicked.

✿ Drink a cup of hot milk with wild honey, or an herbal infusion like St.-John's-wort, chamomile, or valerian. Valerian smells like a horse stable but it knocks you out cold.

✿ Read a fat little book—but not the kind that will keep you turning pages till dawn. Perhaps a Latin American saga or a meaty Russian classic—a novel whose characters' names are impossible to pronounce and family trees are dense and require frequent cross-referencing.

✿ Do a ten-minute deep-relaxation exercise before sleep: Lie flat on the mattress, breathing slowly and deeply in and out of your nostrils. Starting with your feet, tighten then release each muscle in the body—the legs, torso, arms, shoulders, etc. Feel your body growing heavier and heavier, sinking deeper into the mattress.

✿ Beat the "pumpkin hour." They say the hours before twelve are twice as restful as those after.

✿ Distance yourself from alarm clocks or other objects that glow in the dark and make you fret about the lateness of the hour or the responsibilities of the next day.

✿ Music can get you into dreamland. I like nasal, growly baritones. Leonard Cohen does it for me every time (*Recent Songs* features dreamy violins), and when I'm really desperate I dip into James Taylor circa 1975.

✿ Concoct a dream before sleep. Visualize the landscape, characters, and colors. Drifting deep into the imagination may open the door to real dreaming.

✿ Before going to bed, make a list of everything you need to achieve the next day as well as the other niggly pressures that are eating at you. Make the list very official looking, pin it above your desk, and doze off knowing your organized twin will sort it all out mañana.

SOUL FOOD

Everyone needs beauty—a live symphony concert that transports you, a walk through an orchard in bloom, the comforting smell of apples stewing, an hour near the sea capturing it all with oil pastels, Mary J. Blige howling straight into your heart, or a tender movie that moves your compassion. Make sure you get a daily blast of beauty and let it blossom inside you. The soul cries out for it, and the body can't flourish without it.

A Love Letter to Your Bottom

My bottom is my delinquent daughter. I lavish praise upon her cheeks when she's well behaved and when she gets out of control, I pretend she isn't mine. The amount of time women waste loathing perfectly decent arms, legs, and bellies makes me furious. The filthy looks I've given my own derriere for over twenty years makes me laugh. This notion of dividing a female body into good bits and wicked ghastly bits is an ingrained habit: Modern women are not whole, we are mapped instead into warring factions, and the site of our daily civil war is the full-length mirror. This mirror throws back a forensically detailed version of our bodies. And what we see is haunted by a host of distorted voices—*too fat, too short, lopsided,*

boobs like hazelnuts, thighs like Jell-O, unpopular, unfit, ungainly, sad, life's victim, last place in the global bikini pageant, O tragic wench of Sloth! In chorus with the mocking voices is the barrage of "good advice" passed on by a gloating media, insensitive workmates, and the cellulite police. Beauticians tell us to rub seaweed into our jiggly thighs to firm them up. And our mothers buy us control-top pantyhose for a big job interview. Gee, thanks.

No wonder our ideas about the body are so distorted. Clothing is now designed to permanently squash us into (someone else's) shape: Stretch denim flattening our behinds and foam-rubber Miracle Bras giving us homogeneously rounded Barbie breasts. And this is where the real problems of body image begin: The ideal is static but the female body is constantly changing—bloating with the moon, drooping with melancholy, blossoming with love, breasts shrinking like raisins when we diet and falling to earth the second we suckle offspring, skin getting rough in winter and gradually damaged in the summer sun. Given the ideal and the plastic surgery promoted to remedy our supposed flaws, it really is hard to love our bodies the way they are—ingrown pubic hairs, lilac-colored bruises, underarm flipflop, and all. But love them we must! The body, the mind, and the spirit are of the same dimension. Insult one and we damage all. Thought manifests.

In many respects poor body image constitutes a sort of inverse vanity. We can't stop scrutinizing ourselves

Thank You, César

Are you tall and thin and slim as a twig?
Is your arse flat as a pancake or round as a fig?
Do you greet the day with a self-loathing whimper?
Or strut ample thighs with a smug little simper?
Do you really believe that men prefer height?
Has your summer been ruined by cellulite?

Do you wish you were shorter, just by a bit?
Do you want to shift puppy fat from hipbone to tit?
Have you wasted long hours cursing your belly?
Is your idea of diet all doughnut, no jelly?
Do you want a snub nose, a straight spine, or small ears?
Is your morale a mélange of self-loathing and fears?
If you've wasted a decade cursing your bits,
Take the advice of good César Ritz.
To flatter each woman that God ever made,

He warmed her complexion with silk apricot shades.
As they sat down to dine with a coo or a creak,
Those who sat opposite were helpless to speak.
Bedazzled by beauty, deprived of all speech,
Mr. Ritz made his ladies glow like a peach.
With his pleated lamp shades be-trimmed with a tassel,
Ritz declared, "Makeup?! Who needs the hassle . . .
"Let your bottom grow soft and shift all the blame,
"Glow in my limelight and drink pink champagne!"

but in the worst possible light. It's negative narcissism on a gargantuan scale. To reclaim our bodies for ourselves, we need nothing short of a seismic mind-shift. Basically we have to say to ourselves, "Get over it," or, more accurately, "Get into it." And begin to experience ourselves in the flesh that we actually occupy. Next time you feel yourself berating your physical appearance or obsessing over a few centimeters of plump softness, think deep into the center of your body. The strength of your continuous heartbeat over one lifetime has the power to shift a continent (Ben Okri said that); the female body has the potential to both create and sustain human life as well as house the profound and infinite energy of the spirit. When you think in these terms, all the focus on being a size two or a size six surely rings hollow.

BODY-IMAGE BOOSTERS

✿ Write a love letter to your bottom or your ankles or some other maligned and dejected region of your physique.

✿ When you look in the mirror, don't home in on what you perceive to be your faults. The body is a whole, not a field of sex-object "highlights" or isolated "problem areas." Instead approach the mirror lovingly. Would you let someone else observe you as harshly as you observe and judge yourself?

✿ Next time you get a big premenstrual belly and sore, puffy breasts, stroke them with affection instead of cursing your period.

✿ Think about the great beauties of history. Raphael's Madonna, Rubens's timorous fleshy nudes, Frida Kahlo's passionate self-portraits, Titian's Venus, Cranach's pot-bellied, narrow-shouldered little Eve. What is considered beautiful today is not a timeless ideal.

✿ Cherish your body more. A sensual oil bath strewn with rose petals honors the vitality and delicacy of your body at the end of a long day. When you have less time, a brief oil massage or loofah body scrub will get the circulation and energy moving.

✿ Lying down or seated comfortably, breathe deeply and slowly in regular inhalations and exhalations through your nostrils. Consider your body internally as well as externally. How do your organs feel? Your spine? Your muscles? With each in-breath draw vital energy to every part of the body, and with each out-breath release tension from wherever you are holding it (and you'd be amazed where it's lurking).

✿ Exercise for the joy of it and don't monitor your body for overnight results (weighing yourself, looking in the mirror, and so on). Are paparazzi hiding in the bushes outside your place?

✿ Walk tall and stand up straight. Try not to hunch to conceal large breasts or stoop to shrink your height. Pride of carriage generates optimism.

✿ Encourage your lover to cherish your body in a way that celebrates you just as you are. In the same spirit, try to accept compliments for those areas of your body you still haven't reconciled with your own self-image. Beauty as well as lessons in self-acceptance *can* be in the eye of the beholder.

✿ Let your body grow up! The figure you had at seventeen was a girl's body; twenty years later it is the body of

a woman. A woman's body has weight. Not just physical weight, but an aura of solidity and sureness. You're not a twig about to bloom, you are full-blossoming. Trying to hang on to the lissome beauty of girlhood can often have sad results: Too-thin bodies over forty look scrawny, not nubile. Ditto baby fashions on fully grown babes.

✿ Fat is still a feminist issue. Until recently *fat* has been both a pejorative term and an abstract threat used to oppress women and diminish their sense of pride in a fuller figure. A few courageous (and glamorously curvy) women are turning the tables and reclaiming their fat as a positive beauty asset. In her memoir *Wake Up, I'm Fat!* actress Camryn Manheim asserts herself as a "woman of weight" fed up with the stereotypes. On her TV series *The Practice* she demanded sensual love scenes like any other beautiful actress and won an Emmy for her efforts. There are fashion magazines, Web sites, and underground zines for, as Camryn puts it, "women of all sizes of large."

✿ Visualize your body at its most blissful moment, the time in your life when you felt most vibrant and free. To get back to that beautiful, unself-conscious state, try to remember your body before you were fully grown, before it became loaded with social baggage and sexual shame. You pedal your bike so fast that all you can feel is the wind rushing through your skin and you are melting into the wind, you can climb a tree or dive into a creek without fear, you don't have to speak softly or be sugary nice,

Nobody Needs the Gym!

Christiane Northrup, M.D., puts it in *Women's Bodies, Women's Selves,* "If we carry generations of shame about the processes of our female bodies we cannot hope to pass on to our daughters a sense of love for their own bodies."

✿ Wear clothes that flatter and comfort rather than challenge your shape. Don't buy clothes you need to diet into or fashions that make your body feel vulnerable. One or two flimsy dresses are fine in summer, but a whole wardrobe of clothes that are so sheer or tight they demand a G-string is too much hard work. Don't feel stifled by the conservatism of a long skirt or a covered cleavage—dignity, modesty, and mystery have their own grace. Even if you love your body, you are not obliged to be on show twenty-four hours a day.

you don't wear makeup or look in mirrors, you talk to animals and they understand you, you sing out loud when you feel sad, you dance to songs no one else can hear, you can study a cobweb for hours, you have all the time in the world, you are as strong as a boy and laugh at anyone who says otherwise. You are the happiest woman who ever became a child.

✿ Think to the future. The way you view your body right now affects generations of women to come. As

PS: Looser doesn't have to imply frumpier or WASPier. Choose fabrics that are body friendly and of high quality: Cotton and silk knits suggest the body without strangling it, washed silk (acres of it) feels like a hundred little hands dancing on your thighs, a crisp cotton organdy shirt dress is bandbox fresh, and suede stands firm on hips that jiggle.

NUTRITION

Soul Food

Many women have a weird relationship with food. We buy magazines that feature stick-thin models on one page and delicious recipes on the next. This famine-and-feast outlook isn't helped by the culture we live in. Food is relegated to a dualistic landscape with the so-called good (anything that makes you floss) battling the mortal enemy (yummy fattening stuff). What a waste!

To eat well you need to love what you're eating, and you must dispel the idea that healthy food is flavorless mush or a virtuous chore to prepare. Nutrition experts recommend a daily minimum of one serving of protein, five servings of carbohydrates, five servings of fresh fruits and vegetables, and three servings of dairy or other high-calcium foods. This can sound like a lot of work, potentially turning you into a kitchen slave or a rabbit constantly chewing through a pile of raw produce. It needn't.

Eating healthy asks you to reexamine your own personal philosophy of food. Food carries moral weight and emotional resonance. Certain foods connect you to your family and have the power to comfort the heart. Some foods—from foie gras to quinoa—might strike you as odd or outside your class and culture; other foods, like legumes, seem dreary when they are actually what your body needs most.

The trick to eating well is finding the foods that offer the feel-good factor yet are actually good for you. You can build healthy habits from there. If Mom baked muffins and their warm, earthy aroma delighted you as a child, then whip up your own batch with oat bran, walnuts, honey, and organic eggs. If Sunday is incomplete without a roast, put a little spin on tradition by roasting a pile of seasonal veggies with olive oil, a handful of rosemary, and a sprinkling of coarse sea salt.

Improving your diet doesn't mean eating less or eating more expensively; rather it is a matter of choosing foods that have the optimum levels of nutrients, flavor, and sensual appeal. Food that is overcooked or stripped of its skin can suffer a significant loss of vitamins. Processed or refined foods lack the fiber necessary to push food through your system at a brisk, cleansing pace. Junk food or caffeine-heavy snacks like chocolate

and cola give the body a quick jolt of energy or a blast of pleasure-inducing serotonin, but these quick-hit foods gradually tax the body by leaching vitamins and affecting your ability to calm down. Now, about those habits.

NOT PASTA AGAIN!

It's easy to eat the same foods every day or even, when you're busy, to forget to eat. Pasta is a fallback, but too many hyperhectic girls default to it day after day. Whole food groups tend to go missing when you are under duress, especially those food groups that aren't readily available or require thought.

Eating better is about breaking bad habits. To put it in gym terms, you've got to cross-train across the food groups. Often the body will tell you what you need: Dandruff may indicate a lack of vitamin C, dry lips may convey a need to purify the liver, overly oily hair points to an excess of refined sugar. Picking up on these subtle cues isn't easy when you're living on mushy convenience foods like pasta and canned soup. To break your own obsessive habits, consult the Superhealing Foods chart on page 23, and figure out what you're missing.

You can't change what you eat overnight, but you can establish better habits over time. To do this you need to set up a kitchen that's a luscious playpen for you to work in—one strewn with hearty staple ingredients, clean implements, and vibrant color. Learn a little about the healing properties of food and gradually start to change your wanton ways. See it in fashion terms as accessorizing monotonous basics or in tantric terms as adding depth and spiritual energy to an already sacred act.

✿ Mama mia! Not the pasta! Spaghetti is good food, but dream up some starch alternatives that feature more fiber and different textures—brown rice, glass noodles, barley, roasted yams, or that quickie stuff we love: couscous.

✿ Get in the soup! Healthful legumes, like lentils and split peas, make delectable soups that are rich in flavor and nutritional value—and they keep practically forever. Soups are also the perfect way to empty your crisper drawer of veggies and benefit from all their nutrients—you keep the skin and you don't lose the water they were cooked in. For flavorful soups, make up big batches of vegetable, chicken, or fish stock and freeze them. They'll be ready when you are for a stew, a risotto, or a light Asian broth.

✿ Salad is anything you choose to toss in a bowl. Salade Niçoise (boiled egg, canned or fresh tuna, black olives, grilled onion, fresh greens, and baby potatoes) is a good protein and calcium hit. Chopped red cabbage, red bell pepper, corn, and cilantro tossed in tamari and lemon tastes amazing in a baked potato.

✿ Break up the blandscape. Stock your pantry with aromatic, enticing, versatile goodies like five-spice powder, curry pastes, dried chilies, herb, nut, and lemon oils, balsamic vinegar, tamari, and Asian marinade sauces.

✿ Play with your food! Experiment. Start timidly by adding a new and untried herb or ingredient to an established recipe. Use pasta or rice as a base for unusual combinations of beans, herbs, meats, and vegetables. See what you can do with a bunch of spinach, an orange, a fennel bulb, a serrano chile, and a cup of couscous. Food is raw material for art; you hold the vision for abstract creation.

P.S. Use caution with the peanut butter and honey.

❀ Look at your cooking methods and your cooking implements. If you're eating organic, a wire brush is all you need to clean a carrot. If you want the most vitamins from your veggies, you need to steam them or at the very least parboil. Stir-frying is okay if you don't let everything gel into a watery mess; the faster you cook things, the more goodies you retain. This goes for tomato-based sauces as well! To keep a tomato sauce fresh but not sour, cook for less time than usual (eight minutes) and add a grated carrot to sweeten the natural tang.

❀ Bake a batch of muffins using oat bran or buckwheat pancake mix and play around with your ingredients—try chopped walnuts, applesauce, chunks of pear, stewed dried apricots, and nutmeg. These low-fat, high-fiber snacks make great breakfast food and help out during the daily 4 P.M. sugar craving.

❀ Legumes and lentils, butter beans, and green peas get a dud rap. Because they need soaking and then stewing they are easily labeled "weird hippie food." But just adding a bean salad or mixed bean soup to your weekly menu is a great way to add low-calorie energy, protein, and iron. If you're a dairy-free vegetarian, they'll help balance out your nutritional needs. If you're a meat-and-potatoes kind of girl, beans could cut down on the fat factor and help out with fiber, too. In brief, beans rock.

OLD FOR NEW: A WORKSHOP TO BUILD BETTER FOOD HABITS

Eating well is a matter of planning, beginning with having healthy food on hand so you don't fall back into a junk-food morass. At home it's comforting to know that your fridge is your friend, with low-fat treats that won't weigh you down and a freezer full of healthy dinner ideas like lima bean soup or organic chicken. Out in the world the lure of snack foods demands a stronger will and a bit of creative intelligence. Okay, okay, I am the first to admit that there is *no* miracle counterfeit for the taste of chocolate, but for every other junk-food craving there is an alternative choice or healthier cooking method! Wean yourself from your wicked ways slowly by exchanging old habits for new. The following are nutritious, way scrumptious, and not at all dreary substitutes.

OLD HABIT / NEW HABIT

OLD HABIT	NEW HABIT
ALCOHOL	Substitute one glass of really good wine for three cheap drinks. Have a nonalcoholic aperitif instead of hard liquor.
SUGARY BREAKFAST CERALS	Fruit with yogurt. Muesli. Oats. Organic puffed wheat or rice.
CHOCOLATE OR SUGAR CRAVINGS	Mixed fruit. Dried figs, ricotta, and raw honey on walnut toast. Homemade oat muffins. Rhubarb crumble with soy milk. Banana with honey.
COFFEE	Almond, chicory, or roasted dandelion tea. Bancha, ginseng, or soy chai tea.
GREASY FRIED BREAKFAST	Poached eggs with steamed spinach. Grilled tomatoes on whole-grain bread. Miso soup with noodles. Scrambled egg whites on a bagel.
FAST FOOD OR FROZEN DINNERS	Fast food doesn't have to mean junk— add fresh elements like herbs to canned soup or eggs or vegetables to noodles or rice. Drizzle olive oil over a stack of vegetables and roast them. Make diverse salads and keep ingredients like cooked brown rice and organic tofu in the fridge for a quick stir-fry.
FRENCH FRIES	Sweet-potato chips (cut thin and placed on the grill with lightest smear of olive oil). Baked vegetables. Grilled zucchini.

OLD HABIT / NEW HABIT

OLD HABIT	NEW HABIT
HIGH-FAT SNACKS (chips, cookies, pastries)	Fresh fruit. Bean salad. Organic, baked blue corn chips. Carrot sticks.
MARGARINE AND PROCESSED OILS	Cold-pressed olive oil. Vegetable oils. Safflower oil. Flaxseed oil. Blended butter.
MAYONNAISE	Soy mayonnaise. Yogurt and herb dressings. Tahini. Hummus. Ricotta.
MEAT	Fish. Eggs. Tofu. Tempeh. Dark green leafy vegetables. Legumes and grains. Field mushroom goulash.
PASTA	Salade Niçoise. Soup. Risotto. Stir-fried vegetables.
PROCESSED CHEESE	Brie. Goat cheese. Soy cheese.
SOFT DRINKS	Mineral water with fruit juice or dash of lime. Carbonated fruit juice.
WHITE BREAD	Whole-grain bread. Seeded bread. Rye bread. Rice cakes. Organic stone-ground corn bread.
WHITE RICE	Brown, long-grain aromatic, jasmine, or wild rice.
WHITE SUGAR	Rice syrup. Fructose. Honey.

THE VITAMIN MYTH

Don't be fooled into thinking that swallowing a stack of supplements will give you the vitamins you need. Instead, try to get them from the food you eat. Calcium, for example, is best absorbed by the body when it's obtained from food; too much (in the form of a supplement) can interfere with the body's ability to absorb iron and zinc. Women under fifty need a thousand milligrams of calcium a day, and twelve to fifteen hundred milligrams when they're breast feeding. So it's handy to know how much certain foods contain when you're planning meals. There are, for example, one thousand milligrams of calcium in two servings of plain yogurt, three glasses of milk, or one serving of salmon with two servings of winter greens.

Certain food combinations help boost vitamin absorption. For example, if you want to get the most iron out of a watercress salad, garnish with red peppers and drench it in lemon juice; iron loves vitamin C! Calcium absorption can be helped along by the presence of vitamin D (found in oily fish), and may also be triggered by sunlight. If you want zinc and iron from your greens, try eating them with some meat. It's easy to build good vitamin habits. A big spoonful of linseed on your muesli or celery juice in the morning might help you with PMS. Linseed is said to benefit hormonal balance, and celery acts as a mild diuretic for water retention. Amazing, groovy, true.

Vitamins and minerals have varying uses: Iron and folic acid help counter anemia, while potassium regulates the body's fluid levels and helps with high blood pressure. The importance of getting the right vitamins is well documented, and a diet rich in fresh fruits and vegetables can give your looks, immune system, organs, and energy levels a huge boost. Try to eat fruit with the skin on (buy organic if you're concerned about pesticides), and try to cook whole foods as little as possible.

The benefits of vitamins, minerals, and other goodies form an endless list. To make it simple, the table of Superhealing Foods (opposite page), designed to be read at a glance, includes just a few of the vitamins and healing properties found in various foods.

Superhealing Foods

FOOD	HEALING PROPERTIES
APPLE	Rich in potassium, high in fiber, beneficial for reducing cholesterol levels.
APRICOT	Rich in potassium, soluble fiber, beta-carotene, and iron.
ASPARAGUS	Aids digestion, helps with water retention.
BANANA	Rich in potassium, an instant energy booster and mood lifter with vitamin B_6.
BLACKCURRANT	Rich in vitamin C, potassium, and anti-oxidants; a traditional cure for inflammations like rheumatism, eczema, and psoriasis.
BROCCOLI	Superrich in beta-carotene, a good source of folic acid, iron, calcium, zinc, vitamins C and E, and is an anticancer vegetable.
CABBAGE	Superrich in beta-carotene and potassium, and a good source of calcium, B-group vitamins, folic acid, anti-oxidants, and vitamin C; helps reduce the risk of cancer, cataracts, ulcers, and spina bifida.
CELERY	A good source of potassium, rich in sodium, and a calming diuretic that may also be a cellulite buster!
CHERRY	Rich in potassium and vitamin C.
CITRUS FRUIT	Rich in potassium, folic acid, and vitamin C.
CRUCIFEROUS VEGETABLES	Rich in folic acid, potassium, iron, vitamin C, and anti-oxidants (kale, brussels sprouts, cauliflower).
DAIRY PRODUCTS	A great source of calcium.
FENNEL	Rich in potassium, good for digestion, may also regulate estrogen levels.
GARLIC	Nature's antibiotic: good for promoting a healthy heart, fighting colds and flu, and aiding circulation.

FOOD	HEALING PROPERTIES
HONEY	Healing, soothing to the stomach and intestines, and an antibiotic.
LEGUMES AND GRAINS	Rich in potassium, soluble fiber, iron, and folic acid; great to stabilize blood sugar levels, counter anemia, and helps reduce the risk of heart disease.
MEAT	Rich in iron and zinc; boosts the immune system and aids in healing.
OILY FISH	Rich in vitamin D, calcium, iodine, and essential fatty acids; an anticancer food with benefits for the heart, skin, bones, blood pressure, and arthritis.
PUMPKIN	Rich in potassium and vitamins C and E.
PARSLEY	Rich in vitamin C, potassium, carotenes, calcium, folic acid, and anti-oxidants.
RED BELL PEPPER	Has more vitamin C than an orange; rich in anti-oxidants, vitamin E, and carotenes.
SEAWEED	A source of vitamin B_{12}, calcium, magnesium, iodine, iron, and sodium, and may be beneficial for breast cancer prevention.
SOYBEAN	A source of iron, calcium, protein, and soluble and insoluble fiber.
TOMATO	Rich in anti-oxidants, potassium, vitamin E, beta-carotene, and vitamin C.
WALNUT	Rich in alpha-linolenic acid and linoleic acid, which help reduce cholesterol.
WATERCRESS	Rich in iron, vitamins C and E, calcium, and potassium.
WHOLE GRAINS	A good source of selenium, B-group vitamins, potassium, fiber, iron, zinc, and niacin.
YOGURT	Beneficial to gut flora balance, provides immunity against harmful bacteria, a great source of calcium.

SEX ENERGY

Diary of a Super·Sensualist

ex energy isn't just about sex. It may express itself through manic outbursts of creative energy, or through erotic daydreams about fire trucks. It may be triggered by the way your skin feels after an afternoon in the sun; it may be the inspiration of a slip riding up to expose a bare thigh. Sometimes you feel lust for someone you know and sometimes you just feel lust in the abstract. But that power surge that you find riding high just before your period or at other, stranger moments is part of something greater. The same cosmic push that makes flowers open and rivers flow is coursing through your body. Quite simply it is chi or life force. It's all very wholesome and natural and potentially pleasurable, but there are times when that rush of hot energy feels damn inconvenient.

Female sexual energy is also hugely fraught with moral baggage and social taboo. It is deemed conventional for men to go out prowling as King Libido on a Friday night. But when a woman is just as frank about her urge? Well, she winds up on Sex and the City, a sticky mess of heavy eyeliner and heavier one-liners. On the other hand, many of us don't choose to gratify our needs by having casual sex. Some of us crazy old-fashioned fools want to hold out for a meaningful, intimate relationship; some just don't find the zip-free frolic that fulfilling. In the meantime there's still IT—the state the Supremes called "that burning, yearning feeling." What does a woman do with her red-hot life force? I say use IT, express IT, channel IT, and let IT all out. Unleash the beast.

JE SUIS UNE SEX GODDESS

Channeling your sex energy and learning how to tickle your own fancy is not something you can study in continuing ed, but there are courses out there. Once, on the flimsy pretext of journalistic curiosity, I went to a weekend sex workshop called Sluts and Goddesses. The coven, shrouded in nylon lace and ylang ylang incense, was like a camp for wood nymph trainees. On the first day we were commanded to dress up as strumpets in order to find our Inner Slut. Schoolteachers, civil servants, and married moms dutifully rummaged through a dress-up box of stiletto heels, fishnet stockings, whips, and vinyl corsets. Then, before you could say "Kundalini rising," our tantric leader, who chainsmoked between sessions and had a bindi between her eyes, demonstrated a self-stimulated orgasm rather briskly after lunch.

Next day bright and early we donned silk togas and grooved to wild percussive bongo music to find our Inner Goddess. Last but not least we were given vast ostrich plume ticklers and rather cumbersome electronic sex toys to help us locate our Inner Bliss. Yes, it was inner this and inner that as we studiously emoted and begrudgingly confessed utter ignorance of Kegel contractions (that rhythmic scrunching of the most inner part of the Inner Goddess). Some quit after the first round but not me. I still hadn't mastered the Kegel. Besides, the third day of the workshop was G-day, the day when all we had studied and practiced— pagan dance, deep breathing, stripping, strutting, and visualizing wet flowers—was to contribute to an A-student orgasm. The group splintered into quivering

little satellites of private pleasure and the room was a concentrated hush punctuated by the odd low moan.

I lay there in my silky toga and gazed out onto the rolling green turf of the golf course outside the sensuality temple. On the other side of the one-way window I could see middle-aged men putting golf balls noiselessly across a rolling slope of turf. I couldn't reconcile the codgers without and the pagans within. I blushed and rolled around and enjoyed the incense and then I packed up my toys and went home. No big bang.

For cynics the story would end there. NEO-PAGAN TART TENSES UP would run the tabloid banner. Ah, but there's more to this tale. When I got home to my parents' house, I laughed, said I had to go do some homework, and padded up to my attic bedroom. Thinking about the joyful release of all those women (young, old, fat, skinny, freckly, shy, and outrageous) made me smile. Running my gaudy purple plume up the delicate skin on the inside of my arm, I thought, "What the heck?" I acted upon my desire and it felt beautiful.

Feeling sexy alone takes inspiration, sometimes quite a lot. It also takes confindence—the license to say, "I'm sexual without anyone around! I can make my body sing!" For some that just might take a New Age mélange of theme dressing and pseudoprimitivist female bonding; for others it might be as simple as locking the door. Whatever it takes, it's a thrilling discovery. Ladies, start your engines.

SEXY SOLITUDE

Self-seduction *does* sound a bit mad, doesn't it? An afternoon spent bathing, oiling your body, dressing up, eating lush fruits, and retiring to bed with music purring through the fragrant air—all without a single witness—may sound eccentric and self-indulgent. *You are not crazy.* You are, hopefully, charming the pants off yourself, and I want you to keep going. Once you start to feel beautiful and relaxed and a bit spoiled, take the time to explore your body. You may want to run a lazy tongue up the length of the soft skin inside your arms. You may enjoy stroking your own hair or massaging your feet until your whole body is relaxed.

As you grow more aroused you may start to touch your body in an erotic way. At this point it's easy to lose heart and wish you were actually making love with someone else. That's natural, but, in a manner of speaking, press on. Don't pause long enough to get self-conscious. Masturbating with your hands or with an aid like a vibrator or slippery body oil invites you to take your own time and find out what really makes your genitals sing. If you still feel shy, use visualizations to strengthen your union with pleasure. The image of a huge dew-drenched lotus slowly filling with honey or George Clooney clinging to a life raft in soaking-wet boxer shorts may be all you need.

Abandon yourself to the warm blood flowing through your body, to the exquisite scent of your own skin, to the wildness inside you that is being honored and released. Get right into it and keep going. You may not climax at all, or you may explode spectacularly. It doesn't matter. Afterward, relax and spend more gentle time alone. Give yourself time for a second wind. Perhaps a steamy shower and a beautiful brisk walk may follow your little self-love fest.

If it was hard to get in touch with your body and even harder to reach orgasm, don't roll out of bed scowling and light a cigarette like an angry lover. Instead see your ritual as a prelude to other afternoons and evenings. Practice makes purr-fect.

Some of you may be smirking at this point, annoyed and mildly incredulous. You may well ask, "Why not just wait for a partner to turn up and then unleash it all together?" That's a fair argument, but a narrow one. What a woman gains from exploring her own desire is the ability to please herself, a broader erotic imagination, and a keener knowledge of how sex works for her. Next time you take a lover you can confidently lead your *amour* to the secrets of your greatest pleasure and be proud knowing you found the key yourself. Self-seduction is also safe sex and sex without needing the approval and affirmation of another. It's liberating, it's fun, and it may ease the tension of a particularly bad bout of PMS or general rage. It's also free.

EVERYDAY APHRODISIACS

❀ Write a story. When you compose an erotic story you unlock secrets and memories and unleash a raw sort of license. You can be corny, filthy, retrograde, tender, or brutally dominant. You'd probably die if someone else read it, but that's not the point.

❀ Rent a movie. Despite promises of a new wave of arty feminista porn, there isn't a lot of erotica for women that doesn't involve fuzzy lens work and sensitive-looking men with ponytails. European flicks are a cut above, with better soundtracks and fewer false eyelashes. Maybe big dumb singing cowboys turn you on, or perhaps it's the sight of Robert Mitchum looking sleepy in a baggy gray suit. Draw the shades, chill the wine, who cares if the sun hasn't set?

❀ About appliances . . . only very old washing machines with a really aggressive spin cycle can fulfill the cliché of the horny housewife. There are more sophisticated toys available. Men *hate* them; they sulk and make accusations of battery-operated infidelity. Go ahead and keep your secrets.

✿   Expand your library. You don't have to schlep massive airport novels on your daily office commute to enjoy a racy read.

✿   Make time for the pleasurable kinks of life: dancing naked in a pair of marabou slippers, eating a ripe dribbly mango like a supersensualist, shopping for lingerie, swimming naked in a freshwater stream, wearing only a velvet choker to bed, combing your hair very slowly, marinating in body creams, perfumes, and potions like the Queen of Sheba. Okay, so the kids will be home from school in fifteen minutes. Tell them it's ice cream for dinner tonight for everybody!

PS: Go ahead and be selfish about your pleasures. So often sexiness gets confused with being a sex object. We are sexy for the delectation of others but rarely for ourselves. A lot of women don't give much thought to their sexual desires unless they are sexually active with someone else. We live dormant until touched. A new love affair has us out buying a lace thong. An office crush makes us primp in the rest room. We may masturbate in front of a lover but hardly ever rouse the nerve (or find the time) to do it alone. This is a damn waste, and a reality that makes single women in particular feel trapped. "How," you ask, "can I express my sexuality alone?" Feeling awkward, shy, or just plain dowdy, you don't put aside an afternoon to make out with yourself. But of course you can.

Style

CHIC

Untouchable Style

Some think that chic is a form of deprivation—a sort of anorexia of accessories that strips you back to a bare, buffed, and gleaming face set on a frame of sleekly invisible dark-toned coordinates. Others profess that chic is classics—clothing so resolutely conservative and time tested that anyone can scrub up like the Hepburns, Katharine or Audrey. But the principle of chic is more elastic than that. Looking stylish is not a matter of discipline but of adaptation. There are rules but they don't work for everyone, and chic done badly is worse than no chic at all.

Take the twinset, take the little black dress, take pearls, and take beige. Fashion editors since the 1920s have crowed about the big four foundation stones of fashion. This advice is not to be taken literally. Twinsets look best on fine-boned or tall figures. The little black dress is a godsend, but only if you are at a party where everyone else is wearing insipid pastels. Pearls need to be tiny or huge but not in between, and pearl clip earrings edged in gold belong in a display case clearly marked "1980s."

CHANEL
BUNUEL
OH WELL..

Beige works on horsey, honey-colored girls but makes mousy girls look like milky tea and turns pale brunettes consumptive.

Chic may have a code, but personal style takes that code and bends it to circumstance. A woman in a black cocktail dress at a West Texas rodeo is chic, and that same woman at a cocktail party in Madrid wearing the same black cocktail dress and a real cowboy hat is also chic. Diana Vreeland pushed the outer limits of chic with her vermilion scar of a mouth, her custom-made Roman sandals, and her massive dome of lacquered black hair—but that is not a look that can be imitated. Audrey Hepburn, Grace Kelly, and Jackie O. are the holy trinity of chic. They had the bones, they had the grace, they had the money, but most of all they had the restraint to resist some of the worst looks their decades had to offer. They were never seen to make fashion mistakes, and the massive style upheavals of the 1960s never polluted their wardrobes. No safari suits, no white patent-leather go-go boots, no Verushka face paint for them.

Chic vs. Reality

Chic is about leaving well enough alone, but to do that you have to know your body, your face, and your true identity. Posture and pride of carriage make whatever you're wearing look arresting. Josephine Baker looked fully dressed in a skirt made out of bananas and carried her panther's leash the way some girls carry a shopping bag. Chic involves nonchalance but it also demands a certain austerity. The most chic women in history have been known to be fanatical: The music hall queen of the 1920s and 1930s, Gertrude Lawrence, disposed of her wardrobe every six weeks when her perfect pleats and Patou cardigans lost their "bloom." Vreeland had the base of her shoes polished after every wear. Wallis Warfield Simpson's severe Molyneux suits were neat as a pin. No lint. No bra straps. Absolutely no ruffles. When you think about the stars of the best-dressed list it's hard to imagine them naked, or crying, or frowsy in a bad sweater, and that ultimately is the effect of chic. It confers authority.

Chic is not a way to dress every day. Summoning the

sartorial restraint not to wear gold hoop earrings *and* red lipstick day after day would be such a drag! Instead I see chic as a social tool, the sort of unimpeachable elegance you need to face confronting situations: job interviews, weddings, lunch with your ex, a bank loan interview. Every woman should have that well-proportioned little gray suit and buffed pair of pumps ready and waiting in the wardrobe as instant social ammunition. In the other 98 percent of your life there is room for whimsical style, bizarre experiments, and antichic.

Nor is chic for everyone. Some women are night blooms, too exotic for the prissy dictates of a crisp white blouse and a Cartier tank watch. Thank God Ava Gardner and Brigitte Bardot were not chic.

MAXIMS OF CHIC

The trick of chic is to learn the rules and then forget them. Instead of rushing into a room yelling, "Can you believe I found this at Armani at 75 percent off!" maintain your élan and slink in. Even if you're mad about clothes, it doesn't do to make them the central subject of your conversation. *Très vapid.* Can you imagine Lauren Bacall lifting her chin slowly and then spluttering, "Does my ass look too fat in these slacks?" Buy it, wear it, and forget it.

✿ Chic is always half a size bigger than your usual body size. Skimming over your lines, nothing clings— but nothing sags, either.

✿ Chic is clothing that looks sculptural and decisive rather than sloppy or flighty.

✿ Chic never reveals underwear.

✿ Chic limits textures and distractions within a single outfit.

✿ Chic is about details: cigarette pants that make your legs look fluid, a shirt cuff that is crisp but not starchy, anything that adds height, flatters your skin, and suggests rather than advertises your body.

✿ You don't have to be a WASP to be chic, you just have to iron like one.

✿ Chic doesn't have to be expensive: Cheap fabrics look more chic ironed, a cheap cardigan is chic once the plastic buttons are replaced with tiny gold hearts, or mother-of-pearl or enamel ones. A good merino cardigan with the right fall looks more chic than a paper-thin cashmere sweater. Look matters more than label.

✿ Speaking of labels . . . conspicuous display of designer logos is not chic. More than one initial on your body stamps you a fashion victim, and even more subtle designer items need to be rationed. If you are going to flash a La Perla bra under a chiffon YSL blouse and then top it off with a Fendi baguette bag, a Jade Jagger necklace, a vintage Ossie Clark dress, *and* a pair of Anna Molinari boots, you aren't being chic, just greedy. Too many luxurious master strokes in one outfit is less sophisticated lady and more Russian mobster's wife.

UNSPEAKABLE	CHIC-ABLE
G-STRING VISIBLE UNDER WHITE PANTS	Sleek French panties under silk dress
LONG BALL-GOWN SKIRT WORN WITH SHINY BLACK PUMPS	Wafty jaballa with wafer-thin Indian sandals
HANES T-SHIRT AND LEVI'S 501s	Hanes T-shirt and butter-soft leather A-line skirt
SUN DAMAGE	Sunscreen, sun hat, driving gloves
DARK WOOL BLAZER WITH WHITE BLOUSE	Suede blazer with silk knit T-shirt
TRY-HARD CLEAVAGE	Collarbones
KILLER HEELS, SHEER STOCKINGS	1940s wedges, bare summer legs
WHITE AND GOLD	White and silver
WOOL BLAZER, WOOL PULLOVER, WOOL SKIRT	Wool blazer, dress with tiny floral print
CUTOFFS À LA DAISY DUKE	Pareo
WHITE TIGHTS	Sheer, smoke-colored stockings

❀   Chic is having your own scent and sticking to it, whether it is Neroli oil bought in the medina at Fez or a dab of vanilla.

❀   Chic women make one item stand out instead of six.

❀   Chic is classic but it is not conformist. Anyone can buy a ball-gown-length ballerina skirt and a cashmere cardigan; to make it chic there needs to be an element of surprise: amazing satin boots, jade hair ornaments, two delectable deco brooches instead of buttons. Be it the best eyebrows in the room or a bespoke perfume from Florence, chic is in the details.

THE BONES OF CHIC: PROPORTION

It's far easier to tell what is going wrong with an outfit than it is to distill the subtle alchemy of a look that seems effortless. Often the secret is in proportion. The Chanel suit is something of a cliché now but its original inception strove to refine the principles of good proportion. This is the reason that Mme. Chanel labored over her armholes with a mouthful of pins and a calculating pair of scissors until her house models were bleeding. Her rationale? The snugger the sleeve, the slimmer a jacket looks. The flatter a collar sits on a suit, the more your neck looks like an elegant stem instead of a drooping pansy. If a dress is too long or a blouse bunches around your waist like a fistful of lettuce, the proportion is off. When instinct fails, a full-length mirror can really help. Proportion is a study in contrasts—heavy textures balanced with light, a small-print dress with a boldly colored jacket, a long narrow heel with a floaty hemline, a fine stripe against a solid block of color.

HEELS

Different heel heights and shapes rule your line and your legs. Short girls needn't overcompensate with high heels; medium-height, slender heels for evening and low heels for day are more chic. Tall girls look great in flats but needn't fear spike heels if they walk with shoulders pinned back. Experimental heel shapes that look like they are about to hatch larvae or splay at a quirky angle are fine for a season but look cartoonish with very short skirts. Weird shoes and bare legs are antichic, period. Chunky heels look best with pants; wedges show off slim calves; spiky heels need light fabrics or a tailored pencil skirt; ballet slippers love mini skirts and Capri pants; square toes demand crisp suits; Roman sandals and leather thongs suit loose looks (caftans, culottes, summer linens); loafers were born for cigarette pants; low-cut pumps flatter thick ankles; stiletto mules add wit to a summer suit and glamour to a humdrum trek to the supermarket.

HEMLINES

Perennially, the most chic hemline lands just on the knee, wavering in that zone between obvious and frumpy. To make this look work, look at your shoes; look at fabric weight, print, and texture; and look at your knees. If you have really great knees, it makes sense to break the rule and bare them. Chic in the 1960s was all about a higher hemline, but the legs were spry: Jean Shrimpton flashing her coltish legs at the Flemington racetrack in 1965. Chic legs can be bare but they can't look naked; 1960s legs were always brown and twiglike or encased in wicked hosiery.

Don't, however, commit the crime of Paris chic—namely, to wear mini skirts just because you have great legs. There is a saying in France that describes just this sort of woman: Schoolgirl from behind, museum piece from the front. Sacre bleu!

Hem length controls your shape and can transform you from a tulip to a pear in a matter of inches. If your lines are long, then your skirt can be short. It's vertical logic. A pencil skirt worn tight can look sexy (not office party) if worn just a little longer. A-line skirts

HEAVY PETAL

SUBURBAN WEDDING

GLAMOUR AGONY

THE JOB IS YOURS

COMPACTED DISC

that come all the way to the knee need to fit your hips like a glove and then flare gently over your derriere. The longer the skirt, the more definition your hips and waist demand. Ballerina skirts, ball-gown skirts, and long A-line maxi skirts are chic when worn as simply as possible: Team with a boat-necked leotard that shows off your collarbone, a shirtwaisted cashmere cable knit that bares your arms, or (at the height of summer and for those with small bazooms) a tiny white singlet. A cardigan with a long, billowing skirt is chic if you're tall, but make sure the sleeve stops just short of the elbow and is tight to the line of your arm. The secret of mastering proportion is to find a designer who understands your body type. Agnes B. is very chic; she is also very narrow in the hips. I know because none of her skirts have ever fit me. To find clothing that suits your scale, don't just head for the petites section of the department store; actively ignore the sizing on clothing labels. What fits is what looks good and no one but you has to know whether it's a four or a ten. Conventional sizing lies.

CHIC COLOR

The colors that expand your figure instantly are white, yellow, orange, lime green, pink, and purple. The colors that camouflage are the neutrals and pastels—everything from caramel to ice blue. The colors that contain your figure are black, navy, charcoal, and gray. Despite the fact that black frames and slims, it is also hard on your complexion, dull in bright sunlight, and visually heavy. If you want to slim down, use black in the trouble zones (hips, legs, arms, bust) and freshen up the rest of your outfit with color.

❀ Overcoordinating color is the enemy of chic and can look like theme dressing. Chic shoes hardly ever match an outfit. Same-color, same-fabric shoes scream: "Bridesmaid!"

❀ Wear white, but break it up with cherry, aqua, straw,

Hat Proportion Is Easy

Big hat,
little dress

Cloche hat,
long dress

Veiled hat,
sleek dress

and deep neutrals. Forget the ancient dictum that says no white after Labor Day. A white cable-knit dress, a white angora collar, or a long white coat that makes you feel like a Russian princess is gorgeous, highly impractical, and highly chic.

✿   Wear pastels, but not so you're mistaken for the Easter Bunny.

✿   Wear a red dress, but not necessarily matching red lipstick, or red shoes. One hot statement is enough on one body.

✿   Wear black, but not like a Calabrian widow; bare a leg, use sheer fabrics, lighten up. (For more on how to handle black, see below.)

CHIC'S BLACK HOLE

Because black is such easy chic, it's tempting to dip your entire wardrobe in india ink. Well, don't! If you are hell-bent on wearing *all black*, break it up with chic textures—a black silk blouse with wool skirt, sheer pantyhose, and patent shoes is sensual instead of heavy. A cropped cable-knit taffeta slip dress with Wolford retro tights and riding boots is wintry but not bulky. To break the monotony of the little black dress, add a pale blue jacket, a bloodred cardigan, or a summer-weight white silk trench coat.

If you want black to have impact and help you look chic, choose your occasion and use black to really dress up, not just down. Anything predictable isn't chic. Black

needs intervals and ornaments that catch the light—a little black Chinese cardigan beaded with black sequins adds drama, a pale apricot camisole under a black business suit brings warmth back to your skin. Black also has a season. New Yorkers wear it year-round. Let them.

CHIC TOUCHES

ACCESSORIES

✿   Boil the trimmings down to refine your look. One great piece—an art deco bracelet or a Victorian mourning necklace—is better than every gold birthday present you ever received. Jewelry looks best worn for aesthetic rather than sentimental reasons. Scarves should light up your face and not obscure your neck (unless you lack one). Wraps (in voile, crushed velvet, and silk) can be large and dramatic but only when teamed with strong vertical lines (slim overcoat, long-sleeved skinny dress, narrow "smoking" suit).

✿   A very chic and long-neglected accessory is gloves! Remember Rita Hayworth as *Gilda*? Or Audrey Hepburn in *Roman Holiday*? Gloves can be sexy or sprightly but they need never be twee. A short pair in pale kid look fabulous in summer (with a well-cut sheath dress and bare arms), they have erotic charm worn long for evening, and they serve as very practical sun protection. Gloves need to be worn with plain, simple lines, and they have to fit your hands and fingers perfectly—no sausage wrinkles or popping buttons, puh-leeze! Gloves look better without a hat unless you really are going to church. P.S. Leave the diamond bracelet in the safe. Jewelry worn over gloves is "Gilda" but somewhat crass.

❁   It's a myth that the bag has to match the outfit—that is so Mother of the Bride. Choose a bag that fits the theme of your ensemble and let it clash just enough: wild tropical flowers worn with a sand-colored dress, straw with angora, tartan with leather. And don't worry too much about size—a mini-clutch can be for day, a tote for evening: the first for car keys, the second for champagne.

COLLARS AND CUFFS

Renaissance Popes knew how to power-dress. To work the room at the Vatican they would wear a tight little ruff to accent their holy heads and generous falls of lace to accent their massive rings. Nuns' wimples, priests' cassocks, and broad starched schoolgirl cuffs were also the stuff of Coco Chanel's Catholic convent girlhood, and her later designs caught on to the habit. One of her less obvious contributions to chic was a genius for accentuating the face and hands with distinctly ecclesiastic-looking collars and cuffs. A great collar works like a good hat, framing your face and cutting a crisp line. The same goes for jabots.

HAIR

For an image of chic hair, think of a John Singer Sargent society lady with hair swept up and away from her face in a discreet swirl. A 1980s supermodel hairdo—all wisps and gold highlights and tendrils—would look terrible rendered in oils and even worse with a chic ensemble. So take a tip from the great belles of the late nineteenth century: Frame your face, don't festoon it.

❁   Chic hair is never hard looking or overlacquered like a back-combed blancmange.

❁   Chic hair doesn't have to be straight, but it needs to be groomed for maximum shine.

❁   Chignons emphasize the nape of the neck and add volume to the crown. Go Audrey!

❁   Chic hair accessories follow the less is more dictum rigorously: one designer barrette instead of three, one really great faux-diamond-encrusted comb instead of many bobby pins. Scrunchies are for the bathtub.

❁   Chic hair has height. Jackie O. did it with Velcro rollers, but applying some setting lotion onto your roots and blow-drying your hair upside down on a cool setting will add oomph to your coif.

❁   Short hair can be the most chic of all—best for pixie-faced girls with little chins and big eyes.

STYLE PSYCHIC

Chic women know when to adopt a look and when to ditch one. Knowing fashion is like surfing: You watch a wave rise from a perfectly still ocean, feel the swell, ride down the face of the wave, and then leap off before getting dumped. The freaky things that catch the media attention at the Paris shows are definitely *not* what the couture ladies order in bulk. Chic is about taking the best elements of a trendy new look and using it to refresh your inviolate sense of personal style.

Examine the history of design and you'll see the same pattern. Sometimes fashion takes a shocking leap forward (from pencil skirts to mini skirts), but most of the time it is a nostalgic dance. Fifty years ago they said we'd all be sporting silver space suits in the twenty-first century, but it's more probable the ozone will force a return to neck-to-knee swimwear and bonnets to shelter from the sun. The faster we hurtle into the future, the more we mine the past for a romance we feel we've lost or a sense of quality that mass production is rapidly eroding. In the history of chic some looks are just too impractical for modern living—corsets, Dior's New Look crinolines, and massive fresh-flower corsages probably aren't due for a revival soon, while other beautiful relics such as the afternoon tea dress, kid gloves, the parasol, the bowler, the boater, and the top hat patiently await their turn.

Chic women trust their intuitive sartorial urges but blend them with a strong existing look. The reason that the Yves Saint Laurent "smoking" jacket has survived so well since 1969 is that it can be transformed practically every season. A well-cut tuxedo-style jacket looks great with pearls for Thanksgiving and even better with a George Jensen choker for a swanky art opening. If you prefer a more laid-back approach to shifting trends, take a hard look each season at hemlines and hair. Both are easy to change without having to overhaul your wardrobe or spend a lot of money. The subclauses of fashionable chic are not a serious pursuit, but looking your best is. Finally: Never wear clothes at the expense of your dignity or your hips.

Less Is Always More

THREE BLACK SKIRTS

Wardrobe Taming

If you are less concerned with building a personal style legend than with just looking good in everyday situations, you need dress rules that are more practical than prissy. Less a matter of whether to wear diamonds at brunch and more of what's clean and what matches. To have a wardrobe that doesn't laugh at you every time you hit a fashion emergency, you need a balance between basics and luxuries, and you need enough range to accommodate a body that expands in the heat, bloats once month, and shrinks when you fall in love or go to India.

If I had to boil it all down, my ideal wardrobe would pivot around three black skirts: one knee-length (and not waitress tight), for work; one long and slinky, for seduction; and one short and stretchy, for PMS bloat and pigging out. Certain pieces anchor you. These are the building blocks that help you get to work on time, knowing you don't have a visible panty-line problem or a weird color that's impossible to match. Shopping for clothes *ought* to follow the supersensible rationale of foundation stones first, fripperies second. Of course it doesn't. If you have cultivated an antiwardrobe stuffed to the gills with weird accessories made out of satin, felt, and chicken feathers, try this shopping mantra: *Does it fit? Does it match? Does it work for or against me?* With a realistic grasp on your lifestyle (Metropolitan Opera subscription or pickup truck full of horse feed?), try to funnel your funds into the best-quality basic wardrobe you can afford. Be tough on yourself. If you can't see yourself in more than five completely different situations in an item, don't buy it—unless it's a G-string or a wedding dress. Black is a good starting point for your essential capsule wardrobe but can look a little heavy during spring and summer. Use color as a transseasonal infusion of energy. A pink scarf lights up your face like a votive candle.

Three Black Skirts

One to Seduce

One to Succeed

One to Slob Out

THE SUPER BASIC WARDROBE

✿ **Three black skirts**

✿ **A jacket that matches your business skirt (read: suit)**

✿ **Three pairs of pants—denim, evening, stretch**

✿ **One very well-cut, lightweight cardigan in your favorite color**

✿ **Three tops—a crisp white blouse, a lined sleeveless shell top, a leotard**

✿ **Three pairs of quality shoes—flat ballet slippers or loafers, a pair of boots (your call on the style), and a pair of black evening shoes**

✿ **One little black dress**

✿ **Three bras—one to run in, one that looks pretty under white, and one that makes your breasts look twice their natural size**

Of course you also need a good overcoat, sneakers, and enough cotton underwear to last a week. Some women have their own uniform for living, and it might just be jeans. Period. The fewer places you have to go, the less clothing you need, but don't presume that if you're unemployed you don't need one pair of smart shoes and a simple shift dress. This could be the outfit that lands you your next job. Once you start to build a wardrobe of simple, flattering basics, think carefully about fabrics, laundry care, colors, and value—or cost per wear. Here are some shopping ground rules for a wardrobe that doesn't bite.

STYLE MAXIMS

✿ Avoid colors that remind you of an airport in Florida or a hospital.

✿ Beige actually suits some people, but never wear it just because you think it looks expensive.

✿ Big prints, large polka dots, horizontal knits, pale jodhpurs, patterned leggings, and white tights are highly fattening.

✿ Spend more money on day wear than evening wear. Daytime is when you're paid to look like you have it together; the night transforms a flea-market dress into a statement.

✿ Buy swimwear in the middle of summer (anti-depression tip).

✿ Linen is for ladies with maids. Ditto white suits.

✿ Dry-clean-only clothes should occupy one-eighth of your wardrobe. It's less expensive, less toxic to the environment, and forces you to own three great suits instead of seven average items. Cheap fabrics that need expensive steam and dry cleaning to make them look good are a false economy.

✿ "Made in China" doesn't always mean "just throw it in the washing machine."

✿ Tight dresses in cheap, lightweight fabrics like rayon and poly-cotton have a feeble plastic memory and so bag out very quickly, especially over the derriere.

✿ One hundred percent cotton sweaters lose their shape; look for silk blends and good cuts, but avoid acrylic. It pills like crazy.

WARDROBE WORKSHOP

Making clothes work for you means being able to get dressed for any occasion. Here are some real-life wardrobe conundrums with quick solutions.

WORKAHOLIC MEETS WAGNER:

You're working on a deadline and are beckoned to the opera straight from the office. You feel like a cocktail of copier fluid and stale coffee.

Solution: Stash an instant socializing kit at work. It consists of one much louder lipstick, one pair of low-denier high-quality pantyhose, purse-sized perfume, higher heels (optional), and a slinky black knit cardigan. This can be worn over black trousers for the lounge-suit look, over a 1960s shift for formality, and over a print dress for the more demure.

Tip: Craving some evening class but low on cash? Freshwater seed pearls are a less expensive way to warm up the most exhausted workaholic visage, and cream blush is better for overly air-conditioned skin. For the quickie makeup bag from heaven, see "Looking Damn Fine," page 60.

DIFFERENT WORLDS:

You have a conference all day, a loan interview in the afternoon, dinner with your parents, and then the launch of your lover's first CD in a rock pit at midnight. *How?* Easy.

Solution: Wear well-cut trousers, a suit jacket, a silk blouse, and boots all day. At the eleventh hour ditch the jacket and don a vintage halter top or embroidered velvet jacket. *Or* wear a sensible dress with a tailored leather jacket and classic pumps all day. At the witching hour emerge from the ladies room transformed, courtesy of a floor-length halter-neck dress (with your office shoes invisible beneath the hemline).

Tip: Dimly lit clubs and parties allow for the miracle that is the polyester party dress. This little number can roll up small enough to fit in your briefcase and then unfurl as instant, creaseless glamour.

GROOMING SECRETS OF A LADY'S MAID

All the epigrams and bons mots in the world won't excuse a fallen hem. Elegance is about maintenance, keeping a vigilant eye on not just the style but also the condition of your clothes. It does seem tedious to reiterate commonsense grooming tips, but the speed of life often makes smoking wreckage of a potentially great wardrobe. (Don't even ask me about the lilac linen suit I desecrated with an ink pen that had lost its lid.)

✿ Poorly groomed people are always wearing something they think they can get away with one more time. They can't.

✿ Coat linings need repair the second they rip. Ditto dangling labels. These are what people see when you whisk off your coat and sling it over the back of a chair.

✿ Buff shoes each time you wear them and attend to the heels (even on tiny stilettos) once they wear down. When suede shoes look as if they are covered in talcum powder and outline the shape of your toes, it's time for the trash bin.

✿ White bra straps need to be perfectly white. If you hate scrubbing nylon lace with a toothbrush once a fortnight, then invest in black lingerie only. Gray bra straps—need I say more?

✿ Scotch-taped and safety-pinned hems are cute—in high school.

✿ Schlep not! A big bag isn't better, because it just gets crammed to the brim. Deliberately choose a smaller bag and pare down the contents to the point where you carry the bare minimum. This harsh style discipline is easier on your back and nails, and a lot less klutzy on occasions when you need to impress.

✿ To remove the shine from the seat of trousers, sponge them with ammonia water (one teaspoon in one cup of cold water) before steam-pressing.

✿ Silk should be ironed while still damp. Redampening dried silk results in spotty watermarks. After washing and rinsing, roll the silk item in a bath towel with layers of toweling between the folds until it's evenly damp and dry enough to iron. Press the silk on the wrong side with a moderately hot iron.

✿ Iron lace on the delicate setting, on the wrong side while still slightly damp. Sing loudly while you endure the tedium of caring for your delicates.

✿ Be ultracareful what you toss into a laundry basket. Items that needed handwashing can come back to you washed, folded, and child sized.

✿ Trim pilling elbows on sweaters and wool-blend overcoats with a light sweep of a disposable razor blade.

✿ Never iron velvet.

✿ Keep shoes on shoe trees, heels pointing up and out so you can check for repairs. Keep less frequently worn shoes boxed and clearly labeled.

✿ Hang skirts separately on clip hangers; folding them or dangling them by the loops creates wrinkles.

✿ Keep coats separate from lightweight clothes to avoid the squash factor.

✿ Hang sweaters on padded hangers.

✿ Box your special bias-cut items flat and wrap them in tissue. A long beaded evening dress cut on the bias or even a lighter-weight bias-cut slip dress will start to develop a lopsided droop at the hem if it's hung for too long.

✿ To prevent mildew, store clothes in a good strong suitcase rather than in garbage bags under the bed.

✿ Keep leather items (bags, belts, shoes) away from a heat source. Don't put them in a closet near hot water pipes, for instance.

✿ Keep lingerie and stockings in a giant hatbox. Freshen with potpourri bags (and scented love letters).

THE EXPRESS-LANE WARDROBE

✿ The ideal way to organize your closet is seasonally. No one wears velvet in July.

✿ Organize outfits in terms of your lifestyle. Office clothes can hang together, and different looks can be color-blocked for easier access. If your wardrobe is dominated by one color (let me guess? Black!) hang according to use: day, evening, casual.

✿ Accessories get worn when you can see them in context with clothes. If you are very busy, team outfits with their accessories a day or two in advance. Like that great character in *Women on the Verge of a Nervous Breakdown*, you can fling on your cherry red suit complete with brooch without even thinking about it.

✿ Bijous such as rings, bracelets, and earrings are the glittery nomads of any wardrobe. Store them in a plastic divider tray. Hang necklaces on hooks or dangle them from a horizontal rod inside your closet.

✿ Use spring and fall to ritually purge and update your wardrobe.

LOOKING DAMN FINE

Unsnooty Beauty

Looking good is not a matter of being beautiful, it's about being alive. Beauty is not something you can really contrive or control. Hair and skin and body fat are all mutable entities. Some days it all hangs together and other days you're a Cubist painting without a frame, all weird angles and frayed edges. All you can do in the name of beauty is animate it with your spirit, the spirit that never changes and never ages.

Expect to look beautiful at some of the least-dignified moments of your life: sweating, birthing, battling the odds. Inner spark is the ultimate beautifier.

Still, having said that—if somewhere along the way you find some goo that stops your hair from frizzing, a lipstick that doubles the size of your mouth, or a blusher that makes you look après yoga, use that, too!

THE FOUR AGES OF WOMAN

From thirteen to ninety a woman needs sunscreen, fresh food, water, tender love, and pride of carriage. Beauty can be awkward at times of transition. The day you get your first period is as hard as the day you find your first gray hairs or look in a shop window and suddenly see angular cheekbones and other adult face architecture creeping into a once-nubile visage. The best makeup for women of all ages is fresh makeup: anything that looks like a complement rather than a sculptural imposition. A lot of women get through their twenties with a stump of black eyeliner and a red lipstick only to find ten years later that these tools serve to make them look mean rather than pretty. I think makeup works like a bell curve, with very little to start, very little to finish, and bit of a glamour blast in between at the age where you don't look like Lolita or mutton dressed as Drew Barrymore. Hitting fifty shouldn't mean buying a coral lipstick and a sensible cardigan and throwing in the towel as a beauty queen. *Mais non!* Just look at Catherine Deneuve, still working the pout and the smoky eyes quite late in the day. Instead, it is about refinement and technique. A twenty-one-year-old girl wearing too much eye shadow looks like a messy little orchid; twenty years later she just looks messy. Makeup should change with your skin, getting moister as you get drier and getting sleeker as your style evolves.

TEENS

Young dewy skin can get away with glitter, iridescent eye shadow, superbright lipstick, henna body tattoos, too much eyeliner, or the no-eye-makeup look. Pale pastel and tropical colors also look amazing on baby cheeks and lids.

✿ Despite the fact that you don't want to look like a little girl anymore, the less makeup you wear now, the better. Youth is for the young and the naturally rosy.

✿ If you have breakouts, don't plaster foundation and powder over the top of them. Keep the skin clean and let it breathe. Don't be tempted to fry your face in the sun to clear it up, either. Whatever you do, don't squeeze!

✿ Everyone says, "You're young, you're beautiful, don't worry." They're right.

TWENTIES

This is the age of trying to be taken seriously. Job hunt, love hunt, identity hunt. Don't hide your light under a bushel with drab colors and sensible chignons. There's time for sober looks later.

✿ Enjoy red lipstick; later, fine feather lines will gather around the mouth, and lips will tend to shrink with age. Go the air kiss!

✿ Liquid eyeliner and other dramatic eye makeup styles look great on eyes with no crow's feet. Protect your face from the sun and keep the puffy look down with cool tea bags.

✿ Party on but be frugal with cigarettes, caffeine, junk food, alcohol, and drugs. You feel as if you have limitless energy now, but later the body pays. Shine on, don't burn out.

THIRTIES

✿ Don't go into neutral at the first sight of a line or a crepey eyelid! Colors can lighten up and lipsticks can soften up, but not too radically.

✿ Look at your lipstick. What is it doing for your mouth? Rosy reds, fleshy pinks, and stains and sheers work better when lips start to get leaner. Use a lip pencil as a sealant to disguise fraying edges and avoid matte, powdery lipsticks.

✿ Try using eye shadow instead of a hard, blunt eyeliner to accent the upper and lower lids. The smudge factor requires skill, so apply delicately.

✿ Don't scrimp on health care, skin care, or rest. Try to protect the delicate skin around your eyes.

✿ The thirties are hard on hair. Your mane may start to get thinner, grayer, or generally less lustrous. Stock up on essential fatty acids found in linseed and fish oil and foods rich in vitamin E and B.

✿ If motherhood taxes your hair, skin, and body, look into your diet. Do you need a supplement? Is sleep deprivation killing your looks? Perk up with a sensual bath scented with geranium, orange, or rose oil. Ask your partner to ease expectations in times of stress. And most important, ease your own. Don't expect to look like a babe when you're in the thick of the most responsible time of your life.

✿ Get frisky with a subtle brush of blusher. Better still, get your circulation going with a few headstands. Yoga is a great beautifier.

FORTIES AND BEYOND

Hair matters more at forty than before. For decades you may have gotten away with a scrunchie and some old hair clips, but now is the time to frame your face and define your style.

✿ Look at the colors you're wearing, the shape of your eyebrows, your brand of foundation, and the needs of your lifestyle. Old habits die hard, but that chocolate lip liner looked better in 1983 than it does now.

✿ Enhance everything you love about your face. If you have gray hair, make it dramatic with beautifully shaped brows and a black velvet ribbon. If you have deep cheekbones, highlight them; if you still love red lipstick, then just wear it!

✿ We spend twenty-five years or so hanging on to girl-hood, so now is probably the best time to let go of "cute" affectations. Enjoy womanly perfumes, powerful clothes, and dramatic style, or even complete "in the raw" naturalness. If you're not you now, when will you be?

✿ Let your face breathe. If you've had a lifetime of makeup and want a break for a while, then take it! Some women hit fifty and don't need to primp like teenagers anymore. Many striking older vixens simply choose to cut their hair short and wear wild jewelry.

✿ Playing hide-and-seek with aging has its limits. The most glamorous woman I know in Paris has a deeply lined face. She spent years in the Algerian desert and loves to swim naked in the blazing sun. Her hair is worn blond and naturally curly close to her head, her small, piercing eyes are lined

in kohl that she buys in a market in Morocco, her mouth is kept almost bare, and her perfume is intense and exotic. On her arms she wears tribal bracelets, and on her firm legs she likes African-patterned leggings and foxy little boots. Helene is pushing seventy and she breaks all the rules. Sun damage, swagger, and all, she looks incredibly sexy. Attitude creates its own cachet.

COSMETIC SORCERY

Makeup isn't magic but it *can* have transgressive powers. There's nothing like red lip gloss after a divorce or smudgy black eyeliner on a first date. When you're young, cosmetics cover up your uncertainties, and as you get older they accent the features you've come to love. Makeup is getting more sophisticated and refined but essentially it can never replace healthy skin or good circulation. The more your makeup matches and meshes with your features, the better you look.

When buying makeup, bring along a stub of your favorite lipstick and other makeup bag survivors so you don't buy exactly the same shade, politely ignore offers to be made over like a Kabuki mask, and try not to fall under the sway of in-store promotions. It's hard but you have to imagine a product in natural light (daylight) in the context of your own everyday personal style (which eye shadow matches sweats?) and minus the glitz of packaging and bright lights. Buying makeup is never as much fun as getting it home for girly experiment sessions with friends.

The main conundrum of makeup isn't whether we need it but rather what works. What products and clever little tricks really do have the power to transform a face as plain as a dime? How much is too much, and how can we wear the absolute minimum to look totally gorgeous?

BLUSHER

✿ Fear not the blusher! Pale-faced girls look great with a circle of rose blush on the apples of their cheeks. Tan girls can look even more country with a swipe of coral blush across their noses.

✿ Blusher is also handy for a light dust around the jawline, between the bosoms, and at the temples—basically anywhere you need accent, drama, and a healthy glow. No one wants to look green around the gills.

✿ As you get older, blusher becomes a beauty must-have, especially when working in air-conditioned offices where your "bloom" is threatened. The trouble is, older skin tends to be drier skin, so powder blushers can look heavy and tend to streak when applied over moisturizer. A clever alternative is creme blush, but apply it very lightly. Obvious rouge looks way too demimonde.

COLOR

There is a running theory that if eye shadow compacts, blushers, and smudgy eyeliner pencils were art materials, there would be many more women artists in the world. Rich, luscious color is the central attraction of makeup. Sadly, few women have the daring to expand their palette. Beigey, smoky neutrals are safe bets for eye makeup, prim dusty rose and sandy beige predominate for lips, but there's more out there. Much more.

✿ Color is the first thing that dates a face. Wear the same shade of lipstick for more than three years and you may as well not wear any at all. There is a fine line between a beauty trademark and nondescript complacency. If you can wear a rose-pink silk scarf, you can wear rose-pink lipstick.

✿ You may spend a lifetime avoiding a color that looks great on you. Try something utterly different next time a makeup salesgirl swipes toward you.

✿ Bright blue eye shadow is not illegal, nor is pale pistachio green or deep purple. If you have firm, unlined lids and large bright eyes, you can afford to take risks with color and go beyond the tyranny of taupe. Hint: Very richly colored eye makeup looks best worn sheer with a slightly darker mascara. Try pale ice blue shadow with plenty of black mascara. The trick is not so much in the color as in the quality of the textures you apply. Exploit the very broad range of sheer textures, iridescent finishes, and multitasking (cheek, eye, lip) colored pencils available. A color you might never consider as a powdered shadow—say, deep lilac—could look amazing as a sheer gloss.

✿ The same idea applies to blush: A rich red blush can be worn when it's made in a very sheer formulation.

✿ Lips and eyes shouldn't have to compete for attention. The rule of heavy eyes–soft mouth and soft eyes–painted mouth still applies, but it really depends on the shape of your face and the proportion of your features. The younger and fuller your lips, the less help they need; this is the time to wear sheer gloss, frosted lipstick, and icy pale tones.

✿ Color has the visual power to expand or contract your features. Blue-reds, dark plums, and deep brown shades of lipstick shrink a small mouth, while fleshier, warmer tones give you pout power. Very pale lipsticks look best on chubby-lipped blondes, redheads with pale mouths look good with a cherry stain, and brunettes should exploit their high-contrast potential with more lush colors like violet, rust, and vermilion.

✿ Foundation is the canvas against which all other makeup shades gain their beauty. Finding the right match for your skin is essential. If you go even one tone darker, your face will look both aged and overly made up. For many women, the only way to get a true skin-tone match is to have a foundation custom-made. As far as concealers go, avoid any color that looks radically paler than your skin tone. Better to have slightly darker skin under the eyes than the flashbulb effect, like those celebrities who quite literally sport chalky half moons beneath each eye in the name of looking wide awake.

TOOL TRICKS

Even cheap makeup looks better when applied with good equipment and a deft hand. Throw out the tiny sponge applicators that come with most eye shadows and use small, supple-headed brushes to apply shadow and blend in contours. Also invest in a big, fat, generous blush brush and give the stiff little brush that comes with blushers to your nieces or little sisters.

✿ Foundation applied with a sponge needs to be

applied very lightly. To avoid globs, use your fingers. Always use small upward strokes and blend well. Beige face + white neck = bad look.

✿ Tweezers are a personal affair; I prefer a slanted-edge wedge, but go with whatever works. Pluck your eyebrows when you feel less sensitive (not before a period, first thing in the morning, or after a day at the beach). Try to avoid tugging and gouging, and know how much brow to leave on your face. Beware overplucking—real eyebrows look better than penciled arches. Unless you have Dietrich's bones, you'll wind up looking like Ronald McDonald.

✿ Eyelash curlers are nasty little inventions but they certainly give you that wide-awake look when the lash stands at attention. Use with prudence. Curl the outer tips of the lashes first, and then clamp the beast down closer to the lid line, but only for about five seconds. *Do not* use with mascara, and keep the little pads on the clamps clean by washing them thoroughly with hot soapy water and then rinsing.

EYES

✿ If you are sloppy with eye shadow, dust your face with powder before applying it; that way any stray spray can simply be brushed off.

✿ Foundation applied to the lid and inside the brow bone helps color adhere and last.

✿ If you want a round-eyed, wide-awake look, line your inner rim with a white eye pencil.

✿ The color of your eye shadow should bring your eyes forward rather than make them recede, raccoonlike, into your face. Some recommend applying neutrals like taupe and coffee-beige to the whole lid as a base, then adding extra drama with a richer shade to the outside wing edge of the eyelid.

✿ Green eyes look amazing with midnight blue eye shadow, bright purple complements brown, and blue-eyed blondes can splash out with tropical green mascara. The trick with eye makeup is emphasis without weight.

✿ A heavy slash of pencil eyeliner isn't as flattering as blended eye shadow for the same look. In applying pencil, many makeup artists insist on wedging the line as close to the lash line as possible. This gives the illusion

PS: Don't overpluck brows. In terms of regrowth, this is the most unpredictable hair on the body. The first time, get them done professionally.

of lashes that are forever.

❈ Liquid eyeliner is an art form that requires a steady hand and large, alert-looking eyes. Nothing points to crow's feet, eye bags, or a hangover more than heavy pussy-cat wings. There are new liner pens that are slightly lighter and practically klutzproof.

❈ Mascara needs to be fat and lush without getting too close to Jacqueline Susann and her *Valley of the Dolls*. Globs, clumpy bits, and long spindles make you look married to the mob. Waterproof mascara is for synchronized swimmers and hard-core beach bunnies only. Water-soluble mascara is easier to remove and involves less tugging of the delicate skin around the eyes.

❈ False eyelashes now come in small, more natural-looking lengths with a self-adhesive strip that eliminates the bother of applying glue. Extra lashes give the eyes a luxurious flutter and look dramatic even on a completely bare face.

❈ It's tempting to have your eyelashes tinted instead of wearing mascara, but this is also a highly dangerous process that can blind or seriously damage the eye if administered incorrectly. The FDA has not approved the natural or synthetic dyes used to tint lashes and brows.

❈ Wearing perfect eye makeup with sloppy brows is like framing a masterpiece cheaply. Even women who wear no makeup should invest in a monthly brow shape.

LIPS

❈ Vivid red lipstick is a real bad-girl barometer. Before movies were in color, you always knew who was wearing the slutty scarlet and who was just petulant in pink. In one particularly hard-boiled B-grade flick, I recall Bette Davis breaking out of prison, marching into a drugstore, and demanding a lipstick. "Gimme any color" she growled savagely, "as long as it's red." Red lipstick still has a rather tawdry cachet. It's the color you buy when you're freshly single or want to provoke someone. Red can be worn for decades if you make subtle changes to the shade (blue-reds are too damn hard on *anyone* over nineteen) and also if you cleverly adapt the texture of your lipstick. If you can't forgo scarlet lips, wear a cherry or vermilion stain rather than a whole matte mouthful.

❈ Lipsticks now come in a huge range of textures. For day you can wear a stain or a tinted lip balm; for evening you may want iridescent sparkle or even a light reflective holographic lip color. Sheer color is very flattering and takes the pressure off maintaining a perfectly drawn and defined mouth.

✿ Lip pencils can be used after the lipstick goes on for a softer look, but this can be messy. If you draw the line before, don't overdo nature's reality.

✿ According to Kevin Aucoin, lips can be exfoliated using a baby toothbrush and a slick of Vaseline. I like to rough mine up on my beloved's stubbly chin. Each to her own.

✿ Most lip balms are made from petroleum-derived ingredients. Look for nonpetroleum lip balm made from natural oils and beeswax instead. Or make your own using one tablespoon of honey and one teaspoon of rosewater. First melt the honey over a bowl of hot water, then stir in the rosewater and bottle it up. Yum!

SKIN CARE

Skin is partly genetic heritage, partly environment, and partly the regime we establish to care for it. The bad habits that we all think we can get away with such as sunbaking "just once a year," going to sleep with our makeup on, squeezing and prodding a pimple, or dragging makeup off with vigorous swipes are all factors that damage skin over the long haul. To encourage a more beautiful skin, we need to be vigilant but not overly complicated. Skin doesn't like to be marinated in too much moisturizer, massaged too roughly, irritated by fruit peels, or dehydrated by bar soaps and strong indoor heating or air-conditioning.

Skin is also a lot more adaptive and changeable than we are made to believe. Instead of believing that you have a definite and unchanging skin type (oily, dry, combination, or the ever-elusive "normal"), look at your skin as an organ that changes with your moods, the seasons, and the transitions of your body and your life. Pregnant skin is different from traveling skin, which is different from depressed or lovesick skin. And all of these states make their own demands. Keeping the face clean, moist, and protected from the elements with products that are simple, unperfumed, and as nurturing as you can find should be your aim.

FACE SAVERS

✿ Drink two quarts of springwater or purified tap water a day. (Mosturize from within.)

✿ Eat a diet rich in fresh greens and fruits, especially foods rich in vitamin C (for collagen), zinc, calcium, and vitamins B, E, and A.

✿ Get plenty of sleep and go to bed relaxed. Why wake up with frown lines?

✿ Shelter from the sun, not only with sunscreens, but also with a sturdy hat. Even weedy-looking winter sun causes damage. Slap on a reliable sunscreen under your base. Carry a purse-sized SPF 30 sunscreen at all times or wear a tinted moisturizer with built-in sunscreen.

✿ Find a cleanser, moisturizer, and eye cream that are low irritant and suit the needs of your skin. These may change with age and with the seasons.

✿ Give your skin treats like a rosewater and geranium refresher spray for the office, a good natural face mask once every two weeks, and a deluxe facial every six. You can find cheap, wholesome skin care at your health food store and go to salons for the stuff you can't concoct (like seaweed masks).

✿ Be beautiful ethically. Think twice about buying products that are tested on animals or using animal products to serve your skin. How do you really feel about sheep placenta being used to reduce eye wrinkles?

✿ Stop smoking, frowning, and drinking heavily. Smoking dehydrates the skin and creates rapid aging. Alcohol is also dehydrating and aging (by virtue of taxing the liver and kidneys).

✿ Breathe deeply and calmly and get regular exercise (three twenty-minute sessions of light aerobic exercise a week is a good start). Circulation of oxygen detoxifies the skin and gets blood pumping through the body.

✿ Never pick, squeeze, burn, or peel the skin. Skin scars easily. Leave deep facials and blackhead extraction to the experts and quit mauling.

✿ Protect your body as you would your face, especially the delicate skin of your chest, neck, and hands. For softer hands, get into gloves (for gardening, dishwashing, and driving). And keep a pump pack of hand cream wherever you keep your water bottles. Reapply as frequently as you drink! The sun devours soft skin, especially in a sheer little sundress. Be vigilant about your décolletage: Wear low-cut dresses only by moonlight.

SKIN MYTHS

A little sun adds healthy color.

This is a favorite line of my mother's, usually uttered from beneath a vast beach umbrella sheltering her Irish porcelain face from a blazing Australian sun. Sun is needed by the body to absorb vitamin D, but that pink "healthy" glow you get after a day at the beach is just burnt skin, pure and simple. If you want the same look, enjoy your sun fully protected (hat and sunscreen, big shirt over your bikini), and wear a bronzing dust or gentle self-tanner. No, you don't have to prove you've been to St. Barths by scorching yourself to a crisp.

Mists and water atomizers keep skin moist during a long plane trip.

Water evaporates. And in dry recycled cabin air, water evaporates even faster. To lock in the refreshing moisture of a face mist, slap on some day cream right after you spritz.

A tight, shiny face is a clean face.

A face that squeaks or feels as tight as a drum is both irritated and dehydrated. Not such a good look.

Soap and water is good enough for my skin.

If you really believe this, you may as well live on bread and water as well. Give your face a chance: Invest in a gentle, water-soluble cleanser. Expensive cleansing bars are still, basically, soap.

Dark skin doesn't burn as easily as fair skin.

Structurally there is no difference between dark and fair skin; both suffer severe burning and damage if overexposed to UV radiation from the sun. African-American skin sometimes has the advantage of looking younger much longer because it's slightly less sensitive to sun damage, but sun ages *all* skin types. You need to protect yourself in all seasons.

Base needs to be applied all over the face.

Being comfortable in your skin means being able to bare more of it. Foundation is a great way to smooth out imperfections, but a sheer minimum will do. If you've been wearing a foundation with a high coverage for years, experiment with a lighter formulation for daytime. Give yourself a make-under and reduce the amount you wear by half. Visible skin is a beautiful thing. Especially if you have freckles!

MAKEUP BAG BASICS

The bare-minimum-go-anywhere makeup bag is a utopian ideal. Movie stars always claim their desert-island needs are mascara and that's it. Ha! This level of austerity is usually augmented by a live-in manicurist. To boil your makeup bag down to the essentials, you need to know where you're going and what you need. Remember to keep your face hydrated and protected from the ravaging, brutalizing elements. If you carried only SPF 15 lip balm and a sunscreen, you'd be just as beauty-smart. Save face!

ABSOLUTE BASICS

- ✿ **one lipstick or lipstick compact**
- ✿ **one concealer**
- ✿ **one foundation, tinted sunscreen, or tinted moisturizer**
- ✿ **one dual pencil (for eyes, lips, brows)**
- ✿ **one blusher**
- ✿ **soothing eye gel (for travel, air-conditioned offices, pollution, and the like)**
- ✿ **an extra tube of sunscreen**
- ✿ **mascara**
- ✿ **one eye shadow trio that gives you options for both day and night**

HOME-MADE BEAUTY RECIPES

FACE

✿ A calming cleanser for oily skin can be made from two teaspoons of natural honey, one teaspoon of lemon juice, and one tablespoon of natural yogurt. After blending thoroughly, work the mixture into your skin gently with upward circular movements, then rinse with cool water and a soft washcloth.

✿ For softening and moisturizing, blend one tablespoon of fresh honey, one teaspoon of fresh wheat germ, and one teaspoon of sunflower seed meal. Allow the mix to set for one minute, then apply and leave on for half an hour. Rinse with warm water.

✿ A mask can be as simple as one ingredient: egg whites tighten pores and firm the face, raw natural yogurt evens the skin tone. For moist, rosy skin, mash half a ripe peach with one tablespoon of heavy cream. Smells delicious and you'll look heavenly after a half hour of daydreaming.

EYES

✿ For puffy eyes, place two cold, wet tea bags on eyelids for ten chilled-out minutes—the tannin reduces redness and the cool moisture depuffs. For those who prefer herbals, try chamomile, fennel, or elderflower tea bags.

❀ Cut two big slices of raw potato or cucumber and gently press them to your eyelids. They're good for bags or eyes that feel slightly bruised.

BODY

❀ Cut a lemon in half and make two little bowls to soak your elbows in. Fruit acids help exfoliate and gently cleanse and rejuvenate the skin. Raw unprocessed honey on the elbows is a powerful moisturizer.

❀ Shins get scaly in winter from wind, dry heat, and constant imprisonment inside tights and pants. Try dabbing on some pure almond or apricot oil at bedtime.

❀ Use your bath as a rejuvenating spa with this sensuous milk bath. Mix half a cup of powdered whole milk with one tablespoon of apricot kernel or grapeseed oil and add to running bathwater. Before you slide in, add eight drops of essential chamomile oil. Deeply moisturizing, deeply Cleopatra.

❀ Mashed avocado is good for sunburn and dry summer skin. Warning: You will turn into monster-guacamole-woman, so lock the bathroom door before applying. Slather it on your hair as well and wrap it in a towel for a half hour.

NAILS

❀ Stop cuticle pushing! The cuticle is the body's protective barrier between the living matrix of the nail bed (where the nail grows) and the exposed, essentially dead fingernail itself. Moisturizing cuticles is a better idea than torturing or trimming them.

❀ Don't shape your nails after leaping out of the shower. Wait till they are dry. Don't use metal files, either; they're way too harsh.

❀ Nail-saving ideas: Type using the pads of your fingers, use scissors instead of your talons to open things, save clawing at the sheets like a wildcat for special occasions.

❀ Foods that benefit your nails: fresh oily fish, almonds, dates, figs, sea vegetables, whole grains, raw fruits and vegetables, and cold-pressed oils like linseed and sesame. All are great beauty boosters for your hair, too.

HAIR

Shiny hair with good elasticity, bounce, and resilience isn't just glamorous—it's a sign of good health. Rapunzel must have been a pure-water, yoga, and whole-foods queen, because hair growth is stimulated by detoxified blood and a healthy supply of nutrients. When we're

BAD HAIR HABIT	GOOD HAIR HABIT
WEARING A SKULL-TIGHT PONYTAIL PUTS STRAIN ON THE SCALP AND CAN LEAD TO PREMATURE THINNING KNOWN AS TRACTION ALOPECIA.	Loose hair grips, slide combs, and a well-supported chignon are better for your hair than a severe ponytail.
WASHING HAIR TILL IT SQUEAKS.	A dessert-spoonful of shampoo is enough, and shampoo only once.
NEVER LETTING YOUR HAIR GET DIRTY.	Natural oils are the best treatment for dry hair. Hide out for a weekend with unwashed hair.
SQUEEZING HAIR ROUGHLY.	Blotting hair softly means less breakage.
GOING AGAINST THE GRAIN.	Straightening your hair is potentially more damaging than perming it. The chemicals in both methods are very drying, so use a deep moisturizing conditioner.

depressed our hair droops with us, when we're stressed hair can take on that frazzled, raw edge. To create happy hair you need to tend it with gentle cleansing and conditioning products, natural treatments (such as egg, milk, or avocado), and minimal chemical treatments such as perming, dyeing, and straightening. To get your hair in silky strong condition you may just need to leave it alone more. Wash it less, brush it less, treat it less. Overshampooing swells the hair follicle, making hair dull. Not rinsing conditioner and shampoo out thoroughly creates buildup, reducing shine. Overwashing hair can create excessive sebum production in the scalp and give you the weird combination of oily scalp and dehydrated hair. Overbrushing breaks hair, and even though you lose an average of one hundred hairs per day, you don't want to lose any more. Because hair is almost all keratin protein, it responds to nourishment (inside and out). A few small changes to your regime and you can forget hair shame forever.

STYLING TRICKS

The trick for pretty hair is knowing your hair type and having the tools to control and enhance it. For most hair problems, there are fast solutions. The static fuzz of frizzy hair responds to a sealing moisturizer and to finger combing instead of brushing. Applying mousse at your roots then a quick blast of the hair dryer gives height and volume to flat hair. Really long hair tends to weigh more

PROBLEM: Martyr Hair
SOLUTION: Pray for hot rollers.

PROBLEM: Scrunch Head
SOLUTION: Remove bathtub do,
bolt door until hair is braided.

PROBLEM: Killer Cornrows
SOLUTION: Too tight is not alright,
choose a soft touch stylist.

PROBLEM: Heavy Metal Pom Pom
SOLUTION: Contain the rage with
super-slick product.

PROBLEM: Anchorwoman Hair
SOLUTION: Permission to use
Scrunchy.

PROBLEM: Curly Bangs à la
Rebecca of Sunnybrook Farm
SOLUTION: Blow dry, plaster with
mousse, or move to Memphis.

and sit flat on the crown; hot rollers with a spritz of setting lotion can create body for the crown of the head, and so do hairstyles that take the weight off like chignons and high ponytails. When choosing a style, go for what flatters the face above all else. Beautiful eyes look great accented with wispy bangs, long hair suits heart-shaped faces, and a high noble forehead looks better with an updo. Accepting the true nature of your natural hair also helps. If you ask a stylist to go against nature and give you a cut that forces natural waves into submission or a cowlick-kiss girl into blow-dried perfection, you are asking for many bad hair days later on. The closer you wear your hair to the way it grows out of your head (corkscrew or dead straight), the better it's going to look.

THE GRAY ZONE

Going gray shouldn't make you want to die or dye straight away. Aesthetically, gray hair can look quite beautiful and chic. Ladies in the eighteenth century powdered their hair to look like Madame de Pompadour, a famous courtesan with silvery ringlets. Christian Lacroix's favorite couture model, Marie Seznec, wears her gray hair elaborately dressed, and many older women look a lot better with a flowing flinty mane than a head that looks like it was dunked in India ink. Choosing to make a dramatic feature of a big stripe of gray, like Susan Sontag did in her 30s, can be glamorous. You can wear gray hair short, cropped, and modern, or long and fluid like Emmylou Harris. It's a romantic look that evokes wise women and Celtic queens.

If you want to wear your hair gray, then rethink your clothes and makeup for a deliberately stylish look. Think chic instead of girlish—gorgeous textural fabrics, bold silver jewelry, great slabs of turquoise, and sleek, minimal modern cuts that don't say, "Twee granny."

PS: If my praise of gray fails to move you and you want to tint your hair, avoid dyes that are too harsh or dramatically dark. Gray hair can often have a wiry consistency and can take on a uniform flatness if it's tinted a strong tone like blue-black.

FUZZ CONTROL: THE PUBIC WARS

The whole thing about hair is that we want tons of it on our head and virtually none anywhere else. Hair shame creates terrible anxiety for Mediterranean girls with dark arm hair or even little Swedish types with thick golden down on their shins. There are potions made of sugar or chemicals that dissolve body hair and procedures to reduce it, but go gently and don't torture yourself . . . and the same goes for downstairs. The great thing about winter is the right to grow body hair. Salty little fur clumps under the arms, shaggy abominable-snowman legs, and a fuzzy Bermuda triangle unhindered by the dictates of swimwear.

✿ Waxing. One-stop beauty has its rewards. It's cheaper and saves time. For the really organized, a facial,

pedicure, and hair trim should be thrown in. Take a bottle of wine or a CD you love along for the journey.

✿ A trimmed cucci for special occasions feels sexy, but having to constantly attend to your bush like topiary is a bore. If a lover complains about regrowth or demands less and less coverage (i.e., Brazilian ultra-plucked), tell him to go look at his face. Men hate

shaving, so why should women work to re-create a pre-pubescent pubic look just to please them? Do as you wish.

☆   Bleaching is great for hair on the upper lip, but don't leave it on too long or you'll have a blond moustache worthy of that salty-dog sailor in *The Ghost and Mrs. Muir.*

☆   For heavier facial hair, a trained beauty therapist or a certified electrologist should be consulted, especially if lasers or permanent removal is involved.

DECOR DIVA

The Casa Question

Up to a certain age a girl can subsist with the bare essentials of decor. A mattress on the floor, an exposed metal clothes rail, and a couple of framed posters will do. If a big art print and crisp, white bed sheets were enough for Jean Seberg in *Breathless*, then, hey *bébé*, they're good enough for me. Trouble is, Jean Seberg's character lived in Paris in the 1960s. Her tiny atelier was filmed by Jean-Luc Godard in grainy, jump-cut black and white. Her balcony looked out onto those crazy streets and she had Jean-Paul Belmondo. Naked under the heavy white sheets. *That* was decor enough. When the decor *chez toi* has reached its Bohemian limit and you're ready to move on from beatnik style, what are you going to do?

For the uninitiated, minor style changes and simple renovations feel like a big deal. The gulf between how an apartment looks in a magazine and how your own little pigpen feels is huge. It doesn't have to be. To explode the decor myth, here is a list of cheap and speedy ways to change your immediate environment and get some style and some soul into your casa.

ORDER OUT OF CHAOS

Rich people are not cleaner than you and me: They have storage. Walk-in closets, vast concealed cupboards, acres of shelving. The first step toward making a house habitable is housing your crap and reducing clutter. Rooms, like outfits, need limited focal points—one amazing object looks better than twenty-seven dusty tchotchkes (trinkets), and color needs a theme. Room by room, find ways to purge what you don't need and hide what you don't want to see.

✿ Be ruthless about the function of each room in your house. If you are living in a studio apartment or an attic, apply the same stringent codes. A bed can double as a couch, but a kitchen table can only be a used as a desk if the dishes and other ephemera of daily life have regular storage spaces. For those lucky souls who actually have spare rooms where junk accumulates, consider the dangers these clutter dens pose to your feng shui. Old stuff you don't use creates areas of blocked energy, and energy needs to flow through your house and your life.

✿ The more dwellings you find for possessions, the clearer a space becomes. With this in mind, only buy cabinets or other storage pieces that are smooth on the outside and big on the inside. Think of these pieces as "room spies" for they hold much and reveal little.

✿ Give yourself a deadline to clean a room, getting the grittiest jobs done first and fastest. Anything that takes longer than two hours means you're obsessing (why are you ironing a stack of linen napkins for next Thanksgiving?).

✿ A good list for cleaning runs like this—clear clutter, clean surfaces, rearrange, and reduce. Carry a big broom and an even bigger garbage bag. That means a room is emptier as well as cleaner once you've left it.

✿ Instead of letting filth mount up, stagger your cleaning.

BATHROOM

✿ It's better to have one medicine chest that holds all your toiletries than to let them sprawl out lazy-girl style. Poke around for an old dental technician's chest or a mirrored wall vanity, or buy a cheap vertical cabinet in chipboard or pine and paint it gloss white or silver.

✿ Bulgy makeup bags, hair dryers, and frilly dressing gowns are the hallmarks of the beauty-school dropout. Exfoliate all fripperies.

✿ For emphasis, invest instead in three beautiful cotton towels, a richly scented square of glycerine soap, a candle (if you have a bathtub with a ledge), and a small vase of flowers. Nothing else, trust me.

✿ The smallest room in the house needn't be the dreariest. Tiny lavatories feel less stifling if there's something beautiful to stare at on the back of the door.

✿ Bathroom medicine chests, the drab little square ones that are plonked on the walls of most older apartments, need design help. Find tinted mirror glass in pale blue, mint green, or even bright red and have it cut to size to fit the inside of your medicine chest. Instantly it looks bigger and shinier in there.

✿ Give your toothbrushes star treatment by housing them in decorated Moroccan glasses.

✿ Show off a richly colored slab of soap by placing it on an ornate tile instead of a dish. You can find these tiles at vintage architectural supply stores, glass stores, and import stores that stock goodies from India, Italy, and Portugal.

BEDROOM

The kitchen might be the heart of the house, but the bedroom is the soul. Go for a feeling of clarity and intimacy. It's important that the place where you dream and face the day feels optimistic, comforting, and ordered. Guard your sanctuary against blocked spaces (overflowing laundry baskets), blocked projects (stacks of unread books), and blocked visuals (anything you can't stand the sight of has to go, negative lovers included). The bedroom is your cocoon, the most personal space in your house. This is the place where auspicious, spiritual, and sensual objects shine and fantasies find expression. Design catalogs say white beds and honey-colored floors are good taste. So are loafers. Do you even like loafers? Sleep in the colors you love, build a gypsy tent around your bed, paint the ceiling silver. Let it rock.

✿ Keep the area closest to your bed as clear as you can. Allow room for a lamp, a teacup, and a book. Nothing else! The reason hotel rooms feel so good is because there isn't a teetering stack of junk staring you in the face first thing in the morning.

✿ Find a way to conceal the clutter of work and clothes. If you have a metal clothes rail, hang four panels of silk or heavy muslin over your trove. Threaded onto thin sticks of bamboo and screwed into the ceiling, these veils will appear to float over your worldly possessions and create a sense of space visually.

✿ Invest in a stack of hard cardboard or light timber boxes for the stuff you can't get away from and don't wish to see (tax receipts, buttons, ribbons, mending). Painted a dark or neutral color and stacked neatly, these work better than see-through containers. Hatboxes work well for lingerie. Painted bamboo baskets (from Asia) are an elegant alternative to wire mesh catchalls.

✿ An old steamer trunk or wooden chest provides ample space for woolly winter sweaters and other bulky clothes. Place it at the end of your bed where it can double as a table.

✿ Keep shoes out of sight. Build a diagonal rack that can slide beneath your bed or suspend a canvas cupboard of sturdy pouches on the back of your closet door.

✿ Choose a bed base with drawers and shelves built in or with space to stash stuff underneath.

✿ Vanities, mirrored dressing tables, and built-in wall units look best with a few beautiful things but not a whole jewelry shop tipped onto them. Powder puffs, tiny picture frames, soft toys, and other sentimental stuff suffocate the eye.

✿ Jazz up the inside of your night table drawers or linen cupboard with beautiful drawer liners. Don't just stick last year's Christmas gift wrap in there. Cut balsa board to size and cover it with luxurious cotton velveteen or cabbage-rose chintz or husky plaid. A beautiful drawer inspires less mess and a feeling of secret luxury.

LIVING ROOM

I hate television. There, I've said it. The way those big black squares lob into any setting like some false oracle. The way chairs and sofas are positioned around them like iron filings around a magnet. The way the multiple functions of a lounge room are utterly subsumed by the box. If you must have a TV, do something unusual with it. Weld it onto a swinging base that sticks out from the wall at a right angle. Embed it into the wall framed with plaster. Cover the thing with an antique sarong. Don't let it just sit there!

✿ Big, chunky black stereos needn't be plonked at the center of a room either. The 1980s are over—no more need to show off that consumer power.

✿ Ditto those towering black CD holders that look like little office buildings. Despise them. Arrange your CDs like books up on your shelves, spine out at eye level.

✿ Invest in a Chinese lacquered chest to conceal your entertainment unit and videos. Under that witty urbane exterior can dwell as many Elvis movies as you like.

✿ Have fun with your bookshelf. Build a unit with

different levels and shapes and use it as a room divider (à la *Bewitched*). Paint the shelves a dramatic color to give them linear definition, or paint their interiors rich shades of bright colors to liven up the spines.

❀ Be harsh with yourself about magazines. When it comes time to move they are heavy and, unlike books, they do not age well. Clip out the articles you really need and file them. Pass the mags on to hospitals or local clinics and friends.

❀ Invest in art and design books instead of magazines. Study Eileen Grey instead of the decor glossies, or grab a great big book on art nouveau glass. Go to the source if you want to find the light of inspiration.

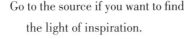

❀ Think beyond the sofa. A daybed festooned with cushions works just as well, or two big round tub chairs and a pouf. Wooden chairs with cushioned seats are easy to reupholster with snappy new fabric. Lazy girls can use upholstery tacks. Kilims, exotic bedspreads, and sari cloths look great over a lackluster couch. Beanbag chairs, flokati rugs, and vacuum-formed plastic pieces from the 1970s work best in very sparse spaces—they're more a rock-video idea than a reality.

❀ Coffee tables can be ugly little ankle-bangers and invariably stack up with cigar ash, party scraps, and phone bills. To capitalize on storage, use a trunk, a big plastic cube, or a gorgeous old low-slung desk.

❀ Drapes! Don't forget the windows. If the view is challenged, cover it with beautiful flowing muslin or groovy Marimekko-style straight blinds. If you have a nice aspect (as the rent vultures call it), frame it sensitively. The window frame itself may also give you ideas. Don't feel dictated to by a particular era. Wooden venetians can hang over an aluminum frame; café curtains can swing gaily over leadlight. Electric chili peppers and fairy lights have their place—for first-date dinners and deep depressions.

DOORS

Door frames create transitions between rooms. Plastic veils of beading look pretty when the light hits them. Vietnamese-restaurant-style bamboo curtains lend that rose-of-the-Orient style to the boudoir. Or hang an embroidered Chinese silk shawl. Gypsy Rose Lee and all that. If you are staring at a door that really bores you, strip and stain it and invest in a vintage enamel doorknob. Removing old knobs is like clipping off boring buttons. Replace knobs with a brilliant gem-colored cut glass from India or Morocco. If you have a door with old-fashioned panels, make a feature of them by painting them with bold solid colors, a bedtime story, a favorite aphorism, or a mermaid.

❀ Think about how a door has the potential to punctuate a space and accent the colors you love. Paint the door to a pale yellow room a bright cornflower blue (à la Monet at Giverny). Or wallpaper an ordinary wooden door with something bold and wonderful to contrast with an austere white room.

❀ My favorite way to use a door is to hang a dress that I love there, but don't let them accumulate—one fantastic item is an aesthetic meditation, three is clutter.

FABRIC

Some of the swankiest interiors conceal their modest origins under a swath of fabulous fabrics. A cheap chipboard table is instantly transformed by a rich damask cloth that sweeps to the floor and a heavy glass vase of white Madonna lilies. Fabric is also the obvious solution for ugly-couch syndrome. Choose fabrics that have

enough weight and visual volume to command the space and experiment with a few upholstery pins to hold your Casbah tent look in place. Go a bit Christo but don't overdo it. Furniture that's knotted at the edges with loose, floppy folds may look like it's wearing a diaper!

Find your fabric everywhere *except* the upholsterers—auction houses, small-town haberdashery stores, and flea markets are good sources for dress fabric, tassels and trims, vintage fabric, recycled bedspreads, and theater backdrops. Wash them first.

❀ Really good lengths of fabric look dramatic as a wall hanging. For the moderno pad, hang a long strip of 1970s-style geometric print fabric behind an equally bold, sexy bit of furniture.

❀ For the romantic shtick, use embroidered organza, sari silk, striped upholstery, taffeta, or batik cut and sewn on as a border to curtains, hung in tent panels around the bed, looped across the ceiling on bits of bamboo.

❀ Dress your bed with textiles—Mexican blankets, Indonesian Ikat cloth, African Kuba cloths, large-scale toile cushions.

❀ Use tablecloths to change the mood of a room—French provincial one day, white damask the next.

FUNCTION

Decorative changes really help an interior, but your house also has to work on a functional level. If the house is a machine for living, you'd better make sure your engine's working.

You don't have to buy new furniture, just rearrange the old! Usually interiors wind up staying the same as they looked the first few weeks after you moved in. Over time you grow oblivious to a poor arrangement and apathetic about the function of things. I spent a year sitting on the floor while I talked on the phone and developed a bad winter flu. All I needed was a $20 extension cord.

Dumb details help you function. List five little things that really bug you and fix them this week—the leaking tap, the dirty shower curtain, the squeaky drawer, the stiff key, the ugly light-switch covers. Use your local hardware store with confidence and definitely assemble a tool kit.

✿ Do you have enough towel racks?

✿ Is your lighting adequate? Are there enough reading lamps? Overhead lighting can be bald and uninviting, while lights placed in the extreme corners of a room and low to the floor generate warmth.

✿ Do you have enough shelving and storage space? If your coffee and bedside tables are groaning with papers, books, and magazines, the answer is no.

✿ I've said this a dozen times and I'll say it again. Find permanent homes for all the bits that make your life run—a regular place for your keys, vitamins, bills, checkbook, condoms, correspondence, sun hat, and favorite hair clips. Where are your socks right now? Do any match? More important, where is your passport?

FURNITURE

Furniture is the one thing that stops people plunging into interior design. It's so serious, so solid, and (often) so expensive. The misconception is that until you can afford a mock neoclassical sleigh bed and a gorgeous little night table with gilt rosebuds trailing down the legs, why decorate? The truth is transformation is much easier, cheaper, and closer at hand than you suspect. Repaint, recover, and, most vital of all, *remove* the unnecessary.

✿ No matter what your personal look, every wardrobe needs basics. Same with your house. Go minimal. Beds should be mostly invisible. Tables need to be simple. Sofas can, on the whole, be avoided or reinvented with great throws and cushions. Armoires need to be light and subtly integrated (pale tones work best) rather than big, dark, vertical coffins or tacky, mirrored wall units.

✿ Strangely enough, chairs are worth investing in. A beautiful little chair right next to your bed makes the best night table. A nineteenth-century Bentwood or a reproduction romantic number with carved spindly legs and faux gilt bits can be found at an auction or an antiques shop for around the same price as a round-trip ticket to Vegas ($120 to $300). Single chairs have character and history. They're poetic.

✿ Beautifully made, modern designer chairs are also great house investments. Investigate the classic office and home designs of Alvar Aalto, Charles Eames, and Knoll.

✿ Before you buy, refine your eye, attend to the proportion, solidity, elegance, and line of a piece of furniture. Study table legs with the same discerning eye that you apply to the heel on a new winter boot.

✿ If you can't afford furniture, beautiful frames and old mirrors look divine above a bed.

✿ Diana Vreeland once said, "A little bad taste is like a splash of paprika—it's hearty, it's healthy, it's physical." Sometimes it's also downright necessary. Some things—modern things like phones, computers, and stereos—can't be concealed, so let them be. If you need to, clump your utilities in one spot.

✿ Think of beautiful oddities—a weathered croquet set, a gold music stand for favorite recipes, an old birdcage to house your Spanish dictionary, a hat block for your windowsill, a brightly painted field altar from Java, a mask from Borneo, a velvet sombrero, a single, apple green Regency teacup.

✿ Auctions are great places to buy unusual pieces, but take your tape measure with you. Don't come home with a white elephant that has to be shoehorned in.

✿ More than three of anything constitutes a collection. Think of clever ways to show off your objects of obsession. An old sewing box is a good house for sunglasses, a glass-fronted cabinet can make a sculptural feature of costume jewelry, and wall-suspended plant holders look great showing off a shoe collection.

✿ Buying new should be informed by the future. Is the piece classic, well-made, and well-designed enough to sustain and delight you for the next fifteen years? Many designers and architects prefer to own one great piece instead of a room full of junk. Fabrics and color are like accessories —transient—but furniture needs to have good bones.

ART

Like electricity, art illuminates a room and gives a house a jolt of energy and warmth. Buying art can start with baby steps. Take your favorite print, varnish it with a clear bright color, and custom-frame it; already you have something with your own touch to put on the walls. Rummage through secondhand stores in the country for old paintings—weird portraits of nameless locals, seascapes, favorite pets, and patron saints have a quirky cachet. Get out to small artist-run galleries on the weekends. Look at new art for at least a month of Sundays and you will start to hone your own tastes and sensibilities.

When artists are starting up they'll sell their work for the price of two pairs of shoes (my favorite economic yardstick), but that isn't the point. The point of buying art is loving it.

Because art is shrouded in cultural snobbery and intellectual mystery and chronicled in rather opaque glossy magazines, it's easy to be put off. Don't be. The best collectors in the world started off very small indeed. My girlfriend Leanne began her now massive collection with four telephone doodles by a famous painter. No one wanted these squibs at auction and Leanne got them for a song. Because she started in miniature, the theme of small works stayed with her, and now she rarely buys a piece that doesn't fit into a small valise. Her walls are a visual poem of moody seascapes painted in oil on board, screenprinted bare-branched trees, tender watercolors, arresting black-and-white photographs, and, in the bedroom, twenty-five different works depicting exotic flowers. What brings her collection together visually is its jewel-like scale. Visiting her house makes the soul sing.

LIGHT

Pretty light fittings perk up a ceiling and, like pillow-cases, they are something you see virtually every day. Secondhand stores have beautiful pendant lights made from glass or porcelain that soften the light in a room. Rice-paper lamp shades look best in bright colors. Asian import stores are often good places to find silk shades and inexpensive hand-painted paper lanterns. If you're lucky enough to have wall fixtures for lights, there are lots of great old pieces designed to dangle. Tiny Thai silk shades in rich colors give

you that Morocco 1940s nightclub feeling. Mini chandelier fittings glitter like earrings and modern fixtures in organic shapes look like glowing sculptures. Standing lamps, like dresses, can be completely reinvented.

If you can sew a seam, you can re-cover a lamp shade. I took three yards of tulle and a fistful of silk roses and even with big, fat, clumsy stitches managed to bunch, ruche, and smunch the net and flowers to my shade in a way that wound up looking positively *My Fair Lady*. If you hate needlework, then all you need is paper, glue, and a little patience. Take a conventional 1960s shade, strip it down to the wire frame, and rehang with sheer, sequined silk. Or re-cover an existing shade with a different fabric (cotton velvet, designer fabric, watered taffeta) using glue.

DESIGN SHORTCUTS

COLOR YOUR WORLD

Color is the fastest way to change a room. A room without exceptional daylight may as well get painted a bright, rich color; then at least it shines in the evening. A rich blue with plenty of violet tones bordered with white gloss suits an apartment near the sea, a golden dandelion-orange for a living room catches the last rays of afternoon sun and enflames them, lavender or pale lilac walls add tranquility to a meditation space.

✿ Color looks best where you don't expect it. Kitchen cupboards that have a solid geometric shape—say, big and square or tall and vertical—are the perfect place to play with contrasting hues. Paint the outer edges of the shelving buttercup yellow and the inside a deep buttery saffron; offset the look with a set of bright blue plates or assembled willow-patterned teacups. Try the same combinations in lipstick red and ivory, lime green and ultramarine blue, or delicate midtones of dusty rose, Naples yellow, parchment, and terra-cotta for that South of France feel.

✿ Van Gogh wasn't really surrounded by electric blue bedposts and bright red rattan chairs, he just imagined it that way. Consult art books for ideas on how to redecorate with color. Notice how Bonnard used a hundred shades of flesh pink and wild lilac; dig the gentle creamy tones in Matisse's paintings of Nice. If you can't find a paint to match your artistic dream, take your books to the paint shop.

✿ Flowers are the most mobile decor around. Buy five bunches of the same flower for a jolt of daffodil yellow or peony red. Put lavender next to your bed for sweeter dreams (lavender relaxes the central nervous system) and is an elegant offset to white linen. Buy vases that suit the colors of your favorite flowers. Baby Campari bottles adorned with single stems look pretty along a windowsill.

ROOM DIVIDERS

✿ Standing screens can create beautiful intervals in a room, especially a bedroom. They're easily re-covered using thumbtacks; you can change the fabric to suit the seasons.

✿ Feature walls are a groovy idea from the 1950s. They float a square of color or wallpaper on a single wall. The contrast this creates works best in a relatively sparse interior. The same principle can be applied to shelving.

✿ A diaphanous fall of muslin looped onto a stick of bamboo works like a veil in place of a proper doorway. This is especially gorgeous in a well-lit room.

WALLPAPER

Wallpaper died out in the 1980s, replaced by the minimalist glamour of tiny glass tiles, stainless steel, and polished plaster. Now wallpaper is back in all its dainty, textural, whimsical, eccentric, and versatile splendor. Wallpaper is a great catalyst for design ideas. Use wallpaper for a mural effect. Paper the entire wall, from floor to ceiling, behind your bed with darting swallows, willow trees, or graphic cherry blossoms. Paint the rest of the room a complementarybut not traditionally matching color.

Light the wall from the side and below for maximum emphasis. Wallpaper demands less furniture and a good sense of scale, but the results are fun and always original. Paper a place you wouldn't think of. The bathroom ceiling is a good place to start. Betsey Johnson covered the ceiling of her entire New York apartment in cabbage-rose-print wallpaper and then lacquered a sheer wash of color over the lot. The effect is like living in a surrealist flower shop. Paper something small in your house—a spice rack, bookshelves, or a window seat—and create color accents with your upholstery and rugs. If you are renting and can't go the whole hog, frame your favorite wallpaper print and hang it up.

STYLE WARS

Like fashion, there are definite looks for houses. You see some girls walking down the street with caramel-colored boot-cut pants and magenta gerbera daisies and you can picture their living room straight away—sparse, clean, low fat. The girl with the trailing slip and a single diamante hoop earring probably finger-painted her futon base and has a goldfish bowl full of pink feathers on her kitchen table. But stereotypes are limited. The notion that owning one black leather Corbusier chair means your whole house has to be painted lab-coat white and nothing but 1960s glass can serve as ornamentation is so literal. In the first place few people can afford a total look, and those who can deserve a slap. Diversify.

Modernism was born to liberate human beings from the overstuffed, stodgy conformity of the Victorian age. Of course, one set of sins was quickly surpassed by another, and today the Bauhaus blueprint has become a diluted generic. Furniture and design outlets provide about five different theme-park styles. Welcome to Italian Leather Lounge World, Chunky Country Blond Wood World, Maharaja Tacky Tasseled Cushion World, Ye Olde Country Ruffle Realm, and 1970s Revival Wood-Grain and Chocolate Brown Leatherland. Heavens, no! To create a nongeneric atmosphere, you have to create your own decor character. Try metallic wallpaper on the ceiling, a jukebox in your bedroom, or a forest of violins pinned to the wall like a corsage. Wheel in the chaise lounge and get fast and loose with the pigment. Burn all furniture catalogs and don't believe that a big white bed makes modern couples happier. Mismatch.

HANDYWOMAN

Get a Grip

The day I found myself trying to whack a three-inch nail into a Masonite wall using the heel of a Stephane Kelian platform shoe, I had an epiphany—every woman should own a hammer. Not just a hammer but also a power drill, screwdrivers, a solid set of pliers, and a wrench.

A basic household toolbox opens up your world. It means not having to wait around for someone else to hang a mirror, fix a screen, or tighten a door hinge. A respectable car needs a manual, maps, a flashlight, and a repair kit, and your handbag should hold a Swiss army knife, a tape measure, a mobile phone, and a mini maglite. With those tools, no matter where you are you can see what you're doing, know where you're going, take the measure of what you need, and be able to open a bottle of wine in the middle of nowhere. Nothing feels better than being able to say, "I can handle this."

ANTIDOTES TO DITZY DEPENDENCY

Being handy is a matter of following simple imperatives—a combination of common sense and practical get-down-on-your-hands-and-knees experience.

✿ Adopt the physician's creed: Do no harm. There's no sense in trying to take apart a bathroom faucet if you can't tell a washer from a valve seat. A botched job may seriously complicate the plumber's task and turn your attempt at thrift into a nasty surprise.

✿ Be realistic. Very intelligent people sometimes believe they can figure out anything, given the inclination. But electrical wiring is not logic or psychology. Learn how. Don't try to wing it.

✿ Find a friend at your hardware store or home supply outlet. The staff in these places are great resources for selecting the right tools and materials for your project, and the good ones will give you tips on doing the job. If you're out to pick an expert's brain, plan your visit for a weekday. (Large discount centers can be problematic on weekends, when they may staff up with less helpful part-timers.)

✿ Read the directions. They may be written in pidgin, but the directions for the tool, adhesive, or replacement part can keep you out of trouble. Ditto diagram.

✿ Own a real toolbox. You need more than the few tools you stuff into your junk drawer. Get yourself a divided toolbox and start filling it with real tools. Don't let anyone sell you a "lady's tool kit." Assemble a basic toolbox like the one given on the facing page, and you'll be equipped to tackle just about anything that needs fixing.

UTILITY SHUTOFFS

As part of your basic training for emergencies, you need to find out where your utility shutoffs are located.

Electric. Inside the house, near where the main power line enters, you'll find an electrical panel. This wall box contains the main shutoff that will turn off all power in the house at once. Open the panel and you'll see rows of either fuses or circuit breakers, which function as safety devices that prevent the electrical circuits from overloading or shorting and igniting. Before you attempt any electrical repairs, you must switch off the appropriate circuit breaker or remove the appropriate fuse, or turn off the main electrical switch.

Water. The water shutoff may be found inside or outside the house, usually near the entry point of the pipe to the house. The valve handle usually turns clockwise to shut off. Each sink or appliance may have its own shutoff, usually located on the feeder pipe beneath the sink, or behind appliances where they connect to the water.

Gas. Next to the gas meter is a pipe that feeds gas into the house. The shutoff valve is located on that pipe. A slot on top of

The Basic Toolbox

For the average handywoman, these basic tools can handle most emergencies:

Claw hammer. The universal adjusting tool, hammers come in several varieties, differentiated by weight and function. This one is designed to pound in and pull out nails. Get a sixteen-ounce hammer—a little tack hammer is not enough for many jobs.

Nail set. Used with a hammer to conceal nail heads by driving them below the surface of the wood. The hole can then be filled with wood putty.

Nails and screws. Both come in several types and sizes. Get common nails (this is a type of nail) or box nails for general use, and finishing nails for woodwork and cabinets. Finishing nails have almost no head; the other two have fairly broad heads that stop the nail at the wood's surface. Screws give greater holding power than nails. The head of the screw is slotted to accept the screwdriver—most common are the straight slot (a single groove across the diameter) and the Phillips (two grooves that form a cross in the center of the head). To avoid splitting the wood, drill a pilot hole (slightly smaller in diameter than the screw or nail), especially when you're using large nails or screws. Screws go in easier when you put wax or paraffin on the threads.

Screwdrivers. Get a standard (straight) tip and a Phillips. You probably need more than one of each: a shorter one for working in close quarters and a long-bladed one for turning power. The size of the tip is also important: It should fit tightly into the grooves in the screw.

Crosscut saw. Most versatile of the several varieties of wood saws.

Three-eighth-inch power drill. It can be cordless or plug-in, variable speed or fixed. Your choice depends upon budget and convenience. Comes with attachments for sanding and buffing.

Carpenter's level. Used to determine if a surface (shelving, appliance, drapery rod) is level.

Adjustable wrench. Basically, a handle with jaws on the end. The lower jaw can be moved up and down to tighten the jaws over the head of a bolt or nut.

Slip-joint pliers. The jaws have only two open positions, with teeth or serrations for grabbing, holding, and turning things.

Utility knife. For cutting almost anything. A retractable blade is housed in a handle that also holds spare blades.

Metal, retracting tape measure.

Hacksaw. Cuts through metal—tubing, nail heads, and the like.

Sandpaper. Comes in different grades designed to handle everything from rough surfaces to final finishing.

Toilet plunger. A rubber cup or bell at the end of a shaft that acts as a suction cup to dislodge blockages in plumbing lines.

Drain auger. For unplugging plumbing clogs. A long, flexible, metal tube with a corkscrew tip is forced through the pipe to find and dislodge the blockage.

Toilet auger. Similar to the drain auger, designed to deal with toilet blockages.

Work gloves (heavy cloth or deerskin) and rubber gloves.

The soundtrack from *The Good, the Bad, and the Ugly*.

the valve is in a vertical position when the gas is on. This valve must be turned with a wrench until the slot is parallel to the ground to turn off the gas.

REPAIRS 101

What follows are some very basic repairs and improvements that are within the grasp of everyone. When you're ready, there are plenty of sources—books, hardware stores, and suppliers—to take you beyond these.

STOPPED-UP DRAINS

If several drains are backing up at the same time, the problem is probably located in the main line, and there is little you can do except call a plumber. But if a lone drain is clogged in the kitchen or bathroom, here's what you can do.

1. Your first line of attack is the plunger. The plunger is a clever device that uses water as a battering ram, and then uses suction to pull at the blockage. This means that you must have a plunger with a bell that fits completely over the drain, and it must form a tight seal. Water must be confined to the drainpipe, so you also must plug all other outlets, such as overflow drains (a damp cloth will work).

First run enough water into the sink to cover the bell of the plunger. Hold the plunger at a slight angle as you put it in the water (so air bubbles don't get trapped), and place it over the drain. Holding the plunger upright, push it down as far as it will go, then pull up to restore the cup to its original position. When you push down, water surges up the pipe into the blockage. Pull up and suction pulls at the clog. Do this vigorously for ten to twenty strokes. If necessary, repeat two or three times until the water flows freely.

2. If the plunger doesn't fix the clog, move to the next, messier, level. The drainpipe beneath the sink has a U-shaped bend in it, called a trap. At the bottom of the U is a clean-out—an entryway into the pipe—which is stopped up with a clean-out plug, usually round or pentagonal, that screws into the clean-out. Place a container under the trap to catch the water, and unscrew the plug with a wrench. As the plug loosens, there will be drips and spurts, so don't get your face too near. Let the water run out, then try to find and clear the blockage, using (gloved) fingers or a coat hanger.

3. If that doesn't work, get your drain auger. Run it through the clean-out hole and alternately push and pull while turning the handle clockwise. If this doesn't get rid of the blockage, bring in the plumber. Hey, you tried.

For kitchen drains, be sure to plug or disable any other drains connected to the sink (double sinks, appliances, overflows), before using a plunger. Plungers don't work with garbage disposals, so start with step 2.

BATHROOM DRAINS

Most sinks have a built-in stopper, which must be removed before you tackle the drain. You do this in one of two ways.

First, look under the sink. If you see two metal rods that are connected in an L-shape (one rod comes straight down from the back of the sink; the other comes out from the drainpipe and is roughly parallel to the floor), you have found the control for the stopper. Remove the nut that connects the two rods, and remove the stopper.

If there is no L under the sink, simply pull the stopper up and out. You may need to twist it a bit to release it.

STOPPED-UP TOILET

Girly accoutrements (like Q-tips, cotton balls, tampons, and rejected love letters) tossed blithely into the bowl can result in a major blockage down in the S-bend of your toilet. Clearing it out ranks among the messiest jobs for the handywoman, but depending on what's wedged down there, it's also pretty simple. Before you do anything, turn off the shutoff valve near the base of the toilet, then follow these steps.

First, try a plunger. With the toilet bowl half filled with water, place the plunger over the outflow (where the flushed water leaves the bowl). Push down (to force the water in the pipe forward), then bring the plunger back to its original position (still covering the outflow). Do this forcefully for eight to twelve repetitions. If too much of the water has drained out of the bowl, add water. If it runs, you're done. If not, repeat another time or two. If this doesn't free the blockage, try the next step.

Insert the toilet auger (plumber's snake) into the outflow, and turn the handle until the auger catches on the clog. Either pull out the clog, or pull back and forth on the auger to break it up. If nothing budges, don't push the obstructing object deeper into the bowl. The moment you remember someone tossing a paperweight into your toilet at your last cocktail party is the moment you call the plumber. Some jobs are too vile and too heavy even for the handywoman.

RUNNING TOILET

The never-ending flush is a simple repair that's more difficult to describe than it is to demonstrate. If you understand what goes on inside the toilet tank, the problem will be easier to find and fix.

Take off the top of the tank and you'll see that the flush handle is attached to a lift arm inside. When you flush, the lift arm rises, and lifts a rubber stopper (attached to the arm by chain, wire, or rod) off its seat, allowing water to run out of the tank and into the toilet. To replenish the supply, there is a water valve that sits atop a pipe or post that's almost as high as the top of the tank. Attached to this valve is a long rod (a lever arm or float arm) that has a large ball on the other end. The ball floats on top of the water. As water runs out, the ball drops, and the lever arm opens the water valve. When the tank empties, the stopper drops back into place, the tank begins to fill, and the ball rises with the water until the lever arm reaches the point where it closes the water valve.

The likeliest sources of problems are stoppers that don't seat properly, and lever arms that don't shut off the water. An old, deteriorated stopper will allow water to seep through and needs to be replaced. If the stopper is slightly off center when it closes, the connection to the lift arm is probably too short or at an angle. Adjust the connection by letting out the chain or by placing it in a different hole on the lift arm. Also check the connection between the flush handle and the lift arm; if it's loose or binding, adjust the nut that holds that assembly together. You can adjust the flow of water by bending the float arm until the water valve shuts off properly.

If none of these things works (it's all quite experimental), you can buy a kit to replace all the inner workings of the tank. Installation is fairly simple.

VIBRATING WASHING MACHINE

Household physics decree: That which shakes has lost its balance. Most appliances have little feet (screws, actually) at each corner; by turning the appropriate screw, you can raise or lower one corner of the machine, or the whole appliance. If your machine is doing a violent bossa nova, adjust the washer's height by turning these little feet. (You may have to support the appliance with blocks to make it easier to adjust the feet.) Use a carpenter's level to determine when it's level, then tighten the lock nut on the feet.

POWER FAILURE

If your entire house goes dark, check your neighbors. If they're blacked out too, there's nothing you can do but wait for the power company.

If a portion of your house goes dark, you may have temporary overload—several power-hungry appliances may have kicked on at the same time—or it may indicate something more serious. Here's how to find out.

1. Look for frayed electrical cords, defective plugs, or smoke or black smudges that single out a defective light or appliance. Repair, replace, or disconnect. A circuit can also overheat if there are too many appliances running at the same time. Try disconnecting or moving a power-eater to another circuit.

Check the fuse box or circuit breakers. If you have a fuse box, look in the glass "windows" of the fuses. A scorch mark or a strip of broken metal means the fuse has blown. Replace the fuse. If you have circuit breakers, find the switch that has tripped into the OFF position, and return it to ON. If the power stays on, you've found the problem.

2. If you didn't find anything in step 1, or if the power goes off immediately, turn off all wall switches and unplug lights and appliances in the affected area. Replace the fuse or reset the circuit breaker. If the fuse blows immediately or the circuit breaker trips off again, you may have a short circuit in the wiring. Call an electrician. If the power stays on, go to step 3.

3. Turn one of the wall switches back on. If that doesn't plunge you into darkness, continue turning on wall switches one by one. If a wall switch blows the power, you may have a short circuit. Call an electrician. If wall switches don't kill the power, test the lamps and appliances one at a time until you turn up the culprit. If power dies as soon as you plug the culprit in, the cord should be replaced. If it doesn't die till you turn it on, the switch may be the problem, or that unit may be one too many for the circuit. Find out by moving it to a different circuit.

MAKING A FIRE

A fireplace needs to be clean of ash and have a chimney flue that's open and unobstructed by soot. (Chimney fires are dangerous and can be avoided with the help of an annual cleaning by a trained chimney sweep.) Clear out the ash, but leave a little of it banked up at the sides and rear of the fireplace. Make a bed of scrunched-up newspaper, topped with small pieces of dry wood and twigs (fatwood is an even better choice, because it burns hotter). Now stack three logs across the andirons or cradled in the grate, making sure that air can circulate around them. If your fireplace doesn't have either, place larger pieces of dry wood in a tent shape, spaced far enough apart that they don't smother the flame. Light the newspaper. In five to ten minutes the logs should sustain their own cheery flame.

FIXING A FLAT

There are two ways to fix a flat. One is very easy, and the other not so easy because directions vary from car to car.

The recommended method is to join AAA (the American Automobile Association). For a modest annual membership fee (around $40), you get free emergency road service for any car trouble, whether it's changing a flat tire (or charging your battery, bringing gas, or towing you to a station).

If you don't belong to AAA, then keep your owner's manual handy. The not-so-easy method is to get out your jack, your lug wrench, and your spare, and follow the manufacturer's directions in the manual.

A word of warning: the spare tire in your trunk is probably not a full-size tire. Most manufactures supply what is called a "donut"—a small expedient to be used only until you can replace it with a regular tire. It shouldn't be driven more than 50 miles at a time and is definitely not intended for high-speed driving.

FINDING A STUD

If you're going to hang a heavy mirror or attach a shelf, it's best to fix your hanger or bolt into a stud—the vertical timber that braces most walls. Lazy girls can find a stud by purchasing a stud finder from the hardware store. No, this is not a device that Joan Collins uses in rodeos and dimly lit wine bars. It's a battery-operated handheld device that uses magnetism to seek out the nails that hold the sheetrock to the stud. Not surprisingly, a stud finder lights up when a stud is found (wouldn't you?).

A less expensive alternative is the "poltergeist" method. Gently knock along the surface of the wall. The wall will sound solid when there is a stud behind it; where there is no stud, it sounds hollow. Drive a thin nail into the wall where you suspect the stud to be lurking. If it's not there, try an inch to either side. (Avoid this method where you might encounter plumbing or electrical wires.) Studs may also be sniffed out by locating the nail holes in the baseboards where the wall meets the floor.

HANGING PICTURES

Your friend at the hardware store will want an idea of the weight to be hung before making recommendations. Lightweight objects (two to ten pounds) can be hung using a standard picture hanger. For medium weights, a molly bolt or butterfly bolt can be used in a hollow wall. You should probably anchor heavy items into a wall stud with a nail or a screw. Start by drilling a hole slightly smaller in diameter than the fastener. Tip: Wear goggles to protect your baby blues from cement dust, splinters, and the like.

PAINTING A ROOM

Painting is a lot like sewing in that it is a skill of sequence. Rush any part of the job and the whole result will suffer. It pays to be patient and mellow at every stage. Play music you love and take long European-style lunch breaks. View each stroke of the roller as a meditation. Do wear a mask if you are working with plastic paints: They are toxic to lungs, eyes, and skin.

Choose your paint according to the room's function and the texture you desire. A little bit of gloss adds light to a room; too much and we're talking 1960s hair salon. Milk paints and nontoxic paints are worth considering if you suffer from allergies or respiratory problems, or have small children. If you are convinced you want *all-white* rooms, consider a subtle tint. White with a hint of mint cools a room, a touch of lavender calms a room, and a flush of pink adds warmth. Choose your color based not only on your decor but also on the light levels. Bright sunlight dances on even the palest hint of color.

There *is* a secret to painting. Read on.

Materials Get a two-inch brush for trim and a tapered sash brush for windows. All-purpose bristles are fine. Rollers with wire frames are preferred. Buy a roller with a threaded end so you can attach an extension for doing ceilings. Buy the best paint you can afford—it's easier to work with, lasts longer, and is more washable (scrub your walls and your bargain paint may wash away with the dirt). For economy, you may want to use an inexpensive primer for the first coat, and a premium paint for the final coat.

When the job is done, take special care of your materials. Brushes and rollers can rise again if they're rinsed well.

Preparation Sometimes preparing to paint is more time-consuming than painting itself. But it'll make the job easier in the long run.

1. Remove pictures, picture hooks, curtains, and brackets from walls. Remove loose paint and plaster, and patch holes.

2. Remove or cover doorknobs, electrical switch plates, and light fixtures. Plastic sandwich bags come in handy. Slip one over a doorknob and tape it into place. Cover radiators, thermostats, and woodwork with plastic sheeting or masking tape. Move furniture and rugs into the center of the room and cover with a drop cloth.

3. Wash walls to get rid of accumulated grime, grease, mildew, and insect remains (yuck). Prime any repairs.

4. Mix your paint. If paint has been sitting for over a week, turn the can upside down for a day or two before opening. To avoid spills, pour some paint off into a separate container. Stir the remaining paint with a wooden paddle until it's well mixed, then gradually add back the paint you've removed and stir until well mixed. Punch a couple of nail holes in the rim so paint drains back into the can rather than running over the edge.

Sequence Work from top to bottom, starting with the ceiling, then the molding, walls, windows, and, lastly, the baseboards and door.

1. Paint across the width of the ceiling squares that are roughly one yard on each side. If you're using a roller, apply paint as a series of connected W's, then fill them in by running the roller across the pattern. Start by pushing the roller away from you (a roller loaded with paint can spritz when put under pressure). Keep a rag handy—dampened with water if you're using latex paint, or paint thinner for alkyds—and clean as you go.

2. Paint the ceiling molding next.

3. Then paint the wall. Start at the ceiling and paint down to the baseboard, working in sections that are about three feet wide. Use a brush to paint in the corners while the wall is still wet, so you can blend brush strokes into the paint from the roller.

4. Windows demand their own sequence. Do sashes first. Raise the inner (bottom) sash and lower the outer (top) sash. Paint the inner sash completely, and paint the exposed surface of the outer sash. Return sashes to their proper positions, but slightly open. Paint the remainder of the outer sash, then do the frame and the sill. When these are dry, paint the inside channels (the surfaces that hold the window in place). Wipe paint drips off the glass, or razor-blade them off once the paint is dry.

5. Paint doors and baseboards last.

The second coat If there are drips or splotches in your first coat, sand them back. The second coat is the one you have to live with, so apply it with concentration and finesse, especially when painting the baseboards. When you're done, try to get out of the house (even the least-toxic paints can irritate skin and lungs). Avoid sleeping in the freshly painted room for at least twenty-four hours.

UNSQUEAK YOUR DOORS

Here's one last facile but extremely handy handywoman skill. If you feel like you're living with Lurch, take a can of WD-40 and squirt your hinges. Super simple, super fast.

BIG   X-SMALL   YOUR SIZE

BIGGER   BIG   DAINTY

See confusing staff for nails & macho stuff..

HEAVY DUTY UNDER COAT

SISSY PASTELS

CAN YOU CARRY THIS LITTLE LADY?

FOURTEEN RULES FOR RENOVATION

Whether you rent or own, the urge to fix the place up a little is a natural one. To approach renovating intelligently, you need a calculator first and a stack of sexy decor magazines second. Knowing exactly how much a job will cost in terms of materials, time, and labor will help you plan your attack. The worst thing you can do with a renovation is get knee-deep in cement dust and then run out of funds, available tradespeople, and time. Renovation is not something to nibble at. Chomp in big time and chew like hell.

1. Plan well. Don't be rushed while you gather as much information and as many quotes as you need. Good advice will save you headaches and money later. Outside help can be horribly confusing. "Minimal," your ex-lover is screaming; "Rococo meets Yucatan chunky plaster," chimes in your best friend; "Overdrawn," says the bank manager.

2. Don't be daunted. The worst mistake a female property owner or first-time renovator can make is to lose control over her own space. Spend time in the space to really work out what you want. Make drawings if you have to. Carry magazine clippings, sketches, fabric swatches, paint samples, and even arty postcards with you as reminders of what you want and start to build your vision. No matter how cheap your renovation or how basic, know that *you* are central to the proceedings, and your choices—from the waste drain to the plaster finish—are your own.

3. Do it fast. Once you know what you want, move quickly. Moving in is messy and disorienting; why make a mess twice? When you move into a place you're full of big ideas and handywoman fantasies. Once the boxes are unpacked, painting and even minor structural change pose problems.

4. Learn about materials so you know what to ask for and to be environmentally responsible. Is your timber from a renewable forest? Are your paints too toxic? If you order wood, will it arrive dressed or raw?

5. Don't forget to express your creativity. Renovation contributes to the value of your property, but it is also about creating a place you really love. If you want pistachio walls, go for it.

6. Do as much as you can yourself. Specialized jobs like plumbing, wiring, complex carpentry, and tiling may be better served by professionals, but once you've experienced a tribe of mucho macho tradesmen you will *want* to do it yourself!

7. Use licensed carpenters and get a guarantee up front. Check the credentials and history of a company, go and inspect their previous jobs if necessary, pay for work only after it is finished, and get an exact quote in writing before any work commences.

8. Measure the cost of tradesmen against the standard of their work. Better to have someone fast and excellent than shoddy and cheap. If you have to breathe down their necks to check on the materials they are using (right down to the nails), do it! Scrimping on materials may take a little off the bill but cost you a lot more in the long run.

9. Allow for renovations to go over budget. Most jobs take twice as long as quoted and go over budget by 30 to 40 percent. Keep a kitty for your expenses that's broad and staggered ahead so as not to eat into your living expenses. The same goes for the materials you choose. Whatever you decide, just be sure to budget for a nice pillowcase and three new towels—all the equipment you'll need for hot baths and tears before bedtime.

10. Allow for trauma. The stress of renovating is up there with death and bad haircuts. It's the thing that breaks up marriages and warps personalities. Why? Because it is incredibly expensive and almost impossible to get right the first time. *Nothing* is

delivered on time; tradesmen can be rude, threatening, ambiguous, incompetent. Everyone is an expert when it comes to renovation, and it's hard to stick to your own plan. Maintain a siege mentality.

11. Allow for damage. The tiler says don't touch the bathroom floor for ten days. The plumber arrives on the eleventh day and scrapes the toilet bowl across it with a masterful arc. "Sorry, honey," he says huskily, "you can't make an omelette without breaking eggs!" Okay, so you can't ask carpenters to tiptoe around like Zen gardeners. You can and should wield a camera, though.

12. Be there—as much as you can! Giving a key to tradesmen while you go to work poses not only security problems but also the chance that you will sustain damage or a poor job. Without the constant vigilant eye of a trained builder supervising the job, you are the foreman responsible for any work that is commissioned. You need to be just as tough.

13. Ask questions. Nothing exists until you ask about it, and many vital details fall between the cracks if you don't press for answers, figures, dimensions, and material samples. From wood beading to spray varnish, if you don't ask for it, you probably won't get it. I didn't.

14. Don't forget the basics. It is depressing to live in more squalor after renovating than before. Spend money on solid basic amenities: taps that work, a good heater, and somewhere to hang your clothes. The Venetian glass chandelier can come later.

MONEY

Less Stress, More Lettuce

It's easy to feel like money is a matter of luck. Some people are born into money, some seem always to be able to attract great tides of cash, and others are clever at making a little money go a long, long way. Despite all the fairy tales about mysterious benefactors and pots of gold at the end of the rainbow, money has little to do with magic; it's almost wholly a matter of discipline and foresight. Barbara Hutton, the heiress to the Woolworth fortune, had today's equivalent of billions during her lifetime. She spent it like water, investing badly and squandering her wealth on men. Barbara was born rich but lost her bundle fast.

Money preoccupies our thoughts much of our adult lives; it can fire ambition, corrupt an ideal, and make or break a marriage or friendship. Money may be used for great good or blown on indulgences and addictions. There is no getting away from the reality of money. Get tight fisted and angry about money and it tends to flee; get organized and clear headed and it starts to keep pace with your plans and aims.

Some lucky women are raised to be sensible about money and others have to learn the hard way. Personally, I've been scorched many times by extravagance, credit-card debt, and the inability to plan beyond whatever is in my pocket. Because money is a finite resource (until the next paycheck), you have to get the most out of it. To do that you need tools, guidelines, and a budget that fits with your goals. Although it's often a taboo subject (too crass, grubby, or divisive), money needs to be discussed—especially between women. You may find that a friend who dresses well is secretly crushed by credit-card debt; you may discover another friend who can teach you how to create a savings plan in a matter of minutes.

Creating a healthy relationship with money means being able to regard it as an ally, rather than the enemy. For years I viewed money as a provider of luxuries, a godsend to get me out of a tight jam, and a source of incredible stress. Obviously, this is a pretty narrow viewpoint. Without a plan or a budget, I wasted a lot of money over the years, but there is no point crying over spilt Chanel No. 5. If you are bad with money you simply need to change your ways. Pronto. If you are in debt you need to pay it off, and not accrue more while you are doing so.

Good money habits feel hideously constraining at first—what do you mean, no more bath oil, taxis, Italian shoes for six months?—but maintaining a lifestyle in which you deny yourself nothing and live on credit is, ultimately, a far greater loss of freedom. The consolation of getting out of debt, establishing a modest little savings plan, and living on a budget is that you can start, perhaps for the first time in your life, to see money as a positive force. If you have a goal that is small (buying a sewing machine) or large (buying property) then becoming financially solvent brings you closer to it. Yes, some people do win the lottery and some people actually marry billionaires (with bad haircuts), but neither windfall can be viewed as a viable financial plan. If you want something to happen, the best way is to make it happen yourself.

MONEY ATTITUDE

Money attitudes go deep. They start in childhood, they percolate through friendships, they are informed by our partners, and they have the power to make life seem expansive or futile. We all have our own powerful internal monologues about money and what we fear often comes to pass. We concentrate on scarcity and remain broke, we spend maniacally and fail to build security, or we try to control every cent and end up with rigid, shrunken spirits. Deluded notions that money is unclean, unfeminine, men's business, someone else's destiny, or just too damn hard hold a lot of women back from having a sensible, prosperous, and enjoyable relationship with money.

Like sexual power, money is something we need to be sure of and calm with. Your confidence increases each time you control the urge to give away your power by overspending, or you keep a cool hand dealing with large sums, or resist the panic that accompanies basic financial choices. Learning to put money in reserve (in savings, a retirement fund, or investments) helps build your composure. Talking openly about money and actively studying the market increases your knowledge and confidence. And facing your debts and diligently reducing them gives back your dignity and self-determination.

Controlling money instead of having it control you is a radical step toward independence, and it takes a radically different mind-set. For years I went around saying, "I'll never have money, so why worry about it?" I thought it was charming and eccentric to pay bills late, be perpetually improvising my income, and at tax time, throwing two dainty hands in the air. It was just irresponsible. A few years later, when I needed a bank loan, this flaky period of my money history came back to bite me on the ass. The bank manager wanted to know *everything* (demanding tax returns, receipts, bank statements, credit-rating documentation, and group certificates), and I had to learn fast and move faster.

Having a positive attitude toward money is probably as important as being able to earn it. Actually, it's more important. A healthy outlook is what makes all the other constructive steps possible. A positive belief in abundance takes courage but also provides invaluable ammunition for survival: Life is incredibly expensive, good jobs are scarce, and college loans send you out into the world with a crippling debt. So stop telling yourself you are "bad with money" and simply get smarter. Don't wait until you have funds to decide how you'll deal with them. Hopefully after setting up a simple budget, planning a debt strategy, boning up on basic money terms, and paying at least the minimum due on your bills on

time, you will be able to look yourself in the eye and say, "I'm not bad with money, I'm good and getting better. I know how to look after myself."

SIXTEEN MONEY RULES

Obviously a course on money goes way beyond the purview of this book, which gives only the very, very basics of money management. For more detailed information about investment, read Susannah Goodman's *Girls Just Want to Have Funds* and *The 9 Steps to Financial Freedom* by Suze Orman. For clarity and deliverance on matters of real estate, taxes, and estate planning, seek out *Money 101* by Debra Wishik Englander.

Sounds like sexy reading, huh? Actually, it is. Given all the time we devote to dissecting relationships, a night spent home reading about stocks, bonds, and interest rates strikes an empowering balance.

Equality is a fiscal issue. Real-life feminism starts at the bank.

1. Budget

Budgeting doesn't have to demand a diet of minute noodles and cornflakes. What it means is balancing what you earn against what you owe (and spend) and making sure that your credit (assets, income, bank balance) exceeds your debit (living expenses, credit-card debts, loans, health insurance, car payments, and so on). A

QUIZ:
Test Your Money Smarts

To get some control over your spending habits, first take a look at your relationship to money.

1. Have you ever taken out a new credit card when your other cards were maxed?

2. Do you shop like crazy using plastic in order not to feel "poor"?

3. Do you refuse to open any envelope that even looks like a bill or a bank or credit-card statement until the last possible moment?

4. Do you lose track of what you spend daily, weekly, monthly?

5. Do you squeeze every dollar until the eagle grins only to find yourself putting more energy into stashing cash than earning it?

6. Do you obsess about being broke but refuse to demand a raise?

7. Are the interest rates and fees charged by your bank, student loan office, or credit-card companies too complicated to bother with?

8. Do you "forget" to balance your checkbook against your bank statement?

Obviously, a run of "yes" answers suggests that an attitude adjustment might be in your horoscope. But this needn't be dire. The solution, as explained in this chapter, is a lot simpler than you imagine.

budget gives you the security of knowing exactly what you have in reserve and how much is really available to spend. If you have never managed your money before, it can be tough for the first few months, but if you want to regain control of your life, you don't have a choice.

2. Balance the books

The best way to build a budget is to compare your monthly expenditures to your income. First gather together all your receipts, bank statements, bills, and invoices. Don't worry if this material is in disarray (setting up a home office is my next subject). If you lack a decent backlog of receipts, dash out and buy a simple office spike and start impaling every cab receipt, dress purchase, and supermarket tape that you can. Do this daily and you have instant chronology. In the meantime use your credit-card statements and check stubs to paint a portrait of your shopping habits. On a blank sheet of paper draw up two columns for the month: INCOME and EXPENSES. Divide the expenses into FIXED and DISCRETIONARY (or VARIABLE). Your lists should look something like the one on the facing page.

When you have listed all your expenses and all your income, add them both up. Once you subtract primary expenses from your income, your enthusiasm may fade as you realize how little is left for the good things of life. But take heart—your budget (over time) will lift you out of debt and put an end to deprivation.

When expenses exceed income (and they usually

My Monthly Budget

INCOME

SALARY (BEFORE TAXES) _____
BONUS _____
OVERTIME _____
NONTAXED INCOME _____
INVESTMENT INCOME (RENTS, DIVIDENDS, ETC.) _____
INTEREST ON BANK ACCOUNTS _____
TAX REFUNDS _____
MISCELLANEOUS _____

FIXED EXPENSES

RENT OR MORTGAGE _____
GROCERIES _____
LOAN PAYMENTS (CAR, EDUCATION, ETC.) _____
CREDIT-CARD PAYMENTS _____
PHONE _____
UTILITIES (ELECTRICITY, GAS, WATER) _____
INSURANCE PREMIUMS (LIFE, HEALTH,
   CAR, HOMEOWNERS OR RENTERS) _____
CAR MAINTENANCE
   (FUEL, OIL, TUNE-UPS, TIRES, ETC.) _____
EDUCATION FEES _____
CHILDREN'S EXPENSES _____
INCOME TAXES (FEDERAL, STATE, LOCAL) _____
PROPERTY TAXES _____
MISCELLANEOUS _____

DISCRETIONARY EXPENSES

CLOTHING _____
COSMETICS _____
HOUSEWARES _____
APPLIANCES _____
GROOMING AND PHARMACEUTICALS _____
ATHLETICS (GYM, SPORTS) _____
ENTERTAINMENT
   (MOVIES, THEATER, CONCERTS, ETC.) _____
RESTAURANTS _____
DRY CLEANING _____
TAXIS _____
GIFTS _____
BOOKS, NEWSPAPERS, MAGAZINES _____
HOLIDAYS AND VACATIONS _____
SAVINGS _____
MISCELLANEOUS _____

TOTAL INCOME _____

MINUS TOTAL OF
FIXED EXPENSES _____

MINUS TOTAL OF
DISCRETIONARY EXPENSES _____

EQUALS _____

do), you need to develop a plan to reduce your debt. To meet expenses you must either find a way to *earn more* or, more likely, devise a strategy to *spend less*. Okay, so now that you realize there's only $2.50 a week left over for discretionary expenses, it's time to start pruning. Rifling through your receipts, you may be shocked at how much money is going into nonessential items and how much of that is financed by credit. Credit is the most expensive money available, and ironically it is what we so often use to buy the most expensive things: handbags, perfume, stereos, plane tickets, sequined slip dresses. Be honest with yourself about what are *needs* and what are *indulgences*. Yes, you need nutritious food, but brown-bagging your lunch is cheaper than takeout. Yes, you need to look smart for work, but didn't Sharon Stone look pretty good wearing Gap to the Oscars? There are intrepid ways to be resourceful; it just takes a little creativity.

Impose your first budget by setting aside the exact amount needed to pay for rent, food, transportation, and utilities. If you can, have your paycheck deposited electronically into your bank account, and then arrange for your bank to pay as many of your bills as possible—loan payments, utility bills, and retirement funds can often be paid electronically. These automatic deductions are a great help in maintaining a budget, because they preempt the illusion of available cash.

Realistically speaking, at least 70 percent of your income will go toward primary expenses. So much of this (health insurance, IRA, loans, and a safe place to live) is not negotiable. What's left over from your primary expenses has to be spent wisely. The mentality needed to survive on a very limited surplus is: "What I have is what I spend, and that's all I spend." Let's say your available spending money is $500 per month. Ouch! That's about $16 a day. Tough call but not impossible—bring lunch from home and you still have enough for a fresh piece of fruit ($1), a video rental ($5),

a lipstick ($9), and a *New York Times* (75 cents).

Living tight doesn't have to mean living Carmelite. If you want to eat out on Friday night, you can scrimp for a few days beforehand. If you want to attend a weekly yoga class, make it an economic priority and resist impulse purchases like incense and massage oil after class. Living on a strict budget might affect the spontaneity of your social life. But if your friends know you are shifting a big debt, saving for something special, or paying off your education with gusto, you should receive their respect, not their pity.

When you get your first real job, there's a temptation to want your world to resemble the funky lofts and endless wardrobe changes on *Friends*. At last you're on your own, out of home, out of college, the world's at your

PS: Budgeting is a skill that will serve you for life. Maintain the tricks you honed so painfully when you had to live on less and you give your money a purpose and a path. The more you earn, the more you'll spend, and raises will get soaked up by expanding appetites—and that's fine as long as your savings increase proportionally. If your income triples, so should your savings. The surest way not to spend money is to put it away where you can't get your hands on it: Pay the maximum into your retirement fund or seek a financial planner to help start a modest investment portfolio.

"Worldly Temptations Shall Befall Thee."

feet—and you're wearing Keds! It's such an injustice. You're young and beautiful and look a lot better in Miu Miu than your boss, but you don't need to go into credit-card debt to prove the point.

Drum it into your head: Savings and investments are acts not of self-restraint but self-preservation. French perfume evaporates, bonds and mutual funds power on.

3. Set up a home office

A home office can live in an accordion folder or a large hatbox, if you so fancy, but it does need to be concentrated in one place. Your personal accounts system should consist of the following: a small desk diary, a spike, a calculator, a three-tiered letter file, some large envelopes, a ruled exercise book, and a paper accordion file. It works like this.

Daily: Ask for a receipt for everything you buy, and at the end of each day place these bits of paper onto your spike. Jot down everything you spend every day in your diary. This works as a backup if you lose a receipt or a checkbook and, like a food diary, tracks your wicked ways.

If you have income, jot down the balance on the page opposite your expenditure.

Place any bank statements, credit-card statements, loan documents, invoices, or sundry bills in a three-tiered letter file, labeled by category:

1. DEBTS (CREDIT-CARD NASTIES, UTILITY BILLS, LOAN DOCUMENTS)

2. ACCOUNTS (BANK STATEMENTS, FUND REPORTS)

3. INCOME (PAY SLIPS, SCHOLARSHIP MONEY, MISCELLANEOUS)

Weekly: Track your bills and balance your checkbook. Know where you are with your payments. One day late on a credit-card debt and you could be slapped with a $29 late fee.

Monthly: At the end of the month separate your receipts and stuff them into large envelopes marked CLOTHES, FOOD, TAXIS, RECREATION, SEX TOYS, and so on. These vital pieces of paper remain in view every month and are not filed until bills are paid and income is accounted for.

Lord, it sounds so dreary, but take heart! Basically you are nagging yourself into financial well-being.

Once a month, collate your accounts. To do this, draw up three columns in your little notebook. The first column is for expenses (your spike reveals all), the second for bills paid (the debit column), and the third for income (probably the shortest column, but do not despair). After diligently noting it all, stuff the lot into the appropriate month, neatly labeled on your accordion file. (Come tax time you have saved yourself hours of hard labor.)

4. Pay yourself first

Pay yourself first and you may be surprised at how quickly you gather together an emergency fund (living expenses in case you get fired or fall ill), a slush fund for a nicer vacation, or,

perhaps more important, a retirement nest egg that you barely notice yourself building.

To start a savings plan, try to bank a minimum of 10 percent of your salary every time you get paid. If this seems like too much, give yourself a smaller goal, say $100 every month. If you have trouble putting aside even the smallest amount, establish a separate account and see if your employer will channel funds straight in. What you don't see, you won't miss, and there's nothing worse than working twelve-hour days and having nothing to show for it by year's end—or, worse, career's end.

5. Be retirement savvy

Retirement—the very word summons images of golf slacks and canasta, or in the worst-case scenario, of having to live on cat food. Planning for your retirement is a responsibility, but it's also one of the easiest ways to learn the basic principles of investment. And you are never too young to start doing either one.

As Suze Orman explains in *The 9 Steps to Financial Freedom*, time creates money. To illustrate her point, she gives a sobering example: "If you're age 45 and start putting $100 a month into an account that averages a 10 percent return, you'll have $71,880 by age 65. If you start ten years earlier, at 35, your $100 a month will have grown to $206,440 by age 65. If you start at 25 you'll have $555,454." Obviously there's a big difference between retiring with seventy grand and retiring with half a million dollars.

In the old days Social Security and pensions provided retirement security. Today, not many companies pay for pension plans. Social Security was intended as a supplement to retirement plans and matches only a portion of your income upon retirement, so women are turning to other, more comprehensive schemes. Your retirement program will be shaped by your line of work (full time or freelance) and by your employer. Many employers offer a 401(k) plan, which allows you to save up to $10,500 of your salary (as of 2000) directly from your paycheck. Some employers will add to your funds by matching a percentage of your contribution. A *simple* plan can be offered by small businesses of one hundred or fewer employees. You may save up to $6,000 of your salary per year, and your employer can match your contribution dollar for dollar up to 3 percent of your salary. Self-employed women or those without a company-sponsored retirement plan can set up an IRA. An IRA is a shield that protects your investment from the IRS. You can put any type of investment behind that shield—stocks, bonds, mutual funds, certificates of deposit.

Many of these plans also serve as a source for inexpensive loans for emergencies or major expenses. Some plan sponsors allow you to borrow money from your retirement savings for things like home repair and higher education.

Building a bonfire out of hundred-dollar bills on payday is for the criminally insane, but neglecting your retirement is just about as destructive. When you put money into a retirement plan you save in two ways: You set money aside and you pay less in taxes. Because your contribution is deducted from your paycheck before taxes are calculated, your taxable income is reduced. You'll eventually have to pay taxes on that money, but not until you actually withdraw funds. And then, because your taxes will be based on your income as a retiree, your taxes will most likely be much lower.

If you are reading this at work, take ten minutes out of your lunch hour to march into personnel and see what schemes are available through your current job. The sooner you start, the more you will save. The golf slacks are optional.

6. Get out of debt

Everyone lives with some level of debt, but just how much debt we shoulder has spiraled out of control in recent years. Since the introduction of the credit card in the 1950s the national credit-card debt has grown to $450 billion, and the average individual credit-card debt is estimated at somewhere between $4,000 and $7,000. We are maxing out not just one card but several at a time, and we have little to show for it—a few dinners here, a vacation there, and a dress we no longer wear—and we're still paying years after the initial buzz of purchase.

Sometimes we have no choice but to live off credit. Fresh out of college with quaking debts ranging from twenty to a hundred grand, graduates have very little cash to live off, and keen credit card companies aggressively target these lambs. Because cards can be acquired with scant credit history, it's easy to feel like they are free money or a ticket to a better lifestyle. Big companies bank on this false sense of freedom, and this is where problems begin. Much to their discredit, some credit providers actually target people who are slow to pay, pay the minimum, or can't make regular payments, knowing that they will carry their balance month to month at crippling interest rates. The card company's rationale? If these folks have trouble paying their bills, they must need credit.

If debt is a fact of life when you're starting out (or even when you're holding down a good job), the strategy you *must* adopt is defensive: Manage the money you owe now and fight like hell against anything that conspires to make you owe more. Debt attracts debt. Once you're in the harness with a student loan, a car payment, and two credit cards, it's easy to get a warped idea about financial responsibility. "What's another

grand when I already owe forty?" you might argue, spending even more borrowed money to forget the debts you already have. It's exactly this state of financial denial, anxious random spending, and ignorance of what you actually owe that makes large escalating debts so pernicious. Everything we have, including time, becomes compressed and devalued when we owe more than we can pay.

The first step in getting out of debt is to face exactly how much you owe, and to whom. Every debt, from that small personal loan from your parents to a massive tuition fee, needs to be accounted for and given immediate attention. If you phone up everyone you owe and arrange for even a minimal repayment plan, you've already made a giant leap. In just a few minutes you've bought yourself time to tackle the next step—deciding your strategy for increasing your income, lowering your overhead, or both. Here are some ideas:

Increase your income. A weekend job or an additional freelance project is sometimes the best way to attack a problem debt. But extra income must be channeled straight into your debt and not frittered away on feel-good pick-me-ups.

Consolidate your debt. By putting all your debts in one basket, you can often save money and cut down the hassle factor. Instead of sending payments to several creditors, you pay only one. Your interest rate may be lower, there's a lot less paperwork, and your credit report looks cleaner immediately.

If you have several credit cards, you can transfer the balances to just one card. To do this you need a clean repayment record and some research to find the best interest rates on offer. The whole point of consolidation is reduction, which means no new debts on any other plastic. In fact, you should cut up and cancel all your cards but one. An alternative is to bypass the cards altogether and apply for a loan from a bank or credit union (or from your retirement fund, as described next). Loans must be paid off faster than credit cards, and the interest rates are much lower. If you are able to get a personal loan to pay off your debts, you move into a classier category of debt. Superficially the bank sees credit-card debits as "bad debt" and other loans as "smart debt." Certainly the organized and streamlined structure of one big debt instead of ten fractured ones feels smarter. The scary part of a consolidated debt is that the bank loan is often a secured loan, meaning that if you default or miss payments, your assets (house, car, and possessions) are at stake.

Borrow against your retirement fund. It is possible to borrow up to 50 percent of the money you have in your 401(k) plan at work. The loan is usually low interest; you have five years to pay it off and the interest you

pay goes back into your fund. (That's right, it goes into your account, but don't be fooled into thinking it's a can't-lose proposition—the amount of interest you pay yourself seldom makes up for revenue lost when you pull chunks of cash out of your investing pool.)

Think twice before borrowing this way. If you leave your job (say, get fired), the sum you've borrowed is due in full; if you can't pay it back, you'll have to pay ordinary income taxes on that money; and if you're under age fifty-nine and a half, you'll pay a 10 percent penalty as well. But if you're drowning in credit-card interest, it may be advantageous to give yourself a clean slate with a much lower interest rate for your repayments.

Sell your assets. When things get really dire you might be tempted to sell off treasured possessions—Grandma's ruby ring, bonds, or investments. Conventional wisdom says to never dispense with an investment whose interest rate is greater than that of your debt. Meaning, if you are earning 15 percent on an investment, and your credit-card interest stands at 12 percent, hang on to your nest egg. This rule is fine until your debt becomes unmanageable. If you have to liquidate, start with the least sacrifice first, and hold what breaks your heart till last.

Seek professional help. Because there are so many people in money trouble, a whole industry has sprung up to help folks deal with bad credit ratings and unmanageable debt. Some companies that claim to "doctor" your credit history or help shift your debt can simply add to your problems by demanding an upfront payment and delivering very little. Nonprofit organizations are safer, and through them you will find moral support as well as solid repayment strategies. If you want to join a twelve-step program to help overcome your debt, contact Debtors Anonymous, General Service Board, P.O. Box 400, Grand Central Station, New York, NY, 10016, to see where you can find a meeting in your area. Your city's public advocate office will be able to help you find non-profit credit counseling services, as will the National Foundation for Consumer Credit (800-388-2227, or on the Web at www.nfcc.org).

Another useful organization is Consumer Credit Counseling Services (800-577-2227).

Declare bankruptcy. When debt exceeds income by 50 percent, bankruptcy is an option, but it should be your absolute last choice. Once you've declared bankruptcy it will be difficult for you to get any kind of credit in the future, and you are still not absolved from paying alimony, child support, student loans, and taxes.

7. Know thyself

Some people handle credit cards sensibly, paying the entire balance each month to avoid interest fees and staying below their credit limit to avoid a penalty. Some use their cards for travel or emergencies only. But many more people use credit cards for things they cannot afford to buy with cash. "I'll charge it," you say grandly at the cash register, completely ignoring the fact that the monthly statement will destroy the illusion. The things you buy on credit do not belong to you until you pay for them. By the time you own them they can cost a lot more, especially if your store credit card's interest rate exceeds 20 percent.

To ascertain your credit personality, take a look at the way you use your card. Do you use it to splurge? Are you more liable to spend using a card than cash? Do you feel like your credit limit is actually a full bank balance? Are you now in credit-card debt over $2,000? Can you re-call how you spent the money? If the answers to these questions disturb you and you are haunted by credit debt, cut yourself free. Literally cut your cards diagonally in half until they are *all* paid off. Whatever you do, don't apply for a new card when all your old cards are maxed to the hilt. If you are still not convinced, read on.

8. Learn how credit cards work

The word *credit* implies money paid. However, what a credit card offers is money extended and then money owed. Credit cards put you in debt, sometimes very quickly. A credit-card debt over $500 needs to be viewed as a loan from the bank, and the interest rates charged on this money are often much higher than those of a conventional loan (usually twice the rate of a home loan). Initially a card seems like a very good idea. You have surplus funds plus some superficial benefits (like frequent flier miles or a limitless balance), and the card provides a method of establishing a credit rating. But miss just a few payments and you blemish your credit rating immediately. The best way to build a credit history *and not a debt* is to acquire a secured credit card. This operates like any other card except that it's secured by a bank deposit. The balance available is the balance you have in your bank account, so essentially you work on a debit rather than a credit system. Another option is to take out a small bank loan and repay it on time.

In their advertising campaigns, card companies associate financial maturity with owning a credit card. But most of us don't have a clue how credit cards work. Tom Waits once said: "The large print giveth and the small print taketh away." With credit cards, details are everything. Special offers to lure new customers can conceal hidden pitfalls in the small print—an inviting grace period or waiver of finance charges might be followed a few months by a huge hike in interest rates. The meter is also running in other areas of your account. Annual fees, late payment fees, cash advance fees, over-the-credit-limit fees all conspire to cost you more. So you can't afford to keep yourself in the dark.

Credit survival tips

✿ If you make only the minimum payment each month, you will deepen your debt very quickly and spend years paying it off. Here's an example of just how bad it can get: If you have an average balance of $1,100

Credit Cards 101

Interest rates and fees vary wildly from one card issuer to another. For example, MasterCard and VISA are issued from a number of different banks, each of which sets its own rates and fees.

Check out how your credit-card companies compute interest. Some issuers begin adding up interest as soon as a purchase is made. So even if you pay your bill in full every month, you still pay substantial interest. Other issuers give you a grace period—no interest on new purchases until after the payment due date of the current billing cycle (usually 25–30 days). If you pay your bill in full every month, you'll pay no interest on your purchases.

With many card companies, annual (or in some case monthly) fees are common, and range from acceptable to disgraceful. Late fees can range from $25 to $40. Most charge a fee if you exceed your balance, and some even charge a fee if you don't use your card!

For information about the best credit card interest rates, quiz your customer service representative. The interest rate you have is probably not the only rate the company offers. Service reps won't talk about lower rates unless pressed. If you can't get enough information, check for credit-card rates on the Web at *Money* magazine (www.pathfinder.com/money) or Kiplinger's (www.kiplinger.com).

on an 18.5 percent card and you pay the minimum of 1.7 percent, it will take you twelve years and six months to pay the debt and $2,480.94 in interest. Pay just $10 per month more on your minimum, and you could cut the repayment time in half and the interest by $676.37.

✿ The minute you get a bill or statement from your credit-card company, open it and attend to it straight away. Pay just a day late and you will be penalized by late fees and an interest rate that can roll over and double. Until you get control over your cards, keep a desk calendar to monitor your due dates.

✿ If you have been turned down for credit, the lender is legally required to tell you the reason credit was denied, and give you the name and address of the credit bureau that supplied derogatory information. You are then entitled to a copy of your credit report, at no charge.

✿ Otherwise, to find out your credit rating, contact the three national credit-reporting bureaus: Equifax (800-685-1111), Experian (800-682-7654), or Trans Union Consumer Disclosure Center (216-779-7200). Call in advance to find out how to submit your request and for the cost of the report.

9. Be penny wise

Central to budgeting is spending less. You will be amazed at the brilliant ways in which you can save money without being a Scrooge. Little luxuries, bad habits, and what you consider treats can eat seriously into your savings. Without wanting to rain on your parade, the pizza you eat too often and that throwaway buzz of a magazine that insults your intelligence end up costing a packet. Consider the math on these everyday indulgences and think hard about where you could economize:

✿ A smoking habit of about a pack a day costs about $34.65 a week and approximately $1,801.80 a year.

✿ One weekly gossip magazine and two monthly glossies add up to $22 a month, or $264 a year.

✿ Five cappuccinos, three chocolate bars, and a scratch lottery ticket per week adds up to $17.50 a week; that's a shocking $910 a year.

Don't sulk! Find alternatives that are good for your health and your budget. One good novel gives you a whole week of riveting train-reading. One homemade cake is less fattening and makes you popular at the office, too. Spending less means pausing and taking stock instead of automatically parting with cash. You can save money on everything from air tickets to mortgage rates by doing a little homework on the Net. Check out the prepurchase research possibilities at www.consumer.world.com, and even interrogate the cost of your phone bill by checking out alternative rates at www.teleworth.com. Play before you pay: Use the Internet to preview CDs, books, and even movies.

If you have a windfall, don't rush out and spend it straight away. Breathe in, sit back, and relax. Look around your house, check out your wardrobe, soul-search, and maybe realize you don't need anything. If that's the case, bank or invest the money for the future or until your imagination catches up with your bank balance.

10. Spend only what you have

Don't carry money in your wallet that you can't afford to spend. This applies to an evening out, a stroll to the supermarket, or a trip interstate. Use a bank debit card in place of a credit card—it functions the same except that the funds you are spending are sitting in your bank balance. Whatever is left after utility bills, debts, and rent is yours, and when it's gone it's gone. Brutal but fair.

11. Have a goal and stick to it

Financial plans can have a life span of a month, six months, a year, or much longer, depending upon your goals. Formulate a plan and remind yourself of it as you chart your own progress. If you need an incentive, keep a photo of a tropical island or a gorgeous dress or a house on your money file. At the end of all this drudgery, there's a reward you have earned by yourself, for yourself.

12. Bank well

What is your bank doing for you? Before you open an account, investigate the interest rates, the fees, any limits placed on fee-free transactions—along with the service and general helpfulness of the organization. Banks provide a service, and you shouldn't lose money getting it. To keep updated, investigate www.bankrate.com, and for goodness' sake read your bank statements.

13. Try a money fast

In a money-driven society, handling currency makes us feel "real." Credit cards provide ID over the counter. Cash flows constantly for hundreds of small transactions. Given the grubbiness and speed of it all, why not behave like the Queen of England for a day and carry no money? Not having and not spending a cent may make you feel utterly naked and insecure, but persist. For your daylong "money fast" have plenty of food at home, walk everywhere, and entertain yourself. See how you feel the next morning. Are you poorer or richer for the experience?

PS: When you're really broke, technique number 13 might prove to be more than an existential exercise. Never let the absence of cash make you feel like a personal failure. You are much more than what you earn or own.

14. Invest well

Investment is a word that intimidates many otherwise competent people. But it shouldn't, because at the most basic level, an investment is simply anything that puts your money to work. The rationale behind investing is that money grows over time; the initial sum you start with isn't important. Starting is.

You can simply put your money into a savings account with your bank—a safe choice, but your money won't earn its keep after taxes and inflation take their toll. Don't think that you have to take terrifying risks when you invest. A good retirement fund is a sound investment that's within reach of any woman who works full time. Real estate is another option, but be aware that the financial rewards are affected not only by market conditions and location, but also by how long you take to pay off the mortgage. Take the slow, easy route, and you wind up paying double: the interest on a house that costs $200,000 at 8 percent over thirty years is a staggering $328,000.

Less expensive places to put your money are stocks, bonds, and mutual funds, but each has its own risks, perks, and drawbacks. If you want to build a small portfolio of stocks, you can enter the market with as little as $500 or less. The three books mentioned earlier (*Money 101, Girls Just Want to Have Funds*, and *The 9 Steps to Financial Freedom*) cover this potentially confusing area of money management with excellent clarity. How you invest your money is as significant as how and where you spend it. Try not to support companies that hurt the environment or exploit or harm fellow human beings. For ethical investment ideas, see Eco Girl, page 223.

15. Reward yourself

If you have been very good and counted your pennies until they are smooth with wear, then indulge in a little splurge. Bring home a beautiful cake as your just desserts, or factor fresh flowers into your weekly grocery budget. Small pleasures feel like extravagances when you've been living frugally. Don't overcompensate for saving by blowing out your funds prematurely. Saving $600 in order to spend $1,000 is a wildly false economy.

16. Give some back

Once you have attended to bills, security, savings, and insurance, you might still have a little extra money kicking around. An inheritance may land in your lap, or you may sell your diary of poems to a big record company and find yourself with a stack of royalties. For girls who have gone without, sudden affluence or even a little extra can feel like a responsibility, and can create even more anxiety than being broke. Relax and do something creative and beautiful with your money. Tithing a portion of your income to a charity or a cause you believe in is tax-free and good for the soul. Giving even a tiny amount creates positive feelings—feelings of abundance, of having enough, and of making a constructive contribution.

SOLUTIONS FOR SHOPAHOLICS

In a consumer culture, Shopping Nirvana represents freedom of choice, abandonment of practicality, creativity, sexy self-invention, and the last frontier of the hunter-gatherer spirit. Why else would they call it retail therapy? If you find a bargain, you feel like a genius; if you find a dress that actually flatters, you feel like an artist.

But there is a price. Shopping is a very expensive way to feel good, and it is subtly addictive. Constant supply feeds the high. This week's brand-new Lurex singlet top is next week's ball at the bottom of the laundry basket, and the hunt goes on. Bigger, better, brighter, shinier, more! When you're caught up on the treadmill of a hard-shopping lifestyle, it's very easy to endow clothes and other objects of desire with an almost spiritual power.

To wean yourself from this fantasy, you need to scale down your expenditures and get more pleasure out of owning less. You need to distinguish between shopping necessities and shopping hits, and if you still feel a need for that buzz, you need to apply a stricter budget. Take $40 to a flea market and see what you can find; enjoy being intrepid and original and know that your credit card is locked safely away at home. Looking a little deeper into that urge, it isn't hard to deduce that shopping can be a form of misspent creative energy. You're out looking for the beautiful *objét* when you could be at home making it yourself; you want to look better in new clothes when really a smile would change everything; you want to be attractive and forget that lovers see auras before they see clothes. That said, I still concede that shopping is a divine pleasure, and as with most pleasures, it comes with a loss of freedom. Here are some ideas to gain power over your passion.

❀ Divert the urge. Spending urges rise and fall like any lust. If you are feeling austere and bony, cook up a big casserole; if you feel starved of luxury, listen to opera, drown yourself in a stack of glossy art and interior-design books at the local library, or eat a bag of fresh figs. The desire for a blast of opulence is not a sin, but you don't have to pay through the nose to sate it.

❀ **Take an inventory.** Pull all your clothes out of the closet and sort out what you never wear and why. Perhaps they need ironing and mending, perhaps they were impulse purchases that really don't match your lifestyle. Perhaps, most important of all, you have great stuff in there that you forgot even existed.

❀ **Swap instead of shop.** Organize a flea-market day at home with your girlfriends. Bring a bag each of handbags, hats, shoes, odd earrings, and old clothes in their most presentable condition, and work out fun swaps.

❀ **Learn the difference between want and need.** You may want thigh-high satin boots but you probably need strong winter shoes that will last a whole season. You may want an expensive trip to a beauty salon but you'll need a hair diffuser to create the same hairdo at home. Spend money on the things you see or use every day— some good pillowcases, a smart bag for work, books, nutritious food—and then build from there.

❀ **Simply spend less.** Materialism can leak into the way you live, especially if you feel the need to keep up. If you get invited to a birthday bash at $70 a head or want to impress someone with opera tickets, think twice. No one should have to bluff a lifestyle she can't afford.

❀ **Don't be ashamed of homemade gifts.** To prepare for Christmas, start making little things throughout the year or have a weekend blowout making jams, curds, and cookies. Thoughtful gifts of your time and skills are often most appreciated: Give a weekend of baby-sitting so friends can escape for some time alone; make up a gift certificate for a massage you will give; prepare and deliver the meals for one day; offer a day of weeding, raking, washing windows, or any other odious chore. You needn't feel embarrassed about giving a homemade gift. If anything, your offering will stand out.

❀ **Next time you go shopping, get groomed and wear your coolest clothes.** Feeling snappy and attractive, you may come to realize that what you have is enough or better and more inventive than what's for sale.

ENTERTAINING

Grace Under Pressure

Remember that scene in *The Doors* where everyone got stoned and left the turkey in the oven until it was a massive charred hunk of smoking coal? That movie always makes me feel better about my own spectacular entertaining mistakes. Today I know that a twenty-six-pound turkey takes between six and six and a half hours to cook when placed in an oven that is preheated to 350°F. And is ready when the kitchen thermometer is gently jabbed into the thigh and reads 180°F. Solid information, recipes that work, and personal style (in place of snobbery) are the keys to entertaining confidence. You don't have to be a great cook to feed people well, and you don't have to worry about elaborate courses and the right silver. If it really is true that 50 percent of American meals are eaten out, then your efforts at home cooking are bound to be appreciated. Put plenty of soul into a dish, serve it generously and quickly, keep the wine and conversation flowing, and the mood and music buoyant. As hostess, stay relaxed enough to actually *enjoy* your guests. The meals we remember most are never about perfect piecrust or precious truffle shavings. Instead they are infused with originality and good feelings.

ESSENTIAL ENTERTAINING

WHAT TO SERVE

The difference between everyday survival cuisine and food for entertaining is significant. You may be able to subsist on simple repasts such as the tofu and broccoli rabe "thing" that is your staple, but your guests shouldn't have to. One boyfriend and five lemons taught me that lesson. When I served my date vegetarian sauce with angel-hair pasta, "Great," he said tonelessly, "student food!" That hurt. Another dinner I overdid the Mediterranean mode and made free with the lemon juice—splattering it over the spinach salad, smothering the marinated chicken, and, finally, submerging the strawberries in a mixture of orange juice, sugar, and even more lemon juice. I did have the sensitivity to serve tea with milk, but by

then it was too late. Five normally friendly people went home sourpussed.

To avoid this and other culinary fiascos, start with one-pot dinners until you have your sea legs, experiment with recipes at least once before inviting the gang over, and make sure a meal—no matter how simple—has abundance, freshness, color, and some element of the visually or texturally unpredictable. A salad of bright red cabbage, mangos, cilantro, and baby sweet corn in a swirl of sesame vinaigrette makes a steak sandwich sexier. A few violets tossed into a simple bowl of endive, avocado, and walnuts delights the eye. Fruit where you don't expect it (in curries and casseroles and savory jams) and dipping sauces that are *not* from the supermarket make your guests feel well loved and well fed. Fancy or rare ingredients are not key to the experience. Place an honest portobello mushroom under the grill with a square of herb butter and you have all the sensual opulence of earthy truffles and velvety chocolate. As Elsa Maxwell put it so well: "Money doesn't make a party. You do."

THE RAW AND THE COOKED

When it comes to breakfast, lunch, dinner, or tea I always combine the raw and the cooked. Something hot satisfies the senses on a primal level and something raw keeps the palette refreshed. Okay, so that's my arty rationale, but in truth it's also an escape route from complex courses and confusing menus. One-pot dishes (curries, pasta, casseroles, hearty soups) and salads take a lot of pressure off the hostess.

On the surface of things salad sounds homely, or as Diana Vreeland put it, "Lettuce is divine, although I'm not sure it's really food." That said, the antidote to generic picnic-style salads is to treat every ingredient, however simple, as a force unto itself. Even fragile watery lettuce comes into its own with slightly oily, creamy

flavors; bitter greens (like watercress, rocket, arugula) come alive dressed with very green fruity olive oil and cracked pepper. You can serve the simplest dishes in the world if you respect the character of each ingredient. Tomatoes need to be bought in season and live outside the refrigerator. Alone, they become a gorgeous simple salad when left to sit in sea salt, sugar, olive oil, and white sherry or balsamic vinegar for ten minutes before serving. My favorite salad of all time is a mix of grilled figs, grilled bacon, chunky firm avocado, and endive tossed in a lemon and olive oil dressing and topped with toasted walnuts. Figs grilled take on a slightly salty taste and the endive balances the rich, oily textures of the bacon and walnut. My mother makes a salad of blue cheese, raw walnuts, mandarin slices, watercress, and the thinnest ribbons of red onion. The dressing is a drizzle of hazelnut oil and fresh orange juice. Sublime!

This brings us to the territory of a warm salad, but that shouldn't drive you back into the pantry whimpering. The parts of a warm salad that need warming are all the ingredients that don't wilt—grilled peppers, squash cut into small chunks and baked, chicken brushed with teriyaki sauce and grilled, celery root sizzled in olive oil, or even sliced duck from a deli in Chinatown. Salad dressings need to be piquant, never too heavy. It's not a sin to buy them ready made (Annie's Natural has a tasteful range), but it's a lot more instructive to make them yourself. Only you know how much mustard, garlic, or horseradish is too much, and only experimentation can teach you how sickly sesame oil can be in excess. For those who find dressing a drama, simply invest in the best virgin olive oil and balsamic vinegar you can afford and use proportions of three to one. For a green salad for four, wipe the salad bowl with three crushed cloves of garlic, then (in a jar) shake up six tablespoons of olive oil with about two tablespoon of balsamic vinegar, cracked black pepper, and sea salt. Scrumptious on fresh Tuscan-style farm bread, too!

For every entertaining emergency there is a simple recipe that can get you out of a bind. Maybe it's not experimental, highbrow, or fancy, but it works. I love minimal recipes that taste complex—a chicken roasted with two lemons or a casserole of lamb and tomatoes—and I love recipes that let you make dinner out of what you have on hand, say in a good curry. Simplicity doesn't have to imply austerity. To distinguish a one-pot dinner from an ordinary home-alone TV-night dinner you need thoughtful touches: sexy chutneys and yogurt raita for the curry; a salad of pine nuts, wild rice, mango, and cilantro for the chicken; a bottle of complex spicy red wine for a simple pasta. Choose the salad you serve as a study in contrasts: something green and sharp for oily or heavy dishes, something sweet for tangy tastes, and something colorful and surprising for a dish that is very traditional.

FOUR RESCUE RECIPES

A BEST FRIEND NEEDS LOVE AND NURTURING:

VEGGIE CURRY

SERVES 2–4

Sometimes the best recipes come on the labels of the products you love. I took this curry recipe from the Thai Kitchen red curry paste jar and added my own little touches. Sometimes I add shrimp, sometimes free-range chicken. But for sensitive girlfriends who want spice and sympathy, I make it like this:

Splash of Asian sesame oil

1 medium red onion, chopped

1 tablespoon Thai Kitchen red curry paste

¼ teaspoon poppy seeds

1 can unsweetened coconut milk (shaken)

¼ cup bamboo shoots

Zest of 1 lemon, grated

2 tablespoons Asian fish sauce

⅓ cup chicken broth

1 can (14½-ounces) plum tomatoes

3 cups butternut squash, cut into 1-inch chunks

1 cup whole button mushrooms

1 large zucchini, sliced ½ inch thick

¼ cup fresh basil

2 tablespoons light brown sugar

Fresh cilantro (for garnish)

Heat the sesame oil in a large skillet over medium heat. Add the onion, curry paste, and poppy seeds, and sauté until onions are translucent. Add the coconut milk and simmer for 5 minutes, stirring constantly. Add the bamboo shoots and lemon zest and simmer for 3 minutes. Add the fish sauce, chicken broth, and tomatoes and stir. Add the vegetables, basil, and brown sugar. Cook on low for about 15 minutes. Before serving, garnish with fresh cilantro. Serve with Texmati rice (also takes 15 minutes), mango chutney, yogurt and cucumber salad, and banana slices rolled in coconut.

THE PARENTS JUST ARRIVED AND WANT DINNER TONIGHT:

CHICKEN WITH TWO LEMONS

SERVES 3-4

Mothers love to feel they have released you into the world with the ability to find love, keep a job, sew a button, and roast a chicken. With this dish (based on a recipe by Marcella Hazan) you can get at least the fourth one right. Serve your bird with authority and patience. Authority because there is very little you can get wrong, and patience because you will probably *still* get a lecture on how to cook a chicken!

1 3½-pound free-range roasting chicken, excess fat removed

Salt and freshly ground black pepper

2 large lemons

Preheat the oven to 350°F. Rinse chicken inside and pat dry with paper towels, then rub salt and pepper all over—both inside and out. Rinse the lemons in scalding water, dry them, and soften them by rolling them between your palms (good preparental-arrival stress relief). Using a toothpick, pierce each lemon in about twenty places. Stick the lemons inside the chicken. Tie the legs together loosely with kitchen string. Place the chicken breast side down in a roasting pan and bake for 15 minutes, then turn it breast side up. Bake for 20 more minutes, then crank the heat to 400°F and cook for another 15 miutes or until a meat thermometer inserted into the innermost part of the thigh registers 180°F.

Serve with creamy mashed potatoes; spinach, bacon, and pine nut salad with a tarragon-mustard dressing; and thick slices of French bread (to sop up the tangy juice!).

PS: Whaddabout Dessert?

If you've gone to the trouble of making the savory stuff, it's perfectly respectable to serve store-bought goodies for dessert. Small (easy) touches keep the flavors fresh—a sprig of mint in a bowl of chilled lychees and vanilla ice cream, your own raspberry coulis (a cup and a half of fresh raspberries, a dash of Grand Marnier, and a dash of sugar pureed in a food processor) drizzled over a Key lime pie, or even just fresh mangos with chocolate sorbet. Guests who demand fancy cheese platters are a little like wine snobs—rarely reinvited.

THE FORTY-MINUTE DINNER PARTY:

RED SNAPPER VERA CRUZ

SERVES 4

2 pounds red snapper fillets

1 teaspoon salt

2 teaspoons butter, melted

1 onion, chopped

1 teaspoon olive oil

1 can (6 ounces) tomato paste

1 can (14½ ounces) plum tomatoes, drained

1 teaspoon hot green chiles (canned)

1 teaspoon capers, drained

1 jar (6 ounces) pitted black olives

Pinch of freshly ground black pepper

Preheat the oven to 350°F. Place the snapper in a shallow, buttered two-quart baking dish. Sprinkle with salt and brush with melted butter. Put the fish in the oven. In a medium skillet, sauté the onion in the olive oil until translucent. Add the tomato paste, tomatoes, chiles, capers, olives, and black pepper and simmer, uncovered, over medium heat for about 20 minutes. Check the fish. If it flakes, it's done. If not, give it 5 more minutes, max. Serve the fish on a large platter, smothered in sauce, and framed with watercress. Rice, fresh steamed asparagus, and a watercress and avocado salad complete the dinner!

THE MOODY MEAT-EATING BOYFRIEND:

DEAD-SIMPLE OSSO BUCO

SERVES 3

6 lamb shanks

1 cup all-purpose flour

2 tablespoons olive oil

1 cup dry red wine (Guigal's Côtes-du-Rhône)

2 cans (14½ ounces each)
Italian plum tomatoes, drained

1 cup fresh Italian parsley, roughly chopped

Salt and patience

This dish tastes a lot more complex than the sum of its parts. Trim all the fat off the shanks, dredge them in flour and shake off excess. Then brown them in olive oil in a deep, heavy-bottomed skillet. When the shanks are golden brown (about 8 minutes), add the wine and reduce the heat to a low simmer. When the meat takes on a drunken, rosy glow (about 10 minutes), add the tomatoes. Make sure that all the meat is covered, then cover and simmer for 2½ hours over very low heat. At the point where he's bellowing, *"J'ai faim, ma chérie,"* toss in a fistful of parsley and salt to taste. And, to keep the lusty peasant spirit sated, serve with lima beans and golden egg noodles tossed with butter and freshly ground black pepper.

AMBIENCE

Ambience is like fresh air: People only notice it when it's missing. Setting the mood means choosing background music that swings when guests arrive (*Way Out West* by Sonny Rollins), purrs while they eat (*Ella Fitzgerald Sings Cole Porter*), and revs up to cut the rug by the time you're brandishing the cognac bottle (*One Hot July* by Tony Joe White). Cocktail parties ask you to take that slightly breathless atmosphere of fresh perfume and even fresher gossip and draw it out. Drinks need to be icy and snacks can't be mushy, runny, or impossible to balance in one hand. Flowers and candles make the best table settings, because you can work in subtle contrasts: gardenias and tall white ecclesiastical candles, potted violets and forest green votive candles, sweetpeas, Julia roses, and dust pink and silver Roman candles. When the budget is tight, use food as a centerpiece. Salads can look electric if composed with color in mind. Trays of peaches, pyramids of apples, and small bowls of cherries form a still life à la Bonnard or Manet. If you entertain a lot, flowering houseplants might be more practical than buying cut flowers every time. Potted gerberas, orchids, and pansies all look scrumptious. Tablecloths and napkins can be bought vintage and starched up easily, or customize your own no-name white napkins with some Indian ribbons or raffia bows. The only dining table rule is that people can reach their food and make eyes at whomever is sitting opposite.

Conversation can't be governed, but it can be steered away from the subjects that upset people (natural disasters, ex-husbands, tabloid nightmares) or alienate and divide (real estate, ex-husbands, Maria Callas). Roman dinner parties demanded high talk because everyone was lying down anyway; as a hostess you are obliged to keep the ball in the air not in the name of contrivance but for the sake of wit. The dirty jokes and bawdy tales that seem to surface at dessert need to be led down a more constructive path. I have a lovely girlfriend in her seventies who, when the going gets raunchy, declares, "Back to beauty!" Everyone straightens up in their chairs and smiles.

Dinner is a forum but it is also a sacrament. Do all you can to make your guests feel inspired, even if it means standing up and reading a poem in honor of the coffee or screening a silent movie on the living room wall and playing your own soundtrack on the piano. Creativity makes people happy.

PRESENTATION

Alice B. Toklas once cooked a fish for Pablo Picasso. She went to a lot of trouble creating a fancy trellis of bright red mayonnaise, jaunty geometric-sieved eggs, truffles, and decorative flourishes of finely chopped herbs. Pablo, the ingrate, merely grunted and said, "Shouldn't this fish be for Henri Matisse?" The moral of this story is not to fuss too much over presentation. Food has to look attractive and vivid but not mauled. If arranging anything on a plate takes longer than a minute, you've got a problem.

Let the way your guests want to eat a meal be your guide. Stacking food works when the ingredients are more solid and substantial. A baby mountain of sweet potato mash topped with caramelized onion topped with a lush lamb cutlet, encircled by a moat of *jus,* and ornamented with fresh Italian parsley makes comfort food look urbane. But try the same stacking method with a watercress salad topped by French toast topped by a poached egg and then a dollop of hollandaise and you've got a Humpty Dumpty situation—a brunch poised to have a great fall. Restaurants make this mistake all the time, presenting dishes that make you wonder if you should eat it or mount it. But you know better.

PS: Wine needn't be an enigmatic conundrum. View your local wine shop as a library and quiz the owner for information about the best years, tannin levels, good buys, the best flavors to match what you're serving, and even how to read a wine label.

A good wine shop will guide you through the different grape varieties and wine-growing regions and will be prepared to sell good-quality bottles for under fifteen bucks. I tend to avoid "big name" vineyards and well-known appellations and try to buy less fashionable grape varieties. When Chardonnay was raging, I found bargains in the Riesling department, and now that Merlot is so big (and often blandly crowd pleasing), I go for more spicy and difficult reds such as Cabernet, Shiraz, and Rioja. Like perfume, you can't "know" a wine until you experience it with your senses.

To serve a bottle of wine you love and feel confident about, it pays to try the wine alone, both with and without food. Men have a tendency to huff around in wine stores and grab the wine menu at restaurants, blabbing on in rarified terms. But the truth is if you have taste buds you have a palette and that palette can be trained to know a granache from a cabernet within a few weeks.

GRACE

You can shop all day, find a rare bottle of Sangiovese, and even dig up a vintage vinyl album of Count Basie. But no matter how much you polish the peaches, there's one thing that crushes the life out of a dinner party: tension. Tense Irritable Hostess Syndrome (or TIZZ) starts in the kitchen and continues throughout the meal when the lady of the *maison* appears thin lipped and pale between courses, watches her guests like a hawk to see how much they are eating, and responds to normal chatty questions with a glazed nervous look. Hostesses with TIZZ don't really enjoy their evening, because they're having an out-of-body experience, floating above the table looking for taste bud responses and wine spills. Well, really! There is just no point in getting this worked up over feeding people. If you're nervous about certain guests (in-laws, ex-lovers, new acquaintances), cook a dish that involves less kitchen time and looks great. Sit down with your guests at the table and realize that no one likes to begin without the chef. *Do not* drink half the cooking wine and start slurring like Dean Martin at a celebrity roast. *Do not* give a chattering, febrile commentary about the meal as it progresses. It's worse than laughing at your own punch lines. Serve it, button it, smile, and have some more wine.

Career

WORKING IT

The Job Huntress

W ork is a big deal. We devote almost two-thirds of our lives to it, it's the source of despair, elation, frustration, and self-definition. And yet we rarely question what we do—or stop to gain some perspective on the work that marks our daily existence. Often it takes a long vacation to make a workaholic realize she's pushing herself way too hard, or a life crisis (like serious illness) to give a woman the courage and perspective to switch careers. Who has a chance to sit down and map out her professional trajectory when life keeps serving up its nonstop demands? At most we are just coping with the very different pressures of motherhood, student loans, a fluctuating job market, and even divorce. Work is something we are expected to juggle with everything else but, like our health or our spiritual life, it is not something we can afford to ignore. You don't want to look up twenty years into a job and realize you're in the wrong place. Nor do you want to overwork to the point where you have no life. For these reasons, it's not self-indulgent to take stock of your work, it's vital.

The definition of a *great* job differs wildly from woman to woman. Not everyone is a manic careerist; some women simply work to pay bills and find their intellectual and emotional spark elsewhere, some women trim their lifestyle down in order to work less, and some women strive for meaningful content in their work. Sometimes these three completely different work profiles can belong to the same woman in one working life. The importance of work shifts radically as our priorities change. When I was twenty-two I was so proud to wear a suit and carry a card with my name on it that I was willing to work twelve-hour days to earn the privilege. A decade or so later the corporate fantasy lacks the same gleam and, like a lot of burnout cases, I sit around scheming up ways to chase fewer invoices and do more yoga.

WHAT WORKS?

So many women go through their lives doing jobs that mean little to them. They're working for money, parental or social expectation, or status while their real vocation remains unrealized. If we spent a little time contemplating a job that could be meaningful, productive, or even more

Love Your Work

fun, the word *career* would be a lot less intimidating and distant. The best job for you may not be the most high profile or even the highest paying. There are women who have had very passionate careers serving food, knitting sweaters, or teaching horseback riding— not prestige jobs but activities that really fulfilled them as people.

It's vital to know when a job is working for you and when it's just a waste of time. If your work seems to tear at your insides, you are probably trying to fit your crazy creative round peg into a company's square hole. So forget everything you've been taught about résumé writing for a moment and make a list instead of your weaknesses, aversions, and foibles. You'll get a clearer idea of the types of jobs you should scrupulously avoid. Admittedly, there are aspects of your work skills you can fix: appearance (see Three Black Skirts, page 43), punctuality (see Time Management, page 133), procrastination (see Discipline, page 136). Feel positive about those areas you know you can improve, then be honest about the stuff that is truly alien to your nature. Nocturnal types suffer horribly in nine-to-five jobs but blossom as freelancers working weird hours (film editor, rock music technician, nightclub hostess, performance poet). Girls with quick minds and quicker tempers might be better at the stock exchange than teaching day care. Know your faults and make them work for you. Once you are doing what you really love, you can soar and succeed.

QUIZ: What's Your V.Q.?

Sick of your job? Find out what you really like to do by taking this easy vocational quiz.

1. What are your skills? What are *all* your skills? (Many may be outside professional conventions— for instance, the multitasking required of a mother of three.)

2. What job would get you out of bed before dawn—smiling?

3. What are your passions now? What were your passions at age ten? Often the secret of job success and fulfillment is buried in a childhood dream.

4. Which job would you still want to do if you were an entirely solvent multimillionaire?

5. What are your commitments? A woman with a mortgage can't just quit an office job and become a yoga teacher; there has to be planning to make the transition.

Your answers to each question may add up not to one job or career path but several. Make a short list of the possible choices your quiz yields and carry them around with you for a week. Look at them on the bus, talk about them with your friends, imagine the changes each job would ask of you and the demands it would make. Don't worry if the result of this quiz seems fuzzy. Every innovation starts as a vague idea.

MAKING IT HAPPEN

The gap between knowing what you want to do and doing it is full of distinctly unglamorous, undreamy pragmatic actions. Starlets get discovered in coffee shops but *you* need more solid strategies. Be excited about knowing you want to change, and then harness that energy and apply it to your plan. Here's how:

Research The more research you do about your career choice, the stronger your plan of attack. Find out what level of education you need, what skills are mandatory, what internships are available, which ways you can fast-track ahead (through intensive courses, summer schools, volunteer work, sheer ingenuity), and what sort of references you'll need. Be realistic: Find out how many positions are available in your chosen field and also where you would have to live.

Saving Putting aside money is a vital prerequisite. You need cash for the job-hunting process, to finance your studies, and even to get you through the hard times of unemployment between jobs. If you know you're making sacrifices for the sake of a short-term goal, then working a night job or going on a tight budget won't feel like such a drag. Factor the money you need into your planning and feel good about it. Every dollar is reshaping your destiny.

Specialized courses and training Be focused about exactly what qualifications and training are required for the position you want. Endless courses can be a form of procrastination. The wrong course will cost you money, and the credentials of your teachers affect your credibility.

Use time off (summer holidays, long weekends, spring break) to study. Devote smaller blocks of time (while driving to work, one evening a week, a quiet Sunday afternoon) to expanding your skills. An extra language, computer literacy, or a public speaking course make you more marketable.

Internships The unspoken age limit for internships is midtwenties. Max. The benefit of taking an internship is the opportunity to see your dream job from the inside and to seek out mentors even if you spend a lot of your time making their coffee. During an internship you are both observing and being observed—try to treat this short span of time (six days to six months) with professionalism and energy. Because you are usually working for free (or for pocket money), an internship is best planned when you are living at home and have adequate savings or some vacation time banked up.

TIPS FOR THE JOB HUNTRESS

❀ Résumés need to be short, honest, visually attractive, and printed on quality paper that doesn't distract. Plain is good. Specific job applications or proposals or project submissions can go for eye-catching packaging, but what you're presenting here is supposed to be the fruit of an ordered mind. Keep it simple. For extra résumé guidance see www.damngood.com, a useful Web site designed by the authors of *The Damn Good Resume Guide*.

❀ Your phone manner should reflect your whole attitude: confident but not cocky, polite but not groveling, alert but not shrill, nice but not insipid. Experts advise making your most important calls standing up and smiling. Spit out your gum.

❀ The way you conduct your job hunt influences your results. Treat it as an actual job with a nine o'clock start, a one-hour lunch break, and a spiffy well-groomed appearance and you will be better prepared when a short-notice interview or temp job lands in your lap. Acting purposeful is a great depression buster, and it tells the world you are ready to work.

❀ For your job interview: Don't make yourself over to the point that the real you disappears. If you never wear pearls and pumps, don't wear them now. Honesty, spunk, and (hopefully) human warmth are qualities employers respond to. Hair spray is optional.

❀ Fronting is about body language. When you're going in for a job interview, walk tall and straight, sit comfortably but don't slump, try not to fidget, and smile only if it's natural. Listen intently and answer naturally. Put yourself in the place of the interviewer and imagine how tetchy she probably feels having to grill you and twenty others. Being fresh and composed counts for a lot.

INSTINCT ALERT

A woman looking for work is often in a vulnerable position. If you're young, speak English as a second language, or are shaky about reentering the workforce, someone unscrupulous may try to take advantage. Remember, just because you are willing to work does not mean you are willing to be exploited. If you have a creepy feeling during a job interview or find yourself answering an ad that was deliberately misworded, get out of there. Report any unpleasant incidents of harassment or discrimination.

Read job ads closely. Some employment agencies, dodgy "modeling" agencies, and so-called talent scouts are smokescreens for far less savory operations. If you have to attend an interview in an unfamiliar place, get a friend with a car to accompany you. Be prudent about what information you divulge in telephone interviews or on forms that seem spurious.

✿ Job interviews are full of little traps, and sometimes the simplest question can stump you. Get comfortable with your professional facts, prepare straightforward answers to awkward questions ("Why were you fired?"), and find ways to link your personal interests to the job that you're applying for. If asked point blank about salary, try to stall for time. You need to gather information about comparable pay and benefits before you answer. The desire to impress a prospective employer musn't be confused with compliance when it comes to your pay.

✿ Keep your pride and your sense of humor. This is probably the most difficult advice of all to follow. It's hard not to take rejection personally when interviews are unsuccessful or calls are not returned, but it is vital to separate professional success and personal acceptance. Being turned down for a job is not the same thing as being rejected as a person. Imagine how actors must feel making the constant rounds of auditions, or models being told that they are too tall, short, pale, or dark for the job. Job hunters can't afford to wear their hearts, self-esteem, ego, or hopes and fears on their sleeves.

I was once so desperate for a job at a bookstore that my mind went blank during the interview. The smug and patronizing store owner asked me over tea, "What are you reading at the moment?" "Umm . . . ," I mumbled like a bimbo, "poetry." I should have said, "I'm reading your mind, you pompous old owl, and if you really had some wits you'd employ me straight away and order us both a platter of cakes to celebrate."

Okay, you need a job, but not so much that you lose your spirit and become a polite little robot. Laugh, pull a face, roll your eyes, breathe out . . . then go into that interview room and knock 'em dead.

YOU ARE NOT WHAT YOU EARN

Often the best and most useful jobs in the world do not reflect their worth in monetary terms. Compare the income of a person who works in a women's shelter with that of a multinational CEO or a trashy radio DJ. The world needs people with consciences in caring employment. This does not imply that you do not deserve a better wage or should not voice the right to equal pay, but sometimes exorbitant salaries involve exorbitant compromise. Know your needs, know your values, and try your best to wed the two.

TACTICS IN THE MEANTIME

Despite your best intentions and most earnest efforts, sometimes you find yourself not just between jobs but totally broke. Being unemployed puts tremendous strain on self-esteem and self-confidence. To get out of this kind of rut takes fortitude and a sack of optimism.

✿ Not having a job or working at one you hate is not a time for inertia and indecision; it's a time for action. So you're working at a supermarket checkout and you want to be a vet? Carry those animal textbooks with you on the bus, and put up a sign offering your services as a dog walker while you're at it. The goal you have may be a long way from the place you are occupying right now, but everything you contribute to it makes a difference.

✿ Keep your wits sharp and try to spot a trend. The Internet and local newspapers present all sorts of career avenues and employment opportunities if you read them with a creative eye. You may see an article about overextended career women who don't have time to cook, and it plants the seed for your own home catering company. Think big.

✿ Think laterally. To get over the awkwardness of your circumstances, let your friends know that you need practical help. For instance, tell your girlfriends you need to get a smart look together for job hunting—if they love you, they'll lend you. Tell your family you are available for baby-sitting, typing, gardening, cooking, and other small jobs that will provide you with cash for day-to-day expenses.

✿ Keep your room or house pristine. Tidying up creates an organized vibe. You know where those résumés are, you know where your subway token is, you know you have a clean blouse and are ready for that impromptu job interview.

✿ Spruce yourself for success. Beauty boosters that can be found at the local drugstore—a pair of tweezers, an emery board, and a $2 sample pack of hair conditioner—will get your extremities dealt with and keep you from turning into "sweatpants woman."

✿ Often finding a job has less to do with actual qualifications and more to do with you as a person. Appearing confident, kind, honest, relaxed, and trustworthy are all advantages in the eyes of an employer. To keep your confidence up, work on your mind-set. Affirmations work for some people. For others it's a matter of feeling not just enthusiastic, but equal to any task set before them. Regard yourself as an asset, pretend you are a double Leo ("I rule"), keep your pride.

STOPGAP JOBS

Money is like an energy field: Once you start earning, prosperity from other sources starts to open up. To get money flowing, you may have to do a job you picture as beneath you. As a journalist fresh back from a long stay abroad and completely broke, I got a job waitressing. Some of the people I served were my old bosses (magazine editors); others were upstart contemporaries who eyed me with more than a touch of snobbery. I was uncoordinated, a bit haughty, and fairly lazy. As a result, I was the worst waitress in the world. Still, in the five months I worked in that café I earned enough to pay my own way, was offered two other jobs by customers who liked my pluck,

gained confidence (it was better than sitting at home worrying about money), got a dancer's leg muscles, and developed lasting respect for the hard physical work that goes on outside of offices. Cappuccino skills are also rather attractive.

Interim jobs like waitressing or retail or telephone sales feel insignificant only if you see them as a dead end. Once you have gained some chutzpah from being back in the workforce, focus your energies on the job you really want. To get out of an in-between job, give yourself a deadline, a modest savings plan, and a strategy.

PS: If you are just looking for a decent, reliable, pay-the-bills job and not a thunderbolt of vision, you should still take a vocational approach. Savvy actresses waitress at eateries where producers do lunch, botany students work in plant shops, aspiring singers work in record stores. A glimmer of personal interest makes the most banal interim job relevant to your résumé, if not your memoir.

KEEPING IT

The Art of Office Survival

La Swank

L anding a job requires diligence and patience; keeping a job requires sustaining that diligence and being able to bend to conditions, demands, and people as they change. Because many small parts make up the whole of your career, even the most minor altercation in the lowliest position of a company can come back to haunt you later on. Build a reputation for being professional and, more important, nice to work with, and you'll have strong references and valuable contacts for life.

Demeanor is important. Diana Vreeland once fired a girl who walked too heavily. The imperious DV claimed that those footsteps sounded angry. "Go to Paris and become a woman!" she declared and promptly dispatched the poor girl from her employ. Now, perhaps this was simple caprice, but it probably held a grain of truth. If you go to work smiling but actually resent everyone present, it's going to show up in strong body language. To work well in an office, it pays to get in touch with your feelings and try to resolve them instead of unconsciously offloading them onto the collective.

THE OBVIOUS STUFF

❀ Be punctual. No ifs or buts.

❀ Be as well dressed as you can afford, but, more important, be appropriately dressed. Think of your company's clients, not your date at cocktail hour.

❀ Be neat. Day-old takeout and coffee-stained invoices do not signify a free spirit. Use your vertical files as a system rather than a paper pigpen. Put memos where you can find them.

❀ Return all phone calls promptly. Use the same pleasant, clear voice for all. A blatant shift in tone (from polite and attentive to brusque and impatient) is the most obvious sign of disrespect. The gatekeepers (at your bank, at the company you want to impress, outside your boss's office) remember who was phone friendly and who wasn't, so be good for goodness' sake.

❀ Hear no evil, see no evil, keep your mouth shut. Unless you've seen something heinous or illegal (corporate espionage, sexual harassment), do not pass it on. Long boring days in a work cubicle tempt us with juicy conversational tidbits, but gossip hurts. What goes around comes around. And fast!

❀ Maintain your privacy—your income, your love life, and your spiritual practice are your business. If you are naturally colorful, coworkers may be tempted to tune in to your life like a daily sitcom. How does that leave you feeling at day's end? Keep you for you.

THE SUBTLE STUFF

❀ Instinct, diplomacy, kindness, patience, and restraint are the unsung emotional skills that are invaluable at work. So is timing. Knowing when to reach out to a workmate and when not to interrupt is a skill well worth cultivating.

❀ Just because you're all girls together doesn't mean you can drop your guard. Build your allies and work relationships slowly. Trust is something that is tested over time.

❀ Try to moderate your moods. If you work from crisis to crisis and have frequent stress-head outbursts, you're exhausting your own energy reserves and putting others on edge. Conflict does not have to be dealt with via fiery confrontational exchanges à la Lady Locklear. It really does make sense to not sweat the small stuff, and relaxed productivity is kinder on everyone.

✿ Envy is the first cousin of resentment, a close personal friend of spite. There will always be someone in the office who pricks your competitive streak or reminds you of your own inadequacies. In the first place, it's not her fault, and in the second, you should know better. Try to learn from those who make you jealous. Concentrate on your own qualities and be a little more generous.

✿ If you are the object of envy, don't try to sugar up your rival; simply contain yourself more. If the boss obviously favors you, play down your advantage and deliberately defer to others during meetings. Good news—a gallery of snapshots of your wedding in a Tuscan villa, huge bouquets arriving daily—isn't always good business. Have mercy! Tone it down.

✿ Make use of criticism. It takes courage not to feel insulted by a home truth or even a lighthearted snipe; it takes intelligence to make use of the information. Don't trash harsh e-mails and critical memos, keep them, and when your head cools down look at them objectively. Better to face your faults and boldly work on improving them than sulk.

✿ Bear in mind that marvelous line from Macbeth and curb "ambition, which o'er-leaps itself." Obsess too much about a promotion or a better lifestyle and your whole demeanor becomes clouded, hungry, and vacant. Don't mistake grasping (quite ugly and hurtful) for drive (very necessary).

TIME MANAGEMENT

How you spend your time dictates how happy and how productive you are, both at work and beyond it.

Workaholics may claim to put in more groaningly long hours than anyone else, they may boast about lugging work home on the weekend, but that doesn't mean they are doing a better job. The current trend toward showy self-sacrifice in the workplace isn't a healthy one. Workaholics don't actually do more. I know from obsessed personal experience. During my desk-slave epoch, I worked fourteen-hour days and started to keep groceries at work. I also worked slower than ever before. I knew I could slack off because I never left my desk. Time became an elastic, monotonous haze, and a distinct lack of personal life intensified the inertia. Small tasks grew into perfectionist orgies of dawdling, and larger tasks became the focal point of all my conversation. Being a workaholic is boring, sad, and inefficient. The antidote to this rut is learning to work harder and more efficiently in less time and developing stronger boundaries between your professional and private selves.

Moira, a senior magazine editor and mother of two, marvels at the time she used to waste before she became a mother. "Basically," she says, "the less time I have now, the better I use it. Before the kids I would indulge in all sorts of professional tangents, indulgent distractions, and elaborate rewrites on stories. Now, because that isn't an option, I work decisively and quickly. I have to work more briskly but I really enjoy it when I'm there. When I get home I leave work at work. It's a more intense way of life but it also serves as a relief to the scatty way I used to work." You don't have to be Supermom to improve your discipline and efficiency; with a little bit of planning and pluck even the laziest gal in town can accrue extra leisure hours. Here's how.

TIME ON YOUR SIDE

Where does your work day go? The only way to find out is to divide it up. Grab a pencil and draw a pie. Divide the pie into eight sections of one hour each and work out precisely how your day is spent—for example, two hours answering e-mail, one hour in meetings, two or more hours on the phone, one hour scrambling to catch up.

Q. Is there something wrong with this picture?

A. Yes!
Three hours on the telephone is lousy time management. (unless you work in PR).

Opposite the pie draw up a list of ten things you need to achieve at work. Now compare the two. How well do they tally up? Could the time you spend communicating be compressed into shorter, more manageable units? Are you using one sort of task to avoid another? Which tasks always get done at the end of the day or, worse, are crammed in outside of your designated eight-hour pie?

❀ For a couple of weeks, keep a time log at work. This is a great way to monitor the flow of your productivity. To get the most from your log, *be honest*. Note every phone call, every interruption, every coffee break, and the actual length of time spent meeting your work commitments. What you find will probably shock you. Use your bad habits to create efficient alternatives.

✿ If you sprawl e-mail and phone correspondence across your working day, reform by designating one hour only to review all voice messages, memos, and e-mails and answer them.

✿ If you have a tendency to chat, tell your workmates that you're on a word diet and ask for their support.

✿ If you see the same work project cropping up again and again on your work log, devote a solid uninterrupted chunk of time to getting it done. Blocked areas of work erode confidence, create pileups, and are always the first thing to be noticed by bosses and supervisors.

✿ If there is an area of your job you'd like to phase out, maybe you can find a way to delegate the tasks that halt your progress.

Now that you've seen where your time is going, spend it wisely. Don't be scared of the word "goal." A goal is anything you need to do embedded in a plan. Goals need to feel doable, not fuzzy and distant.

Once you've set your goals, devise a strategy to meet them. Deadlines are crucial. To make a long-term goal feel real, it has to be attended to regularly. Set aside time (perhaps once a week) for furthering your plans, and get advice when you're stuck.

✿ Use incentives. Instead of going to lunch to escape from a task, get it done and then go out. The anxiety of unfinished work destroys the ease of leisure time. Face it, do it, forget it.

✿ Leave work at the office. Carrying the office in a metaphoric lump in your handbag or hauling it with you on vacation or treasured getaway weekends is more about guilt than it is about diligence. Nine times out of ten the work is ignored and serves only as some sort of physical penance for wasted working hours.

✿ If you really and truly are behind at work, then you have a legitimate reason to work after hours. Catching up may require slightly longer hours for a few weeks. Just don't let it take any longer than that. Use this incentive to crash through it in a short, intense, disciplined sweep: You are buying yourself free time that is truly free.

✿ Pace yourself. I like to use a clock and set certain amounts of time to finish specific tasks. If I know I have limited time to spend, I'll go hard at it. But these periods should be deliberately short—two hours max. If a job is very complex, physically remove every possible distraction. Put the answering machine on, shut your door (nicely), and even put photos of lovers facedown on the desk. Finish things! It's crucial to feel you are completing tasks within a set time.

✿ Know your body clock. If morning is when your pistons are pumping, don't squander it drinking tea; use this time for your most demanding work. If you have a blood sugar slump everyday at 4 P.M., be prepared. Keep a bag of dates in your desk drawer and keep going. Nurturing your performance means nurturing yourself.

✿ Change your self-talk at work. See yourself as a messy, disorganized person and you have plenty of excuses to fall back on. Start to see yourself as reliable, and efficient, and you will change the way others view you. Resist the urge to voice your self-doubts. In a busy office it's actually an enormous relief to work with people who don't demand reassurance or false pity. The more you lift your game, the more your professional confidence blossoms.

✿ Refine your relaxation. How you choose to unwind affects the way you work. Real downtime means restoring, instead of depleting, your energy supply. Typical escape routes such as television, alcohol, coffee, and the phone leave jangled nerves in their wake instead of soothed ones. Of the four opiates, TV and the phone are the biggest time suckers. Try to spend some of your downtime doing something deeply restful like yoga, meditation, gentle exercise, or inspirational reading. Books totally unrelated to work have a funny way of filtering back in subtle, positive ways.

DISCIPLINE

Some years ago I painted myself a sign to hang above my computer in big blue clumsy letters. It read DISIPLINE = FREEDOM. Well, at least I knew how to spell *freedom*. Teachers tried to harness my tardy ways early on, bosses have given up on me making a 9 A.M. meeting, and everything I do, from catching airplanes to mailing Christmas cards, is scraped in at the last possible second. I don't want you to live like that. Dragging your feet is an exhausting way to exist. To tame your fear and meet your aims, you need to address the crucial issue of motivation and the demon seed of procrastination. Work blocks usually stem from a fear of failure. When this feeling seizes you, the thing that you want so very badly starts to slip away from you. Ambitions become millstones. The dream of learning a language slides under a sea of self-doubt; the raise you really need gets shuffled to the back of the deck. Without discipline, organization, and a solid schedule, you are trapped forever in limboland.

GETTING STARTED

Sometimes getting started is a matter of seizing the creative spark, but most of the time it's more prosaic than that. The muse doesn't sing all day long, so in her absence you simply have to get off your bottom and begin.

Motivation is hard. If it were easy the world would be full of prize athletes, prima ballerinas, and serial novelists. The fact is that the world probably is, but 98 percent will never see their dreams realized. Rather, it's the dull, plodding types who have a way of succeeding in life, simply because they stick to things.

To motivate yourself you need:

✿   A plan. Planning contains the fear by breaking down the task into actionable units. If you break down a big job into small bite-sized pieces, you will finish. The brick-by-brick method eases anxiety and helps you focus on each of the small, manageable parts that make up the whole.

✿   A deadline. Deadlines get the fear factor going, and they limit the time you'll spend completing the task.

✿   Visual reminders that trigger motivation. Put corny quotes, Post-it notes, and framed portraits of your personal idols in the places where you go to hide from work.

✿   A reward. Everyone needs the carrot, but not dangled too closely! Long-term rewards force a deadline that's more realistic and give you something to dream of while you grind away.

PS: If you reward yourself with a vacation try to factor in two days of collapsed recovery between meeting your deadline and jetting off. Resort burnout is such a waste.

PROCRASTINATION

Procrastinators work on the panic principle. The delay-button woman will work herself into a corner and then fight her way out, pounding her chest like a hero when the job is done. Her fear of failure translates into something like this: "If I only work at the eleventh hour and it's not a success, well, I didn't have enough time to do a really good job." This habit of winging it starts in school, where last-minute cramming for exams is the norm, but take this attitude into life and it creates problems. If you succeed, you never know if it really was your best shot, and if you fail, you always have a built-in excuse. It takes much more courage to really give yourself a chance at success, to prepare, to spend the necessary time, and then to see what the outcome is. You just might be pleasantly surprised by the result.

When you break with procrastinating, you give your central nervous system, ego, and emotions a chance to breathe out. Creativity blossoms in a nonpressured environment; ideas are able to cruise rather than race. Instead of whipping yourself about not working, you work. Simple. The sheer relief of doing something rather than freaking out about it creates a powerful surge of energy.

Desk Purge

It's said that in an average lifetime we spend one whole year riffling through papers. If your computer is aflutter with Post-its and you can no longer see your desk, purge!

✿ Use your desk for active projects only—the stuff you're working on right now. Your work space needs to be orderly enough for a coworker to find materials in your absence.

✿ Make a list of unfinished tasks, uncomfortable phone calls, and delayed responses to memos. Aim to get the beastly list dealt with within a realistic time frame—three or four days max.

✿ Try to concentrate information. Transfer notes, memos, phone numbers, and flashes of brilliance to one master list on paper, and one on your computer. For larger projects keep relevant numbers, key names, addresses, objectives, aims, and details on one page and in one computer file.

✿ For paper documents, vertical files are better than wire trays.

✿ Give computer files clear, relevant names. Poetic or cryptic names are a nightmare to decode months later.

✿ Use technology intelligently. Learn how to reduce complicated, repetitive tasks to one keystroke. Every office has a techno nerd; buy her lunch and then heed her wisdom. She can save you hours.

✿ If your job entails research and information gathering but you are Internet-ignorant, take an intensive weekend course.

Like diving into a pool swiftly, it is much less agonizing than tarrying at the water's edge.

There is a countertheory about procrastination. Some argue that time spent, for example, musing in the tub is actually a necessary gestation period for an idea to reach fruition. This theory is dangerous to chronic dawdlers and plain nonsense for simple tasks that demand time, not genius. Okay, Charles Darwin went on long, long garden walks to nut out his theory of evolution, and perhaps he even daydreamed, but he didn't go near a TV set! Besides, putting off a task allows its importance to inflate in your mind. If you can't attack a project you dread directly, then at least start nibbling at its edges. Take your reading material into the tub, keep ideas percolating by talking them over with a friend, or make a detailed list before falling asleep. When you finally do have the guts to start, it won't be from absolute scratch.

You'll know that your gestation period has become dangerous procrastination when preparatory notes exceed the length of the assignment or you find yourself scrubbing the grout in your bathroom with a toothbrush. Never let more than an hour pass between think-tank time and action.

HAVING IT ALL?

A Mother of a Job

The idea that women can work, raise children, and still have the energy to make love to their husbands is unreasonable. In fact, it's a fairy tale. But that doesn't stop a lot of women from striving to "have it all"—a social life, a job, a marriage, offspring, intimacy, a spot of tennis. Females are special like that; we can cook couscous, order a magazine subscription on the phone, keep an eye on two kids, and file our nails at the same time. But just because we *can,* does that mean we *should?* The first women's revolution was about the right to do more; the second might be about the desire to do less. Less overachieving, less perfectionism, and less guilt about overstretching ourselves. Every working mother I speak to debunks the myth of having it all. "You have it all," said one, "but you just don't have it all at once. And," she added wryly, "everything you do have is on the run."

While arguments rage about the evils of day care versus the nurturing of stay-at-home parenting, many of us don't have a choice. We work because we have to pay bills. Two generations of women with fulfilling, responsible careers do not bring forth daughters who are content to stay home and knit. We work because we love our jobs. Despite the fact that we have fought for the right to maintain a work life and a home life, not everyone can deal so effortlessly with the intensity of being a mom/wife/girlfriend/crayon artist/chef/corporate diva/carpool driver

The messages out there about combining a career and motherhood are very mixed. There is still an unspoken moral judgment that mothers belong at home. There is also a corporate culture that implies that pregnancy and parenting make a woman go "soft" and lose her professional edge. And there's a lack of compassion about the personal sacrifice involved in trying to do too much. Worst of all is a media culture that depicts women who both work and mother without showing the least strain.

Since I have no tribe of offspring, I talked to eight working mothers who offered their wisdom, insight, and advice on this topic that so many women wrestle with. Not one of them would change the way she lives, yet all of them remain astounded by the complexity of their lives. It's a balancing act that gives birth to a siege men-

tality, a sense of humor, and a wonderful sense of perspective. Who has time to worry about a run in her stockings when she's got ten minutes to make it from a meeting to a day-care center, collecting a bag of frozen peas along the way? Guilt, constant compromise, exhaustion, self-doubt, and joy are the emotions that came up in our conversations, as well as plenty of hard-won grace. Contradiction is part of the job.

LIFE SWAP

For the working mom, time has accelerated to the point that personal milestones become a blur out the window of a speeding train. The skills we are taught in order to succeed at work—planning, structure, discipline, foresight, and rigor—are torn to tatters by the nonlinear chaos of parenting. As my girlfriend Tina put it so well, "I spent the first half of my working life gaining control and the second half losing it."

Watching yourself shift from a goal-oriented life to a just-coping life can come as a slap in the face. "It's a funny switch from working life—you work hard, you get rewards, with kids the work is just being there," says Mimi, an author who works from home. Moira, a mother of two who works full time at a city newspaper, was confronted by the switch on a number of levels. "In the first year I just had to learn to let go. It's important to understand that beyond the logic of work is an emotional realm that has nothing to do with control; instead it's organic, unpredictable, frustrating, and magical."

With multiple demands comes exhaustion. Julie, a mother of three who runs a jewelry business from her rural home, remains astonished by the transformation. "It's not that my plate is fuller, it's more a case of my plate being much, much bigger. I'm stretched thin in a way I never knew possible." Mathilde, also a mother of three, finds that a five-day week in a city office leaves her spent. "My job claims my day and my husband gets the leftovers; sometimes that's not much. I hate cooking, complain bitterly, and fall asleep." Both women talk about extreme emotions ("my crankiness and anger are way too close to the surface") and the physical demands ("I've always got a child on my hip"), but both take pride in how much they can achieve despite the chaos. "I don't know what I used to do with my time before the kids," says Julie. "I'm so much more efficient now. My husband has no concept of what I get done."

For some working moms, having less time forces them to use it more wisely. Mathilde's work hours have decreased but her output is higher. "I can't afford to sweat the small stuff or obsess unduly." Moira's 6 P.M. leave time is nonnegotiable. "One of the coolest things about being a working mom is that it made it easier for me to keep my home and work lives separate. I have to be extremely disciplined and streamlined. My mom said the same thing; she didn't dawdle or procrastinate at work. Having kids made her more focused." For many moms, the office can also be a welcome contrast from domestic mundanity. "I don't know many women who are wishing they were at home," says Mathilde frankly. "Being in the grown-up world gives me a sense of accomplishment."

With that absence from home, however, comes guilt. Moira admits to feeling occasional remorse and anxiety about her divided duties. But she resents the way businesses and advertisers exploit those feelings— urging the purchase of more toys, more entertainment, more specialized care and courses. Moira's solution to external pressure is to do less instead of more. "We spend our weekends lying around, no museums, no movies, no special outings. It's actually a relief not to have to be constructive every minute of the day."

HOMEWORK

For women who work at home, saying "Mommy's busy right now" just isn't enough. When there are toddlers around, long stretches of concentrated time require separation. Lisa Belken, the "Working Life" columnist for the *New York Times*, writes: "The fact is, we can't be fully at home and fully at work at the same time. . . . Being a working parent means having at least one moment of the day when you push your children away."

Even when physical distance is imposed in the form of a separate office, a workroom, or a barn outside the house, splitting the self between working and mothering can be hard. Susan, who works at home and hires a nanny five mornings a week, still finds herself rushing upstairs to check on the kids. "It seems to defeat the purpose of hiring someone to help, but delegating doesn't mean detaching—my children are always at the back of my mind."

Julia's strategy of working once the children have gone to sleep eats into her personal time but affords her the one thing she has missed all day—silence. "I don't have the luxury of being a tortured artist anymore," she says, "but the time I do have to create my work, I really appreciate. Work used to feel like a duty, but lately when I'm finally by myself working in the wee hours, it feels like a reprieve."

For Tina, a puppet maker, writer, and musician, having children meant she "lost time but gained some great leaps of inspiration." For her firstborn she invented a monochromatic mobile to hang above the crib; for her second, a picture book using a human face as a puzzle. Both creations are now popular sellers in the city where she lives. Tina is the first to admit how demanding her sons are, but her workroom and studio time remain sacrosanct. "Taking time to get things done," she says adamantly, "is really a matter of seizing it. Even if you are not officially 'working' at home, it's really important for kids themselves that they don't have your undivided attention all of the time. From a small age they need to know that there are things outside of them that absorb you."

I Need a Wife

SANITY SAVERS

Balancing all the disparate, beautiful, maddening elements of working motherhood isn't just a practical matter, it's philosophical. When it all gets to be too much, take comfort in the fact that there are women all over the planet throwing their hands in the air and reinventing the domestic wheel. No one does this stuff perfectly. My girlfriend Di is the creative director of an advertising agency where twelve-hour days are the norm; she's also raising her teenage daughter alone. When she's not a workaholic, she's a momaholic. Her weekly oil-bath ritual has become a sacred hour without which she feels she'd disappear into the eye of the cyclone. "Listen," she says, "anyone trying to do this much has to keep the engine going or the whole factory shuts down. My strongest advice would be this: Try not to dissolve into your duties, because when the essential 'you' disappears you're no longer any use at home or at work."

Sometimes applying rules helps you survive being a working mother—and other times the opposite is true. "Even if routine is the glue that holds it all together, sometimes you just need to take a break from it," says Janet. Her response is radical. "When it all gets too much I grab the kids and we all play hooky. No school, no work, just us together for a whole day." For Moira, simply recognizing and accepting the profound difference between the professional proficiency asked of her at work and the emotional flexibility needed for mothering was a big step. "You just can't impose work standards on your whole life. As young women we were taught that if you work hard you'll get what you want. That's not true in relationships and it hardly applies to raising kids."

Mess, moments of tender beauty, and moments of abject exhaustion. The sound of howling screams as you try to answer a cell phone with one hand and apply lipstick with the other, the sight of a kitchen littered with crushed crayons and unread cookbooks. This is the landscape of women who do too much—and the vital reality that may await you when you attempt to have it all. The message from the women who survive and even thrive on this balancing act is invariably wry. Mathilde, rushing home to her brood, sums it up with a broad smile on her face: "No one ever has it all. What you have to be grateful for instead are little bits of it all. My hair hasn't seen a comb in three days."

Mood Management

MISERY

Twelve Shades of Blue

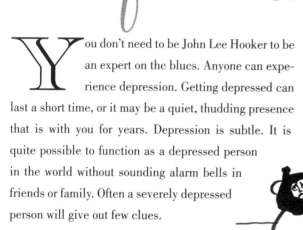

You don't need to be John Lee Hooker to be an expert on the blues. Anyone can experience depression. Getting depressed can last a short time, or it may be a quiet, thudding presence that is with you for years. Depression is subtle. It is quite possible to function as a depressed person in the world without sounding alarm bells in friends or family. Often a severely depressed person will give out few clues.

Internally, the most obvious signs of depression are diminished appetites for the pleasures of life: The world feels colorless, food tastes bland, motivation is low, you either sleep too much or not at all, you may cry for no reason, and you feel little interest in others. It is as if a thick husk has grown over your soul, reducing the world to neutral tones. Without help, depression gets worse and the symptoms become almost physically painful—the body loses its spring and the system grows sluggish, hair becomes limp, the eyes dull. When depressed people say that they feel half alive, it's because in many ways they are. A body suffused with emotion, empathy for others, the desire to reach out and help—all these beautiful human attributes are numbed by depression. To make it worse, feeling low tends to feed on itself; the more inert you become, the less active you are for change. For some people depression is a chronic clinical state that needs the serious attention of both therapy and medication. Antidepressants have become much more widespread in the past two decades, but Western medicine is not the only way to treat depression. Herbal and homeopathic cures are being researched, and many women are finding relief through yoga, meditation, and spiritual practice.

You don't have to be heavily depressed to feel miserable. What doctors call "mild depression" is a state that many women experience without knowing why. Sometimes depression feels shameful because its source is not obvious—you may have a good job and a loving partner and still feel gray hearted; you may be physically beautiful but feel bland and invisible. From experience I have found that depression usually hits hardest when personal fulfillment is blocked or threatened. A cold relationship, a dead-end job, the wrong course of study, or a sludgy malnourished body are all examples of life lived outside its full potential. Seen in this light, depression works as a warning signal—a bland, droning car alarm that asks you to look into your heart to come up with an answer or simply to *act*.

Movement gives depression a great jolt. When you act, you create a chain reaction and you see results. When you exercise, the body releases endorphins—nature's chemical mood lifters. When you eat "happy" foods like serotonin-rich bananas or surround yourself with enlivening colors and scents like geranium or lavender, you are actively pursuing joy. If the larger sources of anxiety in your life feel insurmountable, you need to engage in modest, achievable tasks that shift the sludge. I like to paint a wall or scrub a bathtub; some girls go surfing or memorize a guitar riff. Some sources of depression need more tender solutions or more serious long-term attention. Written from experience rather than medical expertise, here are some thoughts about different kinds of depression. Central to all recovery and healing is a belief in your own resilience. You *can* bounce back.

EVERYDAY EMPTINESS

The French call it *ennui*. That flubby, not altogether palpable feeling of emptiness, repetition, and staleness that we can't quite place. We call it mild depression. Mild depression can come for a spell or last for years. It's a subtle feeling that usually doesn't impair our normal functions; it just guts them of meaning, texture, depth. Doctors give all sorts of explanations why we suffer from melancholia—stress, hormonal fluctuations, poor diet, lack of sunlight or exercise, obesity, and alcohol are all cited as depressants. Poets attribute it to the human condition; sociologists point to a media-saturated, polluted, war-torn, violent, aspiritual, competitive, and unmanageably fast-moving world. These points of view are all valid. The challenges of contemporary life can crush fragile happiness and overwhelm our capacity for joy. Heck, five minutes of TV news is enough to do it.

How then does a girl make her heart hardy and buoy up her spirits? Having a sense of purpose helps. Something to plan for, look forward to, and conceptualize. The smallest project or the greatest fantasy can help pull you through a flat spell. An aim can be something concrete (to build a floor-to-ceiling bookshelf) or something more abstract (to deepen your relationship with a single painting by looking at it every day, to find strength in prayer, to learn to sing). Knowing that you can pull through is another source of solace in the blue times. When none of this works, vigorous physical exercise drags you out of your

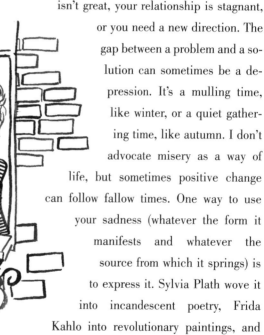

head and into your body. It's hard to feel moody and introspective when a three-foot wave is about to crash over your noggin or you are leaping into the air to spike a volleyball.

Projects and activity are remedies for mild depression, but so is reflection. Sometimes, I think, a spell of melancholy has a function. Stay with the uncomfortable feelings to see what they're trying to tell you—your job isn't great, your relationship is stagnant, or you need a new direction. The gap between a problem and a solution can sometimes be a depression. It's a mulling time, like winter, or a quiet gathering time, like autumn. I don't advocate misery as a way of life, but sometimes positive change can follow fallow times. One way to use your sadness (whatever the form it manifests and whatever the source from which it springs) is to express it. Sylvia Plath wove it into incandescent poetry, Frida Kahlo into revolutionary paintings, and Lucinda Williams into poignant songs. Your droopy spirits might signify something profound or they might point to simple needs—a hug, more vitamin C, more Jerry Lewis videos. Worry less about the symptoms and get creative with the solutions.

WINTER

Lack of sun in winter can make people depressed. Seasonal affective disorder (SAD) pushes many northern Europeans into artificial sunrooms. Other ravages of winter include the flu, the aftermath of which can be a raging, foul outlook. Heavy flu coupled with depression gives you insight into your own mortality. "Oh," you declare glumly, "so that's how I'll look in thirty years' time." This will pass. Eat your fruit! Natural mood lifters for a speedy recovery are sun, vitamin C, strawberries, relaxing herbals, such as St.-John's-wort or Bach Flower Rescue Remedy, and lots of green leafy vegetables to oxygenate the blood. Flu depressions are a very fretful sort of blues; a heavy dose of laughter is crucial, as is the banishment of all mirrors.

POWERLESSNESS

Depression can come to roost when you lose your autonomy. Living at home with your parents, losing a job, depending on someone else financially, being cut off socially or geographically can all plunge you down fast. Whatever your circumstances, the forklift out of this pit is action. If you feel useless, put yourself to use; if you feel isolated, tune in to a great radio show or surf a Web site that links you to the world or, better still, start planning your escape. Perhaps you are not so much depressed about your circumstances as furious.

Sometimes sadness is a veil for suppressed rage. I was living in a basement flat in Glasgow once with the wrong man. Knowing no one, I spent my days reading *Tender is the Night* in front of an electric heater, drinking tea, and crying. The sky was slate gray and I was ready to fling myself into the abyss along with Dick Diver. Sure, I was depressed. I was also full of anger. Entrapment can be subtle, especially when it's happening in a place where you should be safe—in a marriage, with your parents, in an institution you trust like a church or social club. If you suspect you are losing your sense of self through a relationship or job or household that isn't healthy, you might need to fight for your own turf and erect some boundaries. Don't worry about appearing ungrateful, difficult, or not nice. The first step to escaping feelings of futility is admitting that you are unhappy and addressing your own needs.

FAILURE

Big setbacks hurt. Some days many failures converge at once. I remember the day I became poster girl for Losers International: getting fired by the newspaper that ran my weekly column, being turned down for a loan by three banks, contracting bronchial flu, and being dumped by a nasty iceberg of a man all in a matter of hours. If a big depression follows a patch of failure, then you feel doubly feeble. It's easy to lash out and blame the world for your failings—but you are part of the equation, too. Even at the lowest ebb you have to summon the guts to ask yourself why. "Am I pushing too hard? Am I using the right approach? Not to blame the victim, but am I contributing to my own failures?" Sometimes the things you want most come effortlessly when you loosen our grasp and slow the pursuit. This is true of love and it can be true of career and monetary goals. Failure is a risk you take whenever you try for something that appears a little beyond you. If you need to feel better, think of F. Scott Fitzgerald plastering the walls of his room with rejection slips. Sometimes you really do have to "try, try again," wipe the egg off your face, and keep going.

GRIEVING

When my best friend lost her father, it changed her life. Some years have gone by since his death, yet her recollections of the grieving process are still intense and the process is ongoing. Everyone grieves differently, but Karen's account is invaluable to anyone who feels she can't survive the pain of loss. "When my father died, initially I was in shock, and then I went through a time of crying at the drop of a hat. I would cry for what felt like hours and wake up in the middle of the night crying. After the sorrow I became very angry. 'Why has this happened to me?' I thought bitterly. The anger turned into misanthropy and I couldn't stand to have people around me. After that I went into denial, pushing my memories away to stop the pain. I felt I was neglecting his memory and I felt ashamed. When the memories did come back, the pain was so palpable it felt as if someone was pulling out the inside of my chest.

"Grief is not predictable. You can go through all of that and then find it hard to summon a tear at the expected moment. When I went to see Dad's ashes I just went cold and couldn't cry. But if I am alone and watching a family video my chest will tighten and the tears will come. Unless it has happened to you it is so hard to know the reality of grief. When someone dies it is like an absent physical presence that's meant to be there. At my brother's wedding, at the birth of my sister's first child, you just want them to be there."

To cope with the depression that comes with grief it is essential first and foremost to express your feelings. If, like Karen, you need professional counseling, then seek it. Forgiving, loving friends and wise teachers are also essential. A book I have found comforting is *The Tibetan Book of Living and Dying* by Sogyal Rinpoche. Apart from this modest advice, accept the unpredictability of your own feelings and don't censor your responses.

Society allows a pretty narrow range of losses that are appropriate to grieve over. The losses that society finds uncomfortable—miscarriages, crib deaths, abortions, serious operations like a mastectomy or a hysterectomy—remain hushed up. But the grief about them is very real. The depression that follows a deep physical loss like an abortion can be a savage one and should not be ignored. Some women choose to mourn a traumatic, complex, or major event with their own ritual. You might acknowledge the loss by drawing your closest friends near you and mark the occasion by sharing a meal, talking it out, or just having a good hug and a cry. Nothing dramatic that happens to your heart or to your body passes swiftly. Grief is the natural way to deal with pain and loss— not by plastering a smile over hurt, but by letting it rip.

HEARTBREAK

The best way to get over a broken heart is to treat it like a boil. Lance the inflammation, release the pus (and there can be quite a lot), clean the wound, and then let the healing proceed. Amelia Sedley in *Vanity Fair* sniffled into a hanky for fifteen years over a total cad, but Amelia was a piteous wimp and an object of Thackeray's satire. Give it six months to a year and then for goodness' sake contain the wallow. You are not Morrissey or Morisette, so don't moon unless you're being paid royalties to do so. Don't let your past gobble up the potential of your future. You might meet the love of your life at a support group or just hours after you've been kissed off.

Your veil of melancholy will lift—but you must be vigilant. Stringently edit past associations—certain places, certain songs, certain turns of phrase, pet names, and baby talk. Stop idealizing the intimacy you once had and establish new routines. Try not to imagine how your ex-lover would respond to the new you, and don't fall back on wanting that approval. If you get tempted to see your ex—to parade that hard-won, fragile new confidence—

forget about it. You are not changing for your ex. You are changing for yourself.

✿ A haircut is a symbolic action even if it's just a trim. Spruce up with some organic color (henna or Herbatint), have a deep-moisture treatment, cut off your split ends, and kiss your dead-end dreams good-bye. Beware of home jobs with nail scissors.

✿ Be picky about which friends you see. Only the sunny and the sensitive should surround you now. Moaners, back stabbers, and pessimists are unwelcome guests.

✿ Coddle yourself. Burn scented candles, pout beautiful in a lipstick the color of crushed roses, buy some soft angora socks and wear them in bed.

✿ Milk the venom. Resentment, unexpressed anger, hurt, and feelings of violation are like toxins. Left to fester, inside they can harden you for years. Get them out through creative channels or just plain destructive ones—paint it out, wail and smash your pillow. Anything totally absorbing and physically exhausting is good. Later, much later, when you've come down from your cathartic freak-out, you may come to see a hurtful love experience as a lesson. But first set to clearing the darkness out of your heart. Think of the very worst moment and then scream, *"YYYEEEEAAAAAARRRRRGGGGHHHH!"* Or something like that.

LONELINESS

You know you are lonely when you wake up at 2 A.M. in the middle of summer shivering with cold, feeling tiny in an empty bed. You know you are lonely when you haul a bag of groceries home and wonder about all the mindless, solitary, unwitnessed acts that make up your life. Waking, washing, working, schlepping, worrying, waiting—all alone. You know you are *very* lonely when all of your friends are out on a Thursday night and you leave chirpy messages on their machines but really want to cry. You know you're getting desperate when a dog tied up outside a bar looks happier than you do. Loneliness sits about your shoulders like stale perfume. Because the aura of loneliness is so palpable to others, it becomes twice as hard to meet people and alter your circumstances. At lonely times you may be grateful for the attentions of highly unsuitable suitors, not realizing until too late that the worst kind of loneliness is experienced in the wrong relationship.

To salvage pride and break the spell, the lonely need to cleanse their desolate, needy aura. Instead of reaching out, you must reach in and warm your own heart. The first way to do this is learn how to be alone without feeling lonely or unloved. Use your solitude to do the things that make you happy—play music, cook a weird recipe, commune with your spirit, get lost in a project. Step two is to get out of yourself by helping others. Instead of moping around feeling abandoned, volunteer in a soup kitchen, visit a hospital, or just answer the phones a few hours a week for an organization you admire. (See Political Responsibility, page 231.) Feeling useful is a great cure for self-absorption. My ninety-three-year-old friend Thelma helped me through plenty of lonely times by making me feel needed. I made her dinner sometimes, fixed her a whiskey the way she liked it, and even helped her go to the toilet. Sometimes we'd just sit holding hands. Her cool skin and wrinkly smile made me feel warm and connected.

When you look back at the times in your life that you were most alone, you might feel a nostalgic thrill at how you managed to survive. It is much harder to cherish the gift of solitude when you're smack dab in the middle of its thrall. But this is the very best time in your life to meet your self and enjoy her. A good book to build your strength in this area is *Intimacy and Solitude* by Stephanie Dowrick; another is *Peace Is Every Step* by Thich Nhat Hanh. Take inspiration in your own liberty. Okay, living alone or traveling alone can feel cold, but imagine the millions of women across the world who will never be permitted these simple freedoms. If you can sit in a café on a rainy day undisturbed or dance around your shuttered living room in a pair of Ugg boots and nothing else— ENJOY! It's freedom!

POVERTY

The depression that comes with being broke is self-perpetuating. The leaner times get, the more hope diminishes. Poverty, like loneliness, has a scent. I remember friends avoiding me when they knew I needed a loan, potential employers eyeing me harshly, and feeling shabby and flaky in the eyes of the world. To get through this one you need help and a truckload of front. Basically you have to scrape together enough confidence to land a job—any job—and start earning, pure and simple. Being constructive is crucial. Keep away from the TV and don't retreat into late mornings in bed; keep the routine you had as a worker by getting up each day and attacking those want ads. Pay attention to your grooming and, above all, remember that you are a capable woman entitled to gainful, dignified employment.

BIRTHDAY BLUES

I doubt that turning thirty or forty is enough to induce a deep depression, but these milestones can make a girl morose. Thirty makes you panicked about career and confused about how sheer to wear your stockings or your lipstick and whether brief affairs of the heart are an extravagance now. At forty, issues of girlhood take a backseat to career crossroads, huge lifestyle choices, and, for some, the command of the biological clock. You really start to change physically and, unless you're a French actress who never smiles, life's experience starts to show. This isn't a bad thing but it's confronting—and anyone who denies it is fibbing.

Getting older is defined by the beauty industry not as living or growing or even evolving, but as aging. "The visible signs of aging" mentioned in so many ads are obviously to be avoided at all costs, and the costs are damn high. Every new decade a woman enters seems to be accompanied by a new level of beauty-product dependence, an overpriced armory against the "signs." The media is saturated with images of women who slide from decade to decade seemingly untouched—or should I say retouched? Physical ideals of beauty (at any age, really) are unreachable and other ideals—picture-perfect lover, mother, career woman—can be hard on late bloomers and women who do things a little differently.

Take heart in the new breed of role models. The more we see of stupendous, inspiring women who aren't girls anymore, the more encouraged we feel to grow up: unconventional dynamic moms over forty (Melissa Etheridge, Edna O'Brien, Susan Sarandon), sexy performers at forty plus (Helen Mirren, Judith Jamisson, Judy Davis, Jean Moreau, Anouk Aimee, Claudia Cardinale, Jessica Lange), and the spectacles of Tina Turner's mythic legs and the sculptor Louise Bourgeois's gorgeous hands give us quite a lot to look forward to.

After thirty sexuality, energy, wit, and good skin all feel like gifts you finally know how to use. After forty there is no way you will put up with a dumb boss, a dud lay, or subtle putdown without a quickfire response. After fifty you occupy your body with the grace of a woman who knows who she is utterly. And there's a poignant beauty in this loss of self-consciousness. Being comfortable in one's own skin, no matter how long it takes, is the most beautiful thing a woman can be.

Ironically, it is usually the very young who mourn the loss of their youth the loudest, counting every smile line, calling the salon at the sight of the first gray hair, getting botox injections to freeze the natural animation of the face. If you treat your birthday as a big downer each year, how are you living the rest of your life? Commemoration rather than commiseration is the secret of growing up gracefully. Make each decade you turn a celebratory milestone. Buy a tree (not a bonsai) and tend it with love. Wear red. Think about growth instead of gravity. Don't go home with the last man left at the party!

UNFULFILLED DREAMS

Dreams, they say, are for the young. But if you want to go to Perugia and join the backpackers munching Baci and learning Italian at age sixty-four, I say do it. If a dream is still with you long after girlhood, it needs to be realized. Go and make a cup of tea now and list your five burning dreams. Don't censor yourself. Okay, now look at your list. At least one of these dreams will cost nothing (to swim naked, to tell someone you love them), at least one will involve risk (to travel, to get a tattoo, to kiss a stranger). Some of your dreams may be obscenely expensive. Why not start with the ones that cost the least and work your way through? Some visions and life paths take a while to emerge, while others are misfires. You may still want to bleach your hair and start a Blondie cover band, and who's to stop you? Dreaming is free.

REMORSE

Sometimes sadness is a seed lodged within you from a very long time ago. Something as complex as therapy or as simple as a powerful taste or scent might be enough to recover a long-buried memory. Or sometimes you have to work harder to dislodge it. Feelings of remorse that just won't go away need to be faced with compassion and then acted upon. If the people you wish to appease are still living, get up the courage to call them or write them a letter. You may not receive a response, but you have done what you could. If you want to say you're sorry to someone who is dead (and this is more common than you think), go ahead and write a letter as well. In his book *Teachings on Love*, the Buddhist monk and poet Thich Nhat Hanh suggests the ritual of sitting down and writing a long letter as a cleansing gesture of loving kindness and a letting go of old hurt. He's right. Contrition is the first step to self-forgiveness. We all make mistakes, but how good it feels to get them out in the open and then let them go! Say you're sorry without pride, make an offering, and then let love heal your old wounds.

Tickle Your Fancy

Happiness is more than the absence of pain; it is a radical shift from one state into another. It is a subtle transference of energy from darkness into light. It's a smell like jasmine or burnt sugar on the crust of a pie. It's the sound of a zipper on a new dress or the wet sandpaper tongue of a cat: anything that jolts introspection and forces you *up* and *out*. When I want to feel happy I try to change my context—move into a beam of sunlight, thrust through the air on a swing until my toes reach clouds, listen to a whole CD in bed, go to a movie in the middle of the day, or draw a picture of a place I'd rather be. If all else fails I reach for a stack of children's books and let them provide the transport to a realm of lighter spirits. A good picture book makes you laugh and think *and* smile. They give you good impulses: to chase invisible dragons, laugh at your own bad jokes, invent your own rhyming slanguage, paint autumn leaves lime green, wear cowboy boots and tangerine lipstick to the supermarket, or treat a pebble beach like a jewelry store and select faux diamonds and pearls for your moonstone tiara.

Sometimes being true to yourself means looking a little eccentric to the outside world. To do this you need a very supportive circle of imaginary friends. These are mine.

ELOISE

Everyone talks about finding your inner child, but what a dribbly insipid image that summons up. Better to excavate the naughtier incarnation of the inner brat. Eloise is the best brat of all because she has tangled hair, a potbelly, and a bad-girl attitude that makes a mockery of adult ways and leads us back to the sandbox where airy affectations are shed and the most important of all Very Important People is a pet turtle. Eloise is dead sophisticated. She raises pigeons in the bathroom of her suite at the Plaza Hotel, wears a necklace made of champagne corks, orders one raisin and seven spoons from room service, gets her sneakers cleaned and pressed, and reads the *Herald Tribune*. Despite the fact that Eloise dines at Maxim's and has had a dress designed for her by Christian Dior (sans tassels), she's no snob. She knows how to make a pair of skis out of two loaves of French bread and order up a whiskey for her nanny. The best thing about Eloise is that she is an uptown girl with bad hair. Her bons mots sum up a life of insouciant swagger and a flagrant disregard for the banal:

ELOISEISMS

❀ *"You have to eat oatmeal or you'll dry up. Anybody knows that."*
❀ *"Getting bored is not allowed."*
❀ *"Paper cups are very good for talking to Mars."*
❀ *"I always travel incognito."*

OPAL WHITELEY

Opal Whiteley lived at the edge of the woods in the logging town of Cottage Grove, Oregon, at the turn of the twentieth century. Opal was a real person, a child prodigy who wrote her memoirs as she lived them. At age six she started to write a diary using wax crayons on scraps of paper that she hid inside the hollow of a tree. The pages became her nature diary, an extraordinary account of the lives of the animals, trees, plants, and people in her world.

Opal's spelling was phonetic and her grammar and expressions downright strange; still, after a few chapters you fall into the rhythm of her inventive lexicon. Opal would put her ear to a maple tree to "have listens to the sap going up" or stand beneath the tall firs and declare, "I do so love trees. I have thinks I was once a tree, growing in the forest." She wondered whether humans can hear the earth's song carried along by the wind; she made friends with a little girl whom she called "the girl with no seeing." Because her friend was blind, Opal taught her about nature through touch and sound, unpinning her friend's hair so the wind could blow through it.

Opal was eccentric, no doubt, but she was also mystical, perceptive, kind, optimistic, and brave. No matter how many times she got spanked for disappearing into the woods or stealing cheese for her pet rats, Opal always felt blessed. "I am happy," she wrote one evening from her back porch. "I am happy listening to the twilight music of God's good world. I'm real glad I'm alive."

THE MOOMINTROLL

If the Moomintroll were in your class at school he'd be the boy everyone stole lunch from. He's a snow-white troll with a fat bottom, a vulnerable belly, and a great big rounded snout like a hippopotamus. Moomintroll lives at the center of Moomin Valley, a mythical Nordic land skirted by cold deep oceans on one side and dark pointed mountains on the other. Moomintroll's family hibernates throughout the winter, sleeping through the sunless months, but Moomintroll himself wakes up. The poor creature isn't very brave when forced to face the vast snowdrifts and cold gray sky alone. "Some things just are," the story explains, "but one never knows why, and one feels hopelessly apart." The winter, he discovers, is populated by whole tribes of creatures that only emerge when the rest of the world is hibernating. He's plunged into an existential landscape bathed in silence and moonlight and befriended only by the prickly, the hairy,

Read One & Call Me in the Morning

Eloise
by Kay Thompson
SIMON & SCHUSTER

Eloise in Paris
by Kay Thompson
SIMON & SCHUSTER

The Singing Creek Where the Willows Grow: The Mystical Nature Diary of Opal Whiteley
by Opal Whitely
(with a biography and an afterword by Benjamin Hoff)
PENGUIN

Moominland Midwinter
by Tove Jansson
FARRAR, STRAUS & GIROUX

Moominpappa at Sea
by Tove Jansson
FARRAR, STRAUS & GIROUX

The Little Prince
by Antoine de Saint-Exupéry
HARCOURT BRACE

Horton Hatches the Egg
by Dr. Seuss
RANDOM HOUSE

Max Makes a Million
by Maira Kalman
VIKING

Ooh-la-la (Max in Love)
by Maira Kalman
VIKING

and the very weird looking. Unable to wake his mother for advice, he must hold his own counsel when these creatures invade his home, rearrange the furniture, and eat all the jam. As Moomintroll blunders through, he turns to one of his hairy friends, Too-Ticky, for solace. All she tells him is, "One has to discover everything for oneself . . . and get over it all alone." Thanks a bunch, thinks our Moomintroll, but he does just that: surviving a blizzard, learning how to ski, and even summoning the temerity to save his crabby friend Little My from being swept away on a broken shard of the frozen sea.

Tove Jansson, the Finnish author of all the Moomintroll books, lived alone in a lighthouse, and the mood of fruitful introspection and dreamy silence of winter pervade all her books. What makes *Moominland Midwinter* special is the Moomintroll's subtle but remarkable transformation from clumsy and dependent to resourceful and self-contained. By the first day of spring the gentle Moomintroll knows how to be alone, and suddenly he feels happy about it. This book is a comfort to anyone who is afraid of silence, darkness, or emptiness.

THE LITTLE PRINCE

Of all the little boys in children's books, the Little Prince is the greatest heartbreaker, but his tale leaves you happy-sad. Patiently he travels from planet to planet learning grown-up ways, and just as patiently he turns them on their head. The characters he meets in outer space are the shards of human weakness that make up our delusions—the conceited man who wants to be admired, the tippler who drinks to forget that he drinks, the businessman who thinks he owns the stars, the lamplighter who must light and extinguish his lamp every minute, because his planet revolves so quickly. Unfazed by extreme personalities, the Little Prince soldiers on until he reaches the earth. Here he befriends a fox and a man he finds lost in the desert. In typical Little Prince logic the gifts they give each other cannot be seen or touched, only felt. The Prince teaches the man to trust, leading him to a well in the heart of the Sahara. The fox teaches the Prince about attachment, begging the little boy to tame him. No sooner do we get to know the Prince (and like anyone worthwhile, he's hard to get to know) than he has to leave. Before splitting the scene, the Prince asks us to believe that he is not dead but merely traveling back through space. The joy of this book lies in the fact that it covers heavy ground (love, death, yearning) without being earnest or maudlin. Like a good friend, it makes you complicit in a secret language and forces you to be understanding toward peculiar ways. After *The Little Prince* you'll want to draw everything (no matter how clumsily) and question everyone. And you'll never see the stars the same way again.

HORTON

Horton the elephant is left holding the baby when lazy Mayzie the flittery bird skedaddles off to Palm Beach. Somehow, carefully, tenderly, and gently, Horton hauls his bulky butt into the tree and sits it out through storms, snow, and great white hunters to protect his little egg. Horton's creed is patience and fidelity and his motto— "I meant what I said and I said what I meant, an elephant's faithful one hundred percent!"—keeps him going through the hard times. Ridicule, doubt, and even a custody battle with Mayzie ensue until the glorious moment when the little red-and-white polka-dot egg hatches open. Horton's reward is a tiny elephant with the wings of a bird. Dr. Seuss knows when something is right in the universe and he isn't afraid to hammer the point home. Horton has his freaky little offspring and the book sings, "And it should be, it *should* be, it SHOULD be like that! Because Horton was faithful, he sat and he sat." Blessed be the patient and the willfully original.

MAX

You don't have to be a snob to be worldly, you don't have to be sad to write poetry, and you don't have to walk on four legs to be as happy as a dog. These are the lessons taught by Max, the poet-puppy-bon vivant invented by Maira Kalman to show the women of the planet what a real man (I mean mutt) is made of. If Max were a guy we'd all want to date him because he goes through life collecting strange friends and romantic adventures like a hybrid of Jerry Lewis and Jack Kerouac. In the first book, *Max Makes a Million,* our intrepid hero is broke but hopeful. He dreams of going to Paris and in the meantime he proclaims "Someday, fat families and skinny families around the world will be reading my poems and laughing and crying. I feel it in my bones." Max shares his studio with Bruno, an artist who paints invisible paintings. Max's neighborhood is full of sexy, artistic types and every obstacle in his eyes is a blessing: "Sometimes," Max muses, "you make a mistake, or break something or lose a hat and the next thing you know, you get a great idea."

He's obviously a genius! And in fairytales, genius is rewarded quickly and painlessly. Before you can say "hot croissant," Max gets a call from his agent and is informed that he has sold his book for a million bucks. He packs his little brown suitcase, leaves his owners (the Stravinskys), and jets off to Paris to follow his dreams. Any right-minded girl who reads this book wants to join him. Any right-minded girl forgives him for falling in love with a bitch (Crêpe Suzette, the singing canine chanteuse) and eagerly awaits his next adventure. Viva Max! The lucky dog with his dream shoes on.

COMMUNICATION

Can We Talk?

Successful communication is a matter of follow-up—no matter what. A letter after an unsuccessful interview, a thank-you note after a dinner with friends, a hospital visit, or just a silly Post-it poem left on the fridge door for your roommate puts you in contact and back in the driver's seat emotionally by easing that anxious feeling that arises from too many loose ends.

"Keep in touch" is a harmless little request that easily becomes a burden. At fifteen you could hold phone marathons without breaking for food, rest, or breath. Ten years later you have to pinch yourself to make contact once a week. As you get older life splinters: Your friends move away or into relationships, motherhood, or jobs with weird hours or bosses who so unreasonably don't permit those crucial forty-minute catch-up phone calls. In order to maintain friendships and contact, you have to look hard at the limitations of your time and energy and make the best of the media you have available. E-mail, fax, mail, phone, florist, and Internet are your tools, and having friends and family who understand the way you live also helps. Modern living means disappearing for up to three weeks without having to say you're sorry. After a time you're going to realize that your best friends are not the ones who keep a tally pad next to the answering machine but those who see the words "Let's have lunch" in the abstract reality of distant time and space.

STAYING CONNECTED

Unless you sleep using an open Filofax as your pillow or are a double Virgo, you need lists, reminders, and a loose timetable to keep contacts (both intimate and professional) flowing. Make a little list. The top five are your top-priority people (lover, best friend, family, boss, mentor); the next five are people in temporary priority, rotating according to life right now (a specific project manager, doctor, friend with immediate needs, bank manager, coworker); and the rest of your list is a floating tribe. How to apportion your time is personal; some dear friends can subsist on a call a week, and some mothers are hurt if they don't

To: My Special Grandpa
FRONT PORCH, MAIN ST. SAG HARBOR
...iggins Bay
...Australia

hear from you by teatime. The fairest way to deal with people who want an unrealistic amount of contact and attention is to be direct. Tell them when you will contact them and then stick to that. Order your list according to emergency and importance, then take a good look across the span of your social network and ask yourself: "Who am I ignoring?" Your list may reveal a missing thank-you for a great dinner party or a lonely relative waiting for your call. A few minutes on the phone or a quick, loving postcard could mean a lot. Get cracking.

A COMMUNICATION TIMETABLE

Some people and situations demand daily contact and others much less; calling at the appropriate time is also important. Just because you've got fifteen minutes to shoot the breeze doesn't mean everyone else does. Ditto early-morning calls, weekend calls, impromptu drop-in visits, and late-night "emergencies."

Friends with Kids This is the friend who needs a flexible approach and generous, spontaneous help. Her time is stretched and her constant companion is someone who doesn't have a lot of good conversation beyond monosyllables. A face-to-face visit during which you contribute something useful (cooking, a few chores, a box of crayons) is easier on a new mom than a long phone fest—which is easy for you and almost impossible for her.

Girlfriends If your best friend is as busy as you are, she isn't available as a twenty-four-hour counseling service. Attempts to meet on weeknights can also be pushing it. More satisfying, then, is the once-weekly gossiping, dream-sharing, clothes-borrowing, bitching, window-shopping, stretch class. It's better to be there as a really strong shoulder to cry on once a week than to feel overstretched every second day. (For more on friend maintenance, see Friendship, page 173.)

Family Dinner or a long, engaged chat once a week deepens your connection and is probably your mom's ideal. Pity she lives in Alaska. If geography separates you from family, send photos. More than letters, snapshots live in wallets, on the fridge door, and on Grandma's mantelpiece. If a family feud is ongoing, be big enough to keep in touch (there is nothing worse than deathbed regrets). And if nothing separates you—you live close by and get along well—get together to do un-

PS: Don't forget Dad. Many fathers sulk in silence while the mother-daughter phone ritual takes up all available communication time. Call up, ask for Dad, and talk mostly to him. Reassure him that no, you do not need to borrow any money.

usual things like subscribe to the opera or share an exercise class. Parents sometimes get sick of being parents, the old standbys who seemingly don't need stimuli or surprises. It pays to delight them now and then with thoughtful spontaneity. Say, a bunch of flowers for no reason except that you love them.

Significant Others Love has no timetable except that it needs to break routines to stay fresh and sparky. Don't habitually save all of your petty grievances for one big fat snarling outburst over the weekend, or, worse still, roll over and play dead in bed to avoid having to communicate with your turtledove. It's better to take the initiative for brief, clear exchanges than to let resentments or personal needs bank up over time.

To confront your sweetheart with the threatening words "we need to talk" is equal to throwing a bucket of cold water over the desire to listen or talk. People open up when they feel safe. Weird vibes clear up when you take your unrelenting focus off them, and relationships often work better when you don't spend all your time monitoring their progress. Throw something unexpected into the mix: Get out of town, go to a café in a distant neighborhood, jump on a train, cook up a strange new recipe together, play Dean Martin full blast at breakfast, or simply unplug the TV and light a sea of candles. It's corny, but making that quirky, slightly unpredictable space at least every few weeks gives relationships a lift. The heart needs to dream and travel.

Communication in love takes a lot of honesty. The sort of honesty that makes you look hard at yourself before issuing a demand, or admit you're being manipulative when you say "I love you" in a baby voice. They say that men are rational, logical, linear in thought; women are intuitive, emotional, hypersensitive, and real cerebral multitaskers. Left brain, right brain, Sun and Moon, Mars and Venus, et cetera, et cetera . . . None of this means you can't communicate. It just takes patience and practice. Knowing when to simply listen, when to fill in the dots, and when to ask "What the hell did *that* mean?" means refining your sensitivity. Intimacy is built on hearing what someone really says, not just what you want to hear. Half listening, interrupting, breathlessly waiting for your turn to reply are all cardinal sins of couples communication. Shut up and love.

The Boss Depending on your job and the sensitivity, intelligence, and accessibility of your employer, make sure you update the boss on your progress once a week. Bosses are stressed, so don't wait for them to give you feedback first. Try to provide solutions instead of problems. Take the lead.

Workmates The occasional lunch or dinner with a few workmates can brighten up your work life. Out of the office everyone looks and feels more human. Subtleties and feelings tend to get overlooked when people are immersed in the job. A quiet workmate may be lonely or grieving over a broken relationship, an overly loud work-mate may be shy and anxious about her performance, an unbearable office manager may simply need a few gentle tips on human relations. Everyone wants to shine in her work and rivalries and insecurities are natural, but offices where there is care and communication are less stressful places in which to toil.

You All this time on other people—what about you? Getting in touch with yourself doesn't just mean checking out your pore size in the mirror. Meditation, keeping a dream journal, and lying in a bath festooned with frangipani are rituals that bring you back to a quiet place. To make sure you get the time to communicate with yourself (sounds sticky, I know), make sure at least four nights a week are TV-free and twenty minutes a day are purely yours—no phone, no love interest, no worries. (For more on this, see Solitude, page 205, and Spiritual Life, page 213.)

COMMUNICATION ETIQUETTE

✿ "No" is kinder in the long run than "maybe."

✿ Answer the phone politely and clearly; you never know who is on the other end.

✿ Try to remember names by putting a funny little (rhyming) reminder in your mind, like Miss Phipps (skinny hips), or try using association—Mr. Fredericks (of Hollywood). If you go blank at the point of introductions, simply name the people you do know. Really long, tricky names justify an abbreviation; if you can't roll your r's with Catalan finesse, just be honest about it.

✿ Call your mother by her first name in public, especially in boutiques crowded with snotty salesgirls. Imagine being trailed with a long, droning "Mommmmm" for half of your adult life.

✿ If two phones ring at once, tend to one caller and tell the other you'll call back, firmly but politely. No one likes to be second banana.

✿ Not everyone enjoys the phone. Get on, get it sorted, get off. (Warning: With certain men this could inspire love feelings.)

✿ Compliments, at their most honest and unconditional, manifest positive energy and spread verbal sunshine. Isn't it obvious? Hunched over computers, eating bad lunch, and dreaming of a Majorcan swimming pool, everyone needs to hear something nice.

✿ Don't call your boss at home unless your job or her job depends on it.

✿ With a job application: letter first, phone call second.

✿ Make friends with receptionists; they have to be pleasant all day long, you only have to be pleasant once. And they are the gatekeepers.

✿ Answering machine: Record a short, informative, low-decibel message on weekdays; a novelty, musical, or personal outgoing message on weekends (because it's only funny the first time).

WHEN NOT TO SAY YOU'RE SORRY

There are times to be sorry. So sorry that you send a note and flowers or apologize in person. These occasions should be rare and few. But if your conversation is liberally peppered with *"excusez-moi,"* it's time to look at what's motivating your urge to appease. If you are just naturally modest, start replacing the word *sorry* with the words *pardon me.* This awkward little mouthful will make you more aware of verbal cowering and force you to assess the suitability of an apology. If a particular person or context inspires a rash of apologetic mumbling, ask yourself, "Is this really the roommate/lover/boss for me?" Sometimes polite apologies mask less comfortable and less acceptable emotions: anger, guilt, embarrassment, fear. Are you really sorry for spilling the sugar bowl at breakfast or would you like to upend the table? Are you genuinely remorseful for being late for work or do you simply hate your job? Are you saying "sorry" when you really mean "leave me alone"?

To live apologetically is to live in frustration. Frustration swiftly transforms to anger, stifling the urge to confront the situation. Saying you're sorry for this and that becomes a passive-aggressive catchcry, implying that you're polite when you're actually brimming with resentment. Don't be sorry, be honest.

WHEN TO SAY NO

As Dirty Harry almost put it, a woman has to know her limitations. To say no and stick to it takes resolve and realism. Without a calendar next to the phone it's all too easy to accept five invitations and then find yourself gridlocked with obligation. Failure to voice your true feelings about sport or sex or sugar means you could find yourself watching the NBA at 3 A.M., waking up naked next to some gorilla, or eating meringue against your will. The temptation to say yes when you mean "no way in hell!" can be born out of a desire to please and avoid offense. However, a half-baked acceptance always winds up creating more friction than a diplomatic refusal. Use humor, warmth, and a firm tone and try to be honest. The longer the excuse, the flakier the impression, so if you're not being funny, be economical.

It would take eighteen months to genuinely follow through on all the agreements to "meet for coffee" that we so blithely fling at friends, ex-lovers, workmates, family, and pests, so stop saying it. You don't even like coffee, remember?

ARTFUL REFUSALS

Catherine Deneuve once said that men arrange their lives in pen and women in pencil, quickly bending to the needs of their lover. Umph! So much for liberty, fraternity, and equality, but the French ice queen has a point—until you learn to stick to your guns without apology, you are also living a life written in pencil: fuzzy, soft, and ready for last-minute revisions. Saying no gives greater meaning to your yes. The best refusals sound considered but decisive. Never precede a no with an ummmm . . . To extricate you from some of life's stickier wickets, here are a swag of elegant rebuffs and artful dodges. With the right comeback line you can resist everything *including* temptation.

The Gentle Come-On I like you a lot, but I'm not quite ready to drink hot beverages and roll on the carpet. Call me first thing in the morning and tell me your dream.

The Sporty Come-On Yes, it is terribly hot, and if I hadn't just washed my hair I would very gladly take off my clothes and plunge into the hotel swimming pool. How about an air-conditioned movie?

The Heavy Come-On No, I won't come in for coffee, but I would love to see you again in broad daylight, in a room crowded with people, near a taxi stand. Was that a good-night kiss or an invoice?

The Hard Sell No thanks, I have three of those already. Good luck with your sales.

The Eighth Move I can't help you move, but I'm happy to give you the number of a man with a van and a bottle of wine.

The Fattening Hostess I'm actually allergic to chocolate, can you believe that?

The Third Drink Alcohol depletes my ability to detect pheromones, greatly dulling all sensual desire and subsuming my being in a shroud of morose inertia. Mineral water would be lovely, thank you.

PS: To be firm does not imply inflexibility. Once you are strong enough to turn steamy embraces away at midnight, walk past a sale without blinking, refuse chilled French champagne, and guiltlessly ditch a dull dinner party for a night at home with Sam Cook and your Staffordshire terrier, try to strike a balance. Don't be a doormat or a drawbridge—sometimes the stranger invitations in life yield the greatest twists of fate.

FRIENDSHIP

Forget·Me·Nots

It's possible to be good at friendship: a glowing flame at the center of many fluttering social moths. It's much harder to be a good friend. Acquaintances can be kept amused with occasional dinner parties and light phone chats. Friendship demands more. For a friend you have to haul your ass out of bed for the 3 A.M. phone call when she's had three Rolling Rocks too many. For a friend you simply smile when you catch her splashing on the last of your Chanel No. 19 and snap affectionately when she starts up about body fat and the sodium content of hot dogs.

When you ask yourself what kind of friend you are, you come closest to knowing what kinds of friends you want around you. The best friend you can have will challenge you, inspire you, help define you, support you, love you for all your faults, and, if she's a real friend, point out those faults in a way that makes you laugh instead of cry.

Friendships can withstand distance, prolonged silences, and even major fights, but closeness shouldn't breed complacency. Neglect kills love. Being attentive and involved can be hard when life starts to accelerate and fragment. Constant travel, a bout of depression, or even an overly possessive boyfriend can drive a wedge between the closest girlfriends. If you find your friendships starting to splinter, put a night aside to "do the books" and literally account for the special people in your life. Being a great friend takes effort, but it's an engagement that keeps you warm for life.

DOING THE BOOKS

❀ Make a list of all your friends and draw four separate columns next to their names. In the first column note when you last made contact and record the content and tone of your conversation (did you talk or listen?). In the next column write an uncensored account of everything you love and everything you can't stand about each friend. In the next jot down the big life issues, challenges, or problems that each friend is going through. In the fourth list ways in which you could help. This exercise might take hours and it might reveal some uncomfortable facts. You might discover that you have been the

talker and not the listener in dozens of relationships. You might find that you don't really know what challenges your friends are going through, or you might see a friendship that looks a lot worse on paper than you had cared to admit. It's okay to be honest about who you really love and then find better ways to express that affection.

❀ Think about feelings and unspoken thoughts that you may have buried when talking to your friends. Perhaps you sensed the need to express affection or give advice but held back. Next time you speak try to be more open.

CHERISHING ACTS

It's too easy to lavish all of our most thoughtful gestures on lovers. Friends need romancing, too! Use your creativity to make a girlfriend feel fantastic out of the blue.

❀ Send a bouquet to her office with a ludicrously romantic message or profane limerick attached. Great postbreakup remedy.

❀ Celebrate the talents of your friends by supporting what they do. This might involve sitting through a whole tennis match or attending a small art opening after a long day at work. Make that extra effort.

❀ Update your birthday calendar and take note of your best buddies' passions. Personal gestures mean more than expensive ones—a private joke remembered, a favorite song sung over the telephone.

✿ Don't let milestones slip by. If you know a first baby or a fiftieth birthday or a graduation is impending, plan to make it special in a way that is intimate and unique. Write a poem, make a home movie interviewing everyone who knows your friend, or pitch in with others to send her to a spa for a day.

"And the Princess did inherit the castle, the love of three brave knights, a moat full of swans and two black pigs . . . THE END."

✿ If you have many long-distance friends, buy a large map (national or global) and illustrate it with small photographs, drawings, phone numbers, and e-mail addresses. Keep the map near the phone (with relevant long-distance phone-rate specials). *Or* have a stack of stamped, addressed postcards in a handy spot, ready to fill out and send when the mood strikes you.

✿ Pajama parties feel contrived after a certain age, but gatherings of girlfriends create all sorts of magic. Try a homespun karaoke night with vinyl records and potluck or an evening spent swapping clothes or drinking hot chocolate and doing the tarot. Your living room is a coven waiting to happen.

✿ Women together have tremendous constructive power. Use one of your girly nights to attack a shared project or pet cause (see Political Responsibility, page 231); have a working bee to help one of you move, paint a dingy kitchen hot pink, or get psyched up and outfitted for an important job interview. P.S.—Makeovers are a fun bonding activity for a girl's night in, but leave the hair dye to the hairdresser.

LOST AND FOUND: EMOTIONAL HOUSEKEEPING

It came as a shock in my late twenties to realize that I had outgrown several friendships. Growing up, the mantra of the teenage girl is *friends forever*. Later on, the mutability of life creates sometime friends, intense relationships that flare up and then fade away according to the point of your passage. Office friends, gym friends, prenatal class friends, book-group friends—people fall into the categories created by what you do together or what is absorbing you at the time.

There are times when you shed friends in great clumps. This can happen after a move or during a major life change such as a marriage or divorce, a shift in values, a loss of fortune, or even a radical upswing of good fortune. Unlike romantic relationships, there is no civilized way to break up with a friend; instead you tend to slink away, hiding behind workloads, grumpy husbands, and answering machines.

Phasing people out of your life can feel like cruelty, but pretending to be someone's friend is much worse. Toxic friends are the ones who make you feel guilty or heavy on a regular basis, mar your outlook with negativity, or betray your trust. I know I need to curtail a friendship when there's no equality (favors taken but rarely returned), when I feel intimidated and apologetic, or when I have to put on a constant front (of success or manners or happiness) any time that I'm with her.

Sometimes you choose to dump certain friends and other times you are the one who gets turfed. When my friend Michaela divorced recently, she found herself not only rejected by the married couples of her former social world, but snubbed by the friends who decided to side with her husband after the split. Forced to socialize with different people—single mothers, younger women, and unusual types—she found that conversation was more interesting, going beyond the old in-group gossip, and her new friends saw her as an individual rather than the spectral half of a couple. Becoming a social orphan isn't all bad. It means that your life has changed and so have you.

RIFTS AND REPAIRS

Life tests friendships. Rivalries, betrayals, stupid mistakes, or a few thoughtlessly placed words can sometimes wipe out years of intimacy. The saddest thing is to lose a friend over something petty or to let a misunderstanding blow out of proportion. When friends are worth saving, you have to go the distance. If you find yourself treading on eggshells around certain friends, work up the guts to say something. Having a real heart-to-heart clears the air and stops molehills from turning into mountains of resentment. Be honest, play fair, don't let resentments stew, and, most important, don't lend anything you're not prepared to lose: favorite dress, money, boyfriend.

SHALL WE FIGHT? THIRTEEN WAYS TO TEST A FRIENDSHIP

1. WHINING

Problem You call your closest confidante for a light-hearted chat that deteriotes into a massive gripe about your commitment-phobic emotional bonsai of an ex-husband, the hairdresser who gave you squirrel-colored highlights, your aging spaniel who's incontinent, and the fact that Clinique has discontinued Rich & Raspy Red, and . . .

Solution Sooner or later even the most patient friend will develop a whine allergy if all you do is use her as a sounding board. Before you call up your best friend for a massive rambling kvetch, count to seventy-five. Make a list of possible solutions, then make a cup of tea. Doesn't that feel better?

2. UNRELIABILITY

Problem You made it to her wedding but missed the vows, you e-mail her needed résumé advice only hours before the interview, you phone three times on a Sunday to say, "I'll be there soon," but it's dusk by the time you arrive with the croissants.

Solution Being dependable is more important than anything else you have to give a friendship. Respect your friend's time by not claiming it. Simply stop making plans you can't meet and be superdiligent about keeping your word.

3. RIVALRY

Problem You work together, inspire each other, fire off work-relevant e-mails, share contacts, ideas, and even the same personal trainer. You also watch each other like hawks for chinks in the armor and responses from your professional peers. Under the surface of all this camaraderie are two women competing like crazy.

Solution Sometimes admiration between peers slides into something altogether more cutthroat. There is a difference between egging each other on and naked rivalry. If work and friendship are bleeding into each other too aggressively, take steps to revive the interest you share *outside* the office. If that fails, ask yourself what this friendship is really based on.

4. SUCCESS

Problem You get engaged to a honey-colored diving instructor, lose five pounds, and are offered a job as Liam Neeson's personal masseuse in Paris. Suddenly two very close girlfriends are "busy or away from their desk" when you call. It hurts you not to be able to revel in your good news; it hurts them to even think about it.

Solution Share your great news but with sensitivity, and don't let it overshadow the events in the lives of your friends. If you inspire the odd prickle of jealousy, perhaps you're boasting unduly (good fortune can make us momentarily oblivious). True friends stick by you on the ascent as well as the descent in life. They keep you real.

5. DISTANCE

Problem Your hosiery company sends you to Vienna to research the sexual psychology of control tops. You wonder how to send Sacher torte by FedEx and how to gossip telepathically.

Solution If you hate writing and hate the phone, long-distance friendship will be a problem. But even the most perfunctory e-mails can keep a bond alive. What friends need when you're away is to be able to track your life and in some way feel like they are part of the adventure.

6. MONEY

Problem You've sublet your apartment to a friend and she's three weeks behind in the rent. Another friend is perpetually broke and needs you to fork out for taxis, movie tickets, pizza. Yet another has married rich and suggests you meet at expensive restaurants or bars where the cocktails cost more than a French lipstick.

Solution Money is something you need to be clear about with friends, and the less business you conduct with really close ones, the better. If a buddy continually leans on you for small loans, find ways to help her that are not monetary. It's more constructive (and cleaner) to give time instead of cash if it goes toward building economic autonomy (helping her job search, loaning smart clothes, referring her to a debt management agency). When it comes to socializing, it's only common courtesy to take personal budgets into consideration. It should be perfectly okay to need to know how much a birthday party at a restaurant will cost per head, and it is perfectly fine to say, "Precious heavens, I just can't afford Aspen this year, let's hit the ice rink instead." Broke never has to mean landlocked.

7. CHANGE

Problem You have come out as a radical lesbian and your best friend from high school is still living with strict fundamentalist parents. You go out to see bands till 1 A.M. and she's an early riser with kids. You're a vegan and a budding animal rights activist; her idea of bliss is ribs, ranch sauce, and a night at the rodeo. How do you lasso it all together?

Solution Growing apart as individuals is natural; parting because of it seems a waste. Weigh the things you want to salvage from an old friendship against your differences. Those who can't agree with each other sometimes teach each other.

8. TRAVEL

Problem You are a control freak who needs to micromanage each day's schedule right down to prebooking restaurants, and your friend thrives on serendipity and following her nose.

Solution Travel tests compatibility on every front from the grand (she hates the Louvre) to the ridiculous (she is lactose intolerant in Switzerland).

Sit down and talk turkey about your travel MOs, your attitudes toward money, sexuality, comfort zones (is your idea of accommodations five stars or backpacking?), food, and even allergies. The middle of the Amazon rain forest is a hard place to discover your Livingstone has arborphobia.

9. FAVORS

Problem The week you flew off to Sun Valley and asked her to return your library books, check your message machine, and lend you her cherry red cashmere turtleneck on Valentine's Day was the week she screamed, "I have all of the responsibilities and none of the privileges of your damn wife!" and left you standing in the middle of the airport.

Solution No one wants a friend who disappears between favors. If you receive, you have to reciprocate. Keep track of the things you ask for (small and large); make a list if need be. You might be amazed at how long it is.

10. BETRAYAL

Problem Loose lips sink ships. How well can your friends trust you if you have amusing anecdotes about *everyone* you know?

Solution Button it. And while you're sitting there, ask yourself why you need to gossip or generate mini scandals. Do certain friends demand salacious morsels about people you know? Are they worth the price of losing the fidelity of less bitchy buddies?

11. BOREDOM

Problem Routine meeting places, boring rituals, and the same old, same old can get girlfriends into a rut.

Solution Treat your next meeting with the ingenuity of planning a date. Go to a museum instead of the mall followed by high tea in a fancy hotel lobby. If your tête-à-têtes are falling into a vacuous groove, start a two-woman book club, cook a weird feast at your place, or go to a provocative play together. Steer the conversation toward engaging topics. Even if you argue about values and social issues, it sure beats talking about love 24/7.

12. TAKING FRIENDS FOR GRANTED

Problem You made a joke about her lisp (hey, you always josh each other); you borrowed her Kate Spade raincoat (one more time wouldn't hurt) assuming she'd understand. She didn't. What gives?

Solution Taking a friend for granted can be the result of too much rather than too little intimacy. Ditto trampling her boundaries or taking a joke too far. Like old dance partners, you need to swap sides to improve your step and gain perspective.

13. ROLE PLAYING

Problem Maybe you're the clown, or the drama queen, or the ever-patient listening ear. What a bore it is to have to crack a joke when for once you want the luxury of being moody and self-indulgent.

Solution Just like in a family, it's easy to settle into a role with certain friends. To shift the dynamic, try slipping out of character: If you're the relationship counselor, deliberately close up shop; if you're the demanding one, try giving. Stepping out of a role can make others uncomfortable, but it's often the only way to force them to see you in a new, multifaceted light.

CHARLIE BROWN:
*I don't know. I just feel
lonely a lot of the time.*

LUCY: *Why don't you try
taking dance lessons?*

CHARLIE BROWN: *Dance lessons?
What if no one will dance with me?*

LUCY: *Then you'll be a lonely person
who knows how to dance.*

—"Shall We Dance Charlie Brown?"
CHARLES M. SCHULZ

DATING

Perfumed Anxiety

PRINCIPLES OF MODERN COURTSHIP

Dating is supposed to be fun. Easy, romantic, lighthearted, goofy fun. Actually, it's much harder than that. After the initial freedom of teenage dating, where you're just happy to be out of the house, grown-up dating takes a more serious turn. We want to get it right because we want to find the right person, but the best love stories are full of mistakes. Terrible fumbling sex on the first date, turning up at the wrong cinema, spurious first impressions, jokes that fall flat, and accidents with clam sauce. My happiest relationships started with the worst first dates: landing facedown at the ice-rink, arguing in a Thai restaurant, turning up half tanked dressed like a mountaineer, but that doesn't mean you can't have a beautiful beginning.

The trick to dating is to take the heat off. Just because you are looking for someone to love doesn't mean you have to weigh every action and read every nuance of the date with that imperative in mind. The pressure to act like a princess because you want to find a prince has spawned a litter of retrograde dating books that urge unnatural behavior—be available but not that available, be smart but never smarter, answer the phone but only after four rings, be witty but not hilarious and so on. What these books *never* tell you is that it's okay to be insecure and that general rules for love are ridiculous. Making yourself unavailable to someone you really like is unnatural. So is contrivance. Get too tricky about love and you run the risk of blunting your instincts. Look at Emma, Jane Austen's manipulative heroine. She spent so long restructuring the ornamental garden of her romantic sphere that she left her heart under a hedge.

Somewhere amidst all the confusion of intuition, bad aftershave, drawn-out life stories and clammy handholding there is the mystery and excitement of the unknown. Ultimately, the attraction that makes a date zing is subcultural and subconscious, pulsing on the primal plane of scent and rampaging through the ancient turf of tribal archetypes. If you want to break it all down like a chemical compound, you're going to miss something. Don't try to catch the butterflies in your stomach, let 'em ramble. Viva uncertainty!

MEETING THEM

No one wants to feel as if she's actively searching for a date, so most of us assume the mock casual stance of looking but not looking: that slightly schizo mix of nonchalance and fresh lipstick. That willingness to flirt with almost everyone (butcher, baker, cocktail shaker) so we don't lose our touch. Being "open to new things," as they call it, is a highly fictionalized way to look at the world. Suddenly we're considering the intimate potential of perfect strangers. Yes, it's good to be warm and effusive but not so much that you become a freak magnet. I smiled at a Tuscan waiter once and he responded by pressing his mouth to my hand and raining a trail of kisses up to my shoulder à la Pepe Le Pew.

Just one look can be enough to initiate a conversation, but never let flattery ("he's talking to me, he likes me, he's talking to me, at last somebody wants me") get in the way of instinct. You don't want *any* man to ask you out, you want the one who's right for you. If you really want a carpenter who surfs, makes omelettes with home-grown sage, and digs Howlin' Wolf, go to a long-board festival or a craft expo, not a corporate cocktail party. Being in the right place with the right line isn't that hard to arrange. Even the rarest birds have their roosts.

HAPPY HUNTING GROUNDS

You are not alone in your feverish daydream yearnings. Relax in the knowledge that men are out there hunting, too. Ready for love at the hardware store, fantasizing about you at parent-teacher night, joining a yoga class in the vain quest for a tantric partner. Men (if that's what you fancy) are everywhere and they are probably a lot more nervous about finding dates than you suspect. To be able to make contact in spontaneous or awkward situations takes guts and ingenuity. You usually know it's OK to say something if uninterrupted eye contact has happened, but still it's nice to be sure. Personally, I don't buy that myth about meeting future husbands in elevators, but if that lift gets stuck, you have to be able to do more than just stutter. Unless you have considerate friends who throw candlelit pasta nights and invite swags of smolder-ing singles, you have to use your noodle. Here are just some of the places where you can find a date and none of them include the Net. Distrust any medium where you can't sniff your prey. Smell is very important.

SCHLEP SETTINGS

The Supermarket Never underestimate the po-tential for love in aisle three. The Motown muzac, the abundance of comfort food, the sound of your kitten heels clacking on tiles. This is a primal meeting place and a revealing one. Hint: Single guys buy a lot of salsa and corn chips.

YOUR LINE: *"Didn't your Mother tell you to eat your vegetables?"*

Public Transportation This happens in movies, but I once gave a boy a piece of paper that read: YOU WIN FIRST PRIZE FOR THE BEST-LOOKING GUY ON THE SUBWAY. I didn't include my number but the very brazen might.

Hailing a Cab You've got one hand on your hip and one thrust to the sky. You look so bossy, forceful, and ur-bane that any man who wants to share your taxi isn't just looking to save money.

YOUR LINE: *"Going uptown?"*

Moving It's the sweaty, no-makeup thing again added to the sexy new neighbor fantasy. In this scenario you get his details and not the reverse. Safety first!

YOUR LINE: *"What's the best restaurant on this street?"*

ARTY VENUES

Museums Fight your way through the tribes of gluey couples and you may find him, the sensitive art lover alone in front of a far-out installation. Carry a sketchbook; if you can't draw, be writing something.

YOUR LINE: *"Resonant! Powerful! Elemental!"*

Poetry Readings Barnes and Noble is full of single women with the same idea as you, but more obscure readings attract a diverse range of art dudes. If the poet himself is your sonnet made flesh, try this.

YOUR LINE: *"Those words [dreamy pause] are grazing up against the belly of the infinite."*

Film Festival Movie directors are promiscuous meglomaniacs, producers often lack irony. But there are plenty of nice guys in between and fun parties to meet them at. Get to as many screenings as you can so you have instant openers.

YOUR LINE: *"Tell me you don't want to direct."*

OBVIOUS SETTINGS

Wine Bar All you really have to do is walk in and sit down on a barstool; the rest is his story. To feel less sleazy, travel in a pack; to feel less predatory, drink lemonade.

YOUR LINE: *"Don't ask me my star sign!"*

Party Boys in the kitchen aren't shy; they're looking for girls who look good in bright light. Be where the food is and all you have to say is: *"Want some?"*

The Office A million-and-one pretexts for contact are presented by work. Do anything but don't ogle. Men can file for harassment, too.

YOUR LINE: *"Lunch tastes better in natural light—let's get outta here."*

Diners Everyone in diners jokes about the coffee, even the waitress. Diners are full of comfort food and red-blooded American burgers. Capitalize on the nostalgia and think romantic comedy.

YOUR LINE: *"This coffee bites."*

Airplane Talk about a captive audience! If you like what he's reading, if he doesn't hog the available elbow space, if he helps you with your luggage, go ahead.

YOUR LINE: *"I wanted the window seat and instead they gave me you!"*

UNOBVIOUS SETTINGS

Church, Temple, Mosque, Zendo What a hotbed of desire! Hymns! Formal dress! Eye contact! If spiritual life is important to you, this is the place for men who share your values. The community feel means you don't need a contrived introduction.

YOUR LINE: *"Hello, my name is . . ."*

Volunteering A man working in a soup kitchen or helping at a shelter might be the compassionate, intelligent type you've been looking for. See if he's for real.

YOUR LINE: *"How often do you do this?"*

Hiking Trip All you can see is his backpack bobbing up and down, but you sense the primal attraction amid the trees. Pace yourself so you're not gasping, try not to gab too much (bushwalkers dig birdsong) and then offer up your energy bar.

YOUR LINE: *"Can you still feel your legs?"*

Rodeo Buckle bunnies are fierce competition but that doesn't mean you can't be queen of the rodeo. Cowboys, like firemen, are broadly misunderstood and don't always need to be bullwhipped into attraction.

YOUR ACTION: You are not racing toward the pen, but simply relaxing in the bleachers holding two cold beers, you are smiling . . . camera dissolves.

CLASSIC FIRST DATES

Before the flame ignites you have to court the spark. The setting and selected activity of your first date is *molto importanto*.

The Coffee Date Coffee dates are always weird. It's like half a job interview combined with half a compliment. At the basest level, it means a man wants to see you out of the grainy blur of a cocktail lounge memory or stripped of Friday-night disco glitter. Damn him! Arrive in massive sunglasses and take them off dramatically. Or choose to have coffee in a context that has options—a great museum, a grand hotel, an aquarium. That way there's less of an egg timer operating on the attraction stakes and you have something to talk about if it's a fizzer. Coffee is the obvious tryout for the dinner date.

The Dinner Date If anything is going to diffuse the tension of that first *dejeuner* it's laughter. I say order light food (dessert before dinner), talk about anything but life history, emotional patterns, and ex-lovers. Choose a place where you can read the menu (just what is *jus*?), the prices are moderate (you may have to split that bill), and the lights are low but not sepulchral.

The Wacky Date The wildest first date of my life was at an ice-skating rink. No time for moody silences and long confessional outbursts when two bodies are slicing through the abstraction of white space. Bowling, karaoke, a kayak on the Potomac, or a quick half hour in a video arcade are all great icebreakers. There is plenty of time to get serious later on.

The Movie Date Good for sneaking sideways looks, holding hands, even kissing. Bad for talking, even innocent wisecracks whispered in his ear. Do not talk during the movie, since 98 percent of the population see this as a sign of future nagging. Also choose a film that you both really want to see and that sets the right mood. Action flicks are not conducive to sensitive après film cocktails.

FIRST IMPRESSIONS

For the sake of "the quest," we are willing to date unlikely types—men with beards, men who wear cufflinks, men your mother likes, men who say "Yes, Ma'am," men who carry guitars and harmonicas, men who carry Bibles. More often than not, though, breaking the mold of your "type" slides swiftly into comedy. One serial dater put it this way: "Let's face it, everyone knows within the first five minutes if the guy is attractive and interesting. If the date is a disaster he's good for three things—an anecdote for your girlfriends, a footnote in your memoir, or a

PS: A note on first-night jitters: No matter how old you are, standing outside a movie house with perfume behind your knees, a clean cardigan, and a hypernaturalist stance never gets easier. This is good. The point of dating is to delight in the strangeness of it all. But not too strange. Refine your instincts, hone your sniff factor . . . read on.

painful reminder of the man you *really* want."

But first impressions can also lie. Give yourself and him a chance. First to present yourself in a fair light (candles are cheating!) and secondly to know that your date is as nervous as you are. Usually the second date is where the real truths of romance come to pass.

YOURS

✿ The best impression you can make is to be the closest thing to your natural self (with good hair).

✿ Wear beautiful lingerie for good luck (and the strut of an Italian movie star), but otherwise dress comfortably. Cleavage, heels, and a brand-new dress will only make you drink twice as much and talk twice as fast.

✿ Try not to adopt the mien of someone attending a job interview. You are not there to appear reliable, win approval, or deliver a résumé of your private history. Not much.

Don't be a Goldilocks, who whimpered on about her porridge being too hot or too cold. If you're in the middle of a date that's going well, why spoil it by sending back a chunk of unseared tuna? Grow up and eat your vegetables.

HIS

Arrive late enough to see your date waiting for you. Do you like the way he leans against a lamppost? If you hate what he's wearing, try not to show it; he probably bought it that afternoon.

Ever so subtly look at his hands. Are they rough, practical, and strong, or clammy, long, and sensitive? Are they clean(ish)? Does the ring finger have a strange pale stripe as if a wedding ring had been wrenched off for the occasion? It happens.

Without being obvious, look at his shoes:

✿ **Crisp white socks with loafers (lives at home)**

✿ **Socks with sandals (either a marine scientist or a graphic designer)**

✿ **Bare ankles and lace-ups (try-hard casual)**

✿ **Paint-splattered black Oxfords (poets, vagabonds, prize slackers)**

✿ **Brand-new white Birkenstocks and spangly toenail polish (only if he's Beck)**

✿ **Shoes that light up when he walks (what, are you baby-sitting?)**

CHIT CHAT

✿ Initial conversations count for a lot, but they can also be quite deceptive. Attraction makes people say really inane things or blurt out unconscious yearnings during what they believe passes for light banter. A fervent passion for motherhood, therapy, and self-help literature are not great openers.

✿ First dates are the time to listen rather than cathart. You know your life story; what's his? Be prepared to hold back a bit—just a bit—and draw your date out. Why open your heart like an artichoke for an appetizer?

✿ Test your date to see if he's listening, but don't be too harsh: he might be transfixed by the shape of your lips moving at warp speed.

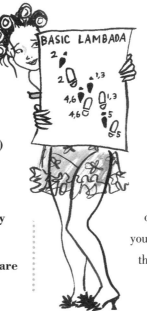

✿ Don't be put off by the fact that your sentences are overlapping like a bad riptide. Enthusiasm breeds bad timing.

✿ Prepare for those inevitable long silent gaps by thinking up some interesting topics of conversation beforehand. Something as simple as reading the newspaper or a compelling book review animates your mind for good discussion and takes the focus off you, you, you.

✿ Question but don't probe. Try to

trust that all will be revealed. Especially regarding sensitive areas: ex-wives, bankruptcy, and religious cults.

❀ Try to put aside self-consciousness about how you are coming across and focus on the person opposite you. Is he compelling? Funny? Kind? Physical attraction fills the ears with cotton wool and can sometimes make submissives out of fire eaters. If your date tells a sexist joke but he is really, really handsome, don't pretend you didn't hear it. Love may be blind but it doesn't have to be deaf. Listen up and then (if necessary) speak up.

❀ Beware the bore factor. Boring men deserve the cool dispatch of Lorelei Lee, the platinum princess of *Gentlemen Prefer Blondes.* Her eyes functioned like traffic lights, widening to invite the oncoming traffic of fascinating millionaires, dim-

ming to convey her obvious disdain for lesser mortals. You know in your stomach if a man is going to bore you senseless. If you want your date to clam up, confront him with a dainty little yawn or be really brazen and go powder your nose. Forever.

❀ Abandon the date who flops back in his chair and declares blandly, "I love a woman who makes me laugh!"; or who states his physical preferences like he's describing a car; or who talks about real estate or his mother for more than five minutes; or who puts your neck in a viselike shoulder grip when you're walking down the street; or who can't distinguish between vulgarity and innuendo.

WARNING SIGNS

Immature Men Men who make long, self-righteous speeches on why they would not bring children into the world and then admit they still live at home.

Miserly Men Men who are stingy with compliments, still carry the wallet they had in high school, and stare at the bill in a coffee shop! Men who complain about child support or ask you nervously if your shoes are new.

Possessive Men Men who hold you by the elbow when you walk, glare at the waiter until he scampers away, wince when you mention a childhood sweetheart, start planning the next date before the entrée arrives.

BORUS TEENAGUS

Still travels by
skateboard

BORUS BACCHUS

Worships wine, women,
and more wine

BORUS POETICUS

Handsome, indolent,
perpetually broke

BORUS ENVIOUS

Jealous of the pillow
you sleep on

BORUS LUSTUS

Smells of exotic perfume,
not yours

BORUS PARSIMONIUS

Penny-pinching Romeo

Complex Types Guys who say, "My emotional pattern up until now has been blah blah," and then look at you for a reply. Dates are not a free form of therapy.

Sulkers His brooding silences last for ten-minute stretches. He stares at you through a cloud of cigarette smoke and self-absorption. Sometimes there are genuine reasons for a man to withdraw emotionally; new relationships can be exhausting, emotions overwhelming, and words inadequate. But the coldness that comes with regular sulky withdrawals is also a very powerful tool of control. If Brutus wants to be alone that's fine. What isn't fine is when he wants to be alone in your company.

SEXUAL ETIQUETTE

There are certain signals in courtship seduction that mean "go forth and frolic." A few telltale signs will show you if he is a keeper or just, in the words of Leonard Cohen, a shining artifact of the past.

THE KISS

✿ Dry, closed-mouth mini pecks. Check if he paid for the popcorn.

THE VERDICT: *tight as a fish's sphincter.*

✿ Torpedo tongue. A kiss this forceful forces you to consider: If this is how his mouth feels, what's going on below?

THE VERDICT: *speed kills.*

✿ Diagonal and super-sloppy. The puppy-love kisser is wet and abstract like a fast-moving sloshy paintbrush. A kiss like this leaves your face as blotchy as an expressionist canvas, a real saliva survivor.

THE VERDICT: *drool is uncool.*

✿ Fast, erratic, and unpredictable. Kissers who stop and start, leap and dart are a bit like trying to sing along with Frank Sinatra—impossible. However, staccato kissers aren't necessarily born to lose. They might be nervous or overexcited, or shy or short-circuiting in their pants.

THE VERDICT: *slow down and stick around.*

✿ Hungry-like-the-wolf kissers who bite. Orson Welles once bit Eartha Kitt on the mouth so fiercely she went on stage bleeding. Even Catwoman herself would despise such bullying. Kissing should bruise but never break. Of all the acts of love, this is the softest and most intimate. Mucho macho fang action brutalizes the mood.

THE VERDICT: *my mouth isn't the main course!*

✿ The full-blown, slow burn. This is the kiss that starts with a soft, tentative smudge of the lips, proceeds with a delicate lick, presses forward with a full-blown kiss, and then retreats to circle the tip of the tongue with agonizing leisure. What follows is a passionate swoon that swirls your pheromones into the realm beyond thought. Sweet, deep, and dreamy, this is the magic kiss that all movies end on.

THE VERDICT: *besame mucho.*

SEX ON THE FIRST DATE

Convention decrees that date three is the lunge and plunge, green-light go, ritually approved lust zone. Some even say it's date five. There are happily entrenched couples who made fast, greedy love on their first meeting and joyous little brides who staunchly waited ten dates. But what about those more premature urges? What about the first date who peels back your soul like an onion and makes you want to do the same with your Wolford stockings? You're standing outside your apartment chin to chin, the moon is shining and it's obviously the "What's New Pussycat Whoa whoa woo woo oh?" Tom Jones moment when a neon sign descends from a starlit sky screaming, "Coffee, tea, or me, baby doll?" You can smell his skin, you've been brushing elbows and knees and wrists all evening long, all you can think about is dissolving inside a velvet kiss. Should you get inside as fast as possible and make love? Maybe yes, maybe no. Entertain your options with considered grace.

"*Waiter! Check! Taxi!*" —*Safety*

✿ No matter how old you are it's good to let your friends, roommates, or parents know where you are going for your first or second date. If you are going on a blind date, don't feel obliged to go alone, especially if you did not meet through mutual friends. Spooky people hang out on the Internet.

✿ Make a first date somewhere fairly public and accessible. A motorbike ride in the country or a meeting in a remote, unfamiliar spot is more dangerous than romantic.

✿ Wear shoes you can walk in; in fact, wear shoes you can run in!

✿ The second you get a weird feeling, listen to it. Never be embarrassed to cut an evening short or leap into a taxi; never feel obliged to receive a lift home or account for your movements and plans.

✿ Never trust the date who stands too close behind you on an escalator or stares goggle-eyed without blinking for longer than you can stand it.

✿ Be wary of unstable types with impeccable manners. Polite is okay, overattentive is creepy. And wanting more information than you are willing to give out is potentially dangerous.

✿ It may feel tarty, but throw a few condoms in your pocketbook. Desire isn't reckless; unsafe sex is.

FIRST-DATE SEX: PROS	FIRST-DATE SEX: CONS
Spontaneity and passion count for a lot.	Are you being a tad greedy?
You need to know if you fit together. What's the point of pursuing someone who kisses diagonally or doesn't know how to use ten agile fingers properly?	You haven't taken the time to get to know each other, so how much can really be revealed by a first, fast fandango?
You want to break down the tension and feel free.	Tension builds desire.
You think this is "The One," so why hold back?	If it's true, why not wait?
You want to wake up in his arms.	You wake in his arms feeling raw, exposed, and vulnerable.
You want to see him body and soul.	You get to see his tattoos, his back hair, his beanbag chairs, and his mother. Still lovesick?
You want him, pure and simple.	Give him a chance to want you just as much.
It is four bloat-free days after your period, you have a tan, you've done a yoga retreat—you may never look this good naked again.	Do you want a deeply shallow lover? Real love is cellulite-blind.
Sex is fun.	Sex is precious and potent.
Maybe this is just an affair. Affairs are fun and a great way to lose ten pounds.	Reread Flaubert's *Madame Bovary* or *Chéri* and *The Last of Chéri* by Colette.
You feel less inhibited with a virtual stranger.	One-night stands last one night.
You want to feel worshiped and hear all those beautiful lies that men tell when the blood ebbs away from their brains.	Fast in, fast out.
Sex makes you briefly forget your huge self-esteem problems. "I'm attractive, I'm desirable," you practice in the mirror . . .	You go home and as you wash off your makeup you smile at yourself in the mirror and declare, "I'm attractive, I'm desirable, *and* I made it home alone without sulking. He'll keep!"

COURTSHIP POSTCOITAL

Even when the dating is going well and you are finally lovers there are points of intimate etiquette that may need polishing. The moments after intimacy are very fragile: a whispered reassurance, a joke, or an affectionate caress brings two lovers back to earth gently. If your turtledove leaps from the futon looking for a packet of cigarette papers or answers a bleating mobile phone, he needs urgent guidance. Leave the *Kama Sutra* lying open at chapter 10, "Of the Way How to Begin and How to End the Congress," or simply read this excerpt aloud:

At the end of the congress, the lovers with modesty, and not looking at each other, should go separately to the washing room. After this, sitting in their own places, they should eat some betel leaves, and the citizen should apply with his own hand to the body of the woman some pure sandal wood ointment, or ointment of some other kind. He should then embrace her with his left arm, and with agreeable words should cause her to drink from a cup held in his own hand or he may give her some water to drink. They can eat sweetmeats . . . the juice of mango fruits . . . or anything that may be liked in different countries, and be known to be sweet, soft and pure. The lovers may also sit on the terrace of the palace or house, and enjoy the moonlight, and carry on agreeable conversation. At this time, too, while the woman lies on his lap, with her face towards the moon, the citizen should show her the different planets, the morning star, the polar star, and the seven Rishis, or Great Bear.
This is the end of sexual union.

We love this. BYO betel leaves.

BEYOND THE VALLEY OF THE DATE

There is a fuzzy zone that exists between "dating" and "a relationship" where you don't yet leave your pajama pants at his house but he *has* stopped phoning before he drops by. It is usually at this point that dates take on a different, slightly anxious, complexion. You begin to watch like a hawk for signs of commitment (use of the word *we*, planning more than a month ahead), you judge every throwaway line with humorless intensity and sulk if his attentiveness wavers. You get touchy and clingy and lie in bed with your eyes wide open while he dozes, obsessing: "Is this love for him or lust or a weird experiment or a passing fling or an unresolved mother issue or what? Am I in love with him or just addicted to the faint trace of cinnamon that scents his skin? Does he really like my body, can he sense that I'm awake? Why is he smiling in his sleep, who could he be dreaming of . . . why I am feeling so hideously needy? Can he tell? Is this love for him or just . . ." and so forth. This is a difficult time to stay cool and trust in the flow of the universe; you want answers! "Women always want to know what's next" men grumble. Damn right we do! Heck, some of us are even asking that question after date one.

It's hard to repress the desire to know *everything* your date is thinking, feeling, wanting, and dreaming, but really this is more information than you need. Obsessing over the subplot of a new romance, rushing home for a postmortem teleconference with your girlfriends, and torturing yourself with what-ifs change the dynamic of dating. Suddenly something magical and slightly unpredictable becomes a serious project and you're too preoccupied to appreciate just how beautiful the awkward instability of a new love is. Not just mutable but fragile and easy to topple.

If you demand answers too soon you'll get them, but they may not be the ones you want to hear. Pronouncements such as "We need to talk" or "*Where* is this relationship going?" asked too early are enough to make anyone feel cornered, pressured, untrusted, or just plain confused. Sometimes there *are* circumstances that give you the right to demand an emotional reality check: If he's booking two tickets to Istanbul after three weeks, if he breathes even one word about bambini or if he wants "space" after two dates. If, on the other hand, things are going fine but not hurtling toward an explicit conclusion, don't panic. Love isn't just a matter of good planning, it's a matter of timing. The things you are ready for now may be six months or six years away for your boyfriend. You might have to be patient or just plain realistic if the timing is off between you or there is a radical difference in age and aspirations. An 18-year-old man is thinking car registry, not bridal.

Not many people come together wanting all of the same things at the same time. They meet when they have divorced or been freshly broken-hearted or just bought a one-way ticket to Rajistan. Love is both tested and forged by such sources of conflict and divergence. Let your subtle powers of intuition feel their way, let yourself really get to know this beautiful stranger, trust your gut instead of your romantic paranoia. Once you silence your doubts or habitual fears you'll be amazed at how much you can feel and perceive. Nothing worth having was ever won by ultimatum.

LOVE

Myth vs. Reality

"Give me, Love, innumerable kisses, bound fast in my hair, and one hundred after that, and after that one thousand one hundred, and after that one thousand one hundred, and after many thousands, three; and then, so as to annoy nobody, let us destroy the accounts and count backwards."

—**CHRISTOBAL DE CASTILLEJO**

Love exists, but it is never the love you read about or expect. It is electrifying and astounding and messes up your best-laid plans. That's the good part. Love is also cruelly unpredictable. It's rarely a matter of justice: You may be virtuous and beautiful only to be brutalized by love. You may be wicked and lazy and inspire orchids and epistles.

To make love happen you have to believe in it all the way and wish audacious good fortune upon your heart. Approaching love with a theory of scarcity is no way to live. Love should never be the last straw; even on a desert island you still have a choice. Of course you do!

Love comes to those who wait and those who date madly, love dwells in every single little thing that makes you smile, and it lies dormant (like a spring bulb) in the worst crisis your life can dish up. Falling in love involves the risk that your feelings will be shattered by rejection—but even *that* is a bearable thought given the hardy nature of love. Picture Marlene Dietrich at seventy odd, lifting her world-weary lids and singing, "Falling in love again, what am I to do, can't help it!" and you know the woman lived every smoky gorgeous word of that song. Love doesn't stop, thank God, and every time you fall you do it a little differently.

To please your heart and answer your own dreams of love you need to abandon appearances and expectations. Forget the turquoise box from Tiffany's, the rose in the plastic cylinder, and being the envy of your girlfriends. You might run away with a climbing instructor twenty years your junior, you might find a passionate flame inside your heart at a religious retreat, or a seventeen-day affair may teach you more about love than a ten-year steady thing. There are no recipes. To enliven the debate and refresh your appetite for the cleansing energy of love, scan this list of clichés, myths, and love lore and feel free to cast your arrow into the void.

LOVE'S MYTHS EXPLODED
Myth No. 1
Love comes when you're not looking and when you least expect it.

Look but don't *look*; seek too hard and you'll be sorry about what you find. These words are profoundly irritating to a single woman. Everything in this society tells you to find love and yet you are supposed to pretend you can blithely live without it and act busy in the meantime. This is crazy. If you see someone at a party and you act on your attraction, is it hunting? I think it's just normal. If you go to extra social events in the hope of meeting someone, is that desperate? Sometimes it's practical.

According to the movies, boy meets girl when girl is inevitably carrying groceries to her brand-new one-bedroom apartment, oblivious to all admirers. Okay, there is some truth in this. Nothing is more attractive (in a man *or* a woman) than strength and containment. However, the idea of being strong, single, and ready for love shouldn't be seen as a weakness or contradiction. Perhaps in place of the old adage there could be an updated homily that goes something like: Love comes when you least expect it, and love comes when you pray all afternoon; love comes when you are wonderfully together, and love comes when you are falling apart. Just have faith that it will come.

Myth No. 2
Treat 'em mean, keep 'em keen.

This may be true early on in a courtship but it's disastrous for an ongoing open, communing love. Games hurt. Inventing a steeplechase romance in which you are the elusive prize and he is the hunter greatly diminishes the experience of love. Frozen to the spot, unable to initiate a kiss, your role as lover becomes passive. Or worse, solely focused on the idea of being won, you lose sight of the person who is pursuing you and (quite possibly) of your own needs. Being able to be yourself should be the greatest privilege and joy of an intimate relationship. Lovers who strategize and toy with emotions in the beginning lay the groundwork for an agonizing relationship throughout. My mother has a saying: "It's either on or it's not!" Stopping, starting, dawdling, and torturing are good signs that your new flame would be better in a bad French movie than in reality.

Myth No. 3
There are plenty of fish in the sea.

This is the last thing the brokenhearted want to hear and in some ways it is an untruth. Some loves really are once in a lifetime, so it pays to think deeply about your choices and your breakups.

Myth No. 4
You can't hurry love.

True and false. Some slow-starting loves are long burners, and others need to spark fast or they fizzle. Try to learn the difference between promise and long-suffering. One girl's classically extended courtship is another's unrequited heartache . . . which leads us to love long distance.

Myth No. 5
Absence makes the heart grow fonder.

Adversity can fuel love, but it can also pulverize it. If you have a pattern of long-distance loves, examine your motivation. To put it more bluntly: What's in it for you? Do you want the relationship or the adventure? Are you frightened to truly reveal yourself in the gritty light of mundane reality? Do you feel more charming over the Net than across the pillow? Lack of physical touch kills love.

Myth No. 6
Your wedding day is the happiest day of your life.

Perhaps, but don't forget the marriage itself. Beyond the dress, the cake, and the flowers, there's the reality of serving eighty years to life with one partner. Glamour and romance are probably the least-enduring aspects of a long haul spent with one person. Instead it's more like packing the dishwasher, conflict, understanding, repetition, desire, patience, aversion, compromise, temptation, routine, tenderness, kids, miracles, frustration, unpacking the dishwasher. Because love is sold as a cruise in a pink Cadillac when it's actually a long commute (with singalongs), there is a high incidence of trade-ins. To keep the engine turning over, create lots of little rituals throughout the year. Honor and celebrate your union over time instead of concentrating on just one big shebang.

Myth No. 7
Love is blind.

You don't have to be. Despite the pheromone rush of attraction, everyone has the privilege of exercising choice; take your time if you need to. Love shouldn't be like the last sale dress in your size. If it's real, it will still be there tomorrow.

Myth No. 8
True love is forever.

Ugh, what a burden. See love as a life sentence and both partners are bound to get clammy and claustrophobic. Even in marriage a couple needs to focus on individual days spent together rather than great heaving chunks of time. Cherish each moment to build up to a whole, and love becomes lighter and more spontaneous. Love is also seasonal, blossoming, shriveling, and rebudding over time. Old married people make love after decades and, quite often, they've put up with a dreadful amount in the meantime. Desire comes and goes. Sometimes you spend so much time with one person that he melts into you and you can't "see" him. Sometimes you trap the person you love into a finite set of rituals and responses and don't accept his change. Give yourself and each other a fighting chance.

Myth No. 9
Love is all you need.

Love is all you need but one lover isn't. To put too much emphasis on a committed long-term relationship as an avenue of salvation (in the absence of religion), as an escape (from self-doubt, poverty, or boredom), as acceptability (in the eyes of society, your family, or the law), or as ultimate fulfillment is very dangerous, not least to the relationship itself. Take the heat off.

Myth No. 10

Love the one you're with.

Or leave him. Don't slug out a relationship for the sake of being in one. Solitaire à deux is the pits—be alone instead of getting good lovin' gone bad.

Myth No. 11

Love means never having to say you're sorry.

No one ever believed this. Without contrition, love is doomed.

Myth No. 12

If you love someone, set them free. If they come back, they're yours; if they don't, they never were.

Those 1970s posters adorned with seagulls and sunsets hold a sickening grain of truth. Possessive love rarely flourishes. Whether it's a child, a husband, or a best friend, people need space to express their feelings. When you fall in love it's hard to loosen that grip and still feel secure, but you must try. Reassurance and open, intimate dialogue will give you the strength you need not to cling, but try not to demand. Before you ask for what you need from a lover, consider deeply what you can give of yourself.

PS: When you really love someone, setting him free or even giving him two weeks of "space" is about as easy as cutting off your hand.

Myth No. 13

(Three little words) "I love you."

In English we are pretty limited in our lovers' lexicon and, reductively, a vast range of emotional expression, expectation, and longing is crammed into one little phrase. "I love you" is the declaration that we all wait to hear. Why is it, then, that when we finally get our wish the phrase falls a bit flat? Often in a courtship, the L word is contraband for some months. Then, once declared, it's bandied about to a pulp. Used day to day in a long-term relationship, "I love you" can mean "I'm sorry," "You owe me," "I need you," or, more often than not, "But do *you* love *me*?" What can we expect if we use "I love you" as an invoice? When issued as an emotional demand the thudding silence that follows these words is its own reward.

Because "I love you" has been exploited by card companies and bad movies, it often doesn't feel *big* or *deep* enough to express a big, deep love and some lovers refuse to use it at all. It's up to us to find our own fresh expressions of intimacy. Showing and sustaining love are a lot harder than declaring it. Savor those three little words, mean them, don't wear them out, and (hardest of all) don't demand to hear them. Learn them in a foreign tongue.

Myth No. 14
There's nothing like the real thing.

I don't believe there is a real substitute for intimate human love and romance. It's natural to miss the heady rush of falling in love—the way it heightens every one of our senses and replaces the monotony of the solitary life with drama and dimension. Once tasted, it is hard to live without. But if you're in between loves, how are you going to live in the meantime? In a dreary self-absorbed vacuum or a vibrant playground? I say, get out the finger paints. Try to see the world for a day as an artist sees it— passionately!

Romancing your life creates energy, energy makes you happy, being happy brings back your sense of humor, and laughing makes you pretty. Everyone is suddenly asking you, "Are you in love?" and all you have to say is, "Yes, in fact, I am in love—with snails and poems and pastry flour and a cloud shaped like Mozart's ponytail and Lyle Lovett's voice and my nephew's big toe and the smell of fresh sheets and the squish of wet earth in the garden and the way I feel singing Etta James on my bicycle on a spring day—but other than that, no, not really."

Myth No. 15
Love is for life.

Many books will tell you that the aim of love is, eventually, to find the person with whom you can settle down, the person who is willing to have a long-term, serious relationship. Not this book. The idea of finding "the one" or the idea that marriage is a superior relationship leaves far too much in its wake. A woman may love four men in her lifetime, and they may not all have been her lovers. A woman may mother a child with one partner but choose to love and live with another woman later on. A woman may have many brief relationships to find that marriage suits her much, much later in life, or not at all. The idea that we must find someone with whom we can share our life is an anachronism, for we are sharing our lives with a broad range of special people at any given time. Focus on the one and we may miss out on the beauty and contribution of the many.

Spirit

SOLITUDE

The Wellspring

When Coco Chanel declared that she stayed in most nights to avoid bad wine and bad conversation, she had good reason. Sometimes a girl needs to coolly withdraw from the frantic pace of life and enjoy an evening or an afternoon of true solitude. Silence may be golden, but solitude is richer still. You need solitude to read, to let thoughts settle, to have strokes of genius and take deep, quiet reflection. Most of all you need solitude to get back to the most private and essential you, stripped of artifice, divorced from external demands, free to dance and dream and blob out to your heart's content. Unlike loneliness (which can be experienced in a relationship or at the throbbing center of a vast dance party), solitude is a chosen state. It's a time when you make a conscious decision to be alone, or when you find yourself alone and don't panic but use the time as a privilege. By spending tranquil time away from others, even for a few minutes a day, the heart starts to heal, creativity blossoms, ideas begin to germinate, and the mind has a chance to rest.

Sadly, many women never get the chance to experience solitude in a positive, creative way. We avoid silence, cluttering up what is perceived to be empty space with long phone conversations or the constant background noise of TV, radio, or loud music. Some only find themselves alone in times of depression—nursing a flu, in the aftermath of a breakup, or sulking during a fight. And most of us are kept in a state of constant movement, meeting the demands of job, love, and children. The only real opportunities for private time are spent sleeping, having a shower, or traveling to and from work. The need for solitude can often be misconstrued by those who are closest to us. In the context of a relationship the words "I just need some time alone" are usually viewed as a threat, a means of bargaining, or the prelude to walking out. And sometimes it isn't until we are at absolute breaking point, physically or emotionally, that we claim even *that* space for ourselves. In the meantime, any spare hours that are left free are not often planned. When we don't know what to do with time alone we waste it— fretting or obsessing, dumbing down in front of the TV, or ordering up from QVC. Ask any woman with kids

about solitude and she'll reply in a heartbeat: "Get it while you can." The real secret of solitude is knowing how to juice every precious minute.

INITIATION RITES

Solitude served straight up can be a freak-out. Once the external layers of distraction—company, chatter, media blurb—are removed, inner voices fill the vacuum and come to haunt you: "What are you doing alone? Don't you have a life? Gosh, you're boring." Anxious thoughts and insecurities surface seemingly from nowhere. "What's happening?" you may well ask. "I thought solitude was all about getting relaxed." To make sense of these uncomfortable feelings, you might compare your first time of solitude to your first facial. When you cleanse the skin and open up all those blocked pores, the results might not immediately be beautiful. Instead your face can break out in spots, releasing pent-up toxins and grime that have been buried beneath the layers. After a few days the complexion settles down and breathes freely in its refreshed, cleansed state. Toxins have to come out, and so do pent-up feelings, dreams, and ideas. The imagination needs excavating.

Like a change in diet or a new exercise regime, introducing solitude needs to be done in a way that is gentle and sympathetic to your lifestyle. Experiment with solitude by biting off little chunks of time alone. Start with a quiet walk twice a week, then add another hour of reading, and another hour of yoga or stretching. Take just fifteen minutes a night before sleep to keep a journal of all the thoughts and "mind noise" that come up. Write freely, without censoring your thoughts. If you're a morning person, keep a dream diary of impressions and images captured immediately upon waking. After a few months, look back through the journals. What is solitude teaching you?

✿ Fight the fear and be alone anyway. Don't be tempted to think that you're a failure, unpopular, or eccentric for spending a Saturday night by yourself. If you find yourself focusing on emptiness and absences (the phone that isn't ringing, the barren interior of your refrigerator), try to propel yourself ten years into the future and finish this sentence: "When I had time to myself I used it to . . ."

✿ Finding out what makes you happy alone—certain songs or colors, planting herbs, reading, cooking, singing, writing letters, matching odd socks—will teach you what makes you happy when you're spending time with other people.

✿ When you've built up to the point that you can spend a whole day alone, treat that time like a menu that satisfies all five senses: A vase of freesias that smell like spring and Earl Grey tea, a muffin of ginger and peach, a lyrical sonata, a new set of buttons for a velvet dress, a dab of moisturizer on your heels and elbows have all of the relaxing benefits of a spa or a brief holiday without the expense.

THE FRUITS OF SOLITUDE

The ability to be self-contained and self-sufficient is a mark of a strong character, but solitude is not just about discipline; it is also a journey. Some of our greatest potential takes time to reveal itself. This doesn't necessarily mean sitting on a cushion waiting for a vision to rise from the mists of time. But perhaps some days it just might. View your time alone as time to polish and improve any area of yourself or your life that has fallen into neglect and shadow and know that you follow a long line of contemplatives, saints, singers, poets, mystics, painters, philosophers, and scientists who did the same.

SELF-UNDERSTANDING

Feel free to talk to yourself. Laugh out loud at your own weaknesses (circular, obsessive thoughts, cravings for certain foods, petty jealousies, irrational fears). Cultivate a gentle, mindful eye that observes anxieties and other thoughts as they arise and just as gently lets them go.

Sometimes we hear small children or very old people chiding themselves with a big smile on their face. "Silly me," they declare without a shred of self-consciousness, able to view themselves with loving detachment and a healthy dose of bemusement. When we are alone with our thoughts is when we have the right (and the need) to take charge of them with a firm but affectionate upper hand. Our thoughts are part of us, but we are not our thoughts. Buddha came up with that revelation after a *lot* of time alone.

PRODUCTIVITY

Sometimes alone time gives rise to a power surge of energy; use it to get things done. Make two huge pots of soup and freeze them, or jar enough stewed fruit or pesto sauce to keep you going through the month. Rearrange your house to make it cleaner, more functional, or more sensual and aesthetic. Sew a stack of pretty pillowcases from vintage dress fabrics or make a new handbag for summer out of hardy denim and polka-dot chintz. Time alone doesn't have to be endured stoically; if you want company after a long day of concentrating on your own needs, celebrate by having a friend over for dinner.

CREATIVITY

Not many girls were raised to spend long stretches alone reading Russian novels, learning how to reassemble a motorcycle engine, or teaching themselves how to build the Eiffel Tower out of matchsticks. Perhaps if we were all less frantically socialized in our early years, there would be more Renaissance women in the world. Creative vision has a way of surfacing during prolonged periods of solitude. Many of the really great artists had a certain amount of isolation thrust upon them before they discovered their true calling. Henri Matisse was convalescing in the hospital when someone brought him a box of watercolors. With hours to spare he began his lifelong love affair with color. Frida Kahlo started painting, drawing, and keeping a journal after a terrible spinal injury and literally created through her pain. And even the hypersocial Diana Vreeland polished her verbal brilliance early through years of reading and reflection. "I know how to be alone," she said plainly, "because I've been so often alone. Maybe that's the secret of life."

SECRECY

There is an ancient fairy tale about a man who finds a princess who lives alone in a castle deep in the forest. Because it's a fairy tale, they fall in love straightaway. The princess invites the man to live with her on one condition: that she be left entirely alone on every Thursday of the week. He must not ask where she has gone, but simply trust that she will return. He respects her wish and they wed and have children. And every Thursday she disappears as agreed. After many years the husband grows curious, even a touch jealous, and he sneaks into the chamber of the castle where his wife has taken her retreat. He finds her in a vast wooden tub of seawater with the tail of a fish. When his wife sees that she has been apprehended in her secret ritual she sheds a single tear and then vanishes forever. The moral of the story? Serves him right for snooping.

Secret spaces, the proverbial room of one's own, and personal rituals are crucial. Men retreat to their clubhouses, cubbyholes, and garage workshops, and it's an idea that women should steal. Of course, the more committed you become to this idea, the more shocked others may be. I had a boyfriend once who came upon some drawings on the back of a bedroom cupboard door. One depicted a naked crimson-skinned she-devil on all fours with pointed teeth and wild blue hair; another was a pair of legs with blood and love hearts trickling out from their center. Fleeting expressions of a wild, hostile, barbaric little mood. The boyfriend was horrified. "What are all those sluts and white witches doing in there? Who are they?" he demanded. "Good question," I replied. "I think they're me."

LOVING LIVING ALONE

Living alone can be the best time of your life or an existential nightmare depending on both your life skills and your outlook. Over ten years of living alone have taught me the following solitude survival prerequisites:

❧ Make your house worth coming home to. Just 'cause no one can see your dishes doesn't mean you shouldn't wash them.

❧ Build an extensive library of mood music—this is the soundtrack to the movie of your life.

❧ Personalize your casa. This may be the last time you will be able to live with ABBA pillowcases and cabbage-rose wallpaper.

❧ Budget your phone use. If you spend more than two hours on the phone or the Web every night, ask yourself if you are truly learning to bear your own company. Try to put aside one night that is just with you, not reaching out but reaching in.

❧ Don't skimp on eating well. Cheerios eaten straight from the box is not dinner. Making the effort to cook solid, attractive food for one is not just a sign of self-esteem, it also keeps you in touch with civilization. Guests hate canned soup.

✿ Celebrate holidays in miniature—a baby Christmas tree, a mini menorah, fairy lights for New Year's.

✿ Don't let your pets rule your life. Your loneliness might lead to dominatrix cat syndrome: a pet becoming more and more demanding and holding you hostage in your own home. If your pets are starting to keep you in, take them day-tripping to an outdoor café or a spot of window shopping. If your cat hisses at your dates and brings up fur balls of emotional blackmail, start thinking deeply about goldfish or plants.

✿ Always have at least three books you love next to the bed. Stash trashy biographies under worthier novels and art magazines for when guests drop in.

✿ Invest in the best Chinese satin pajamas and marabou slippers. The postman only knocks twice.

✿ Live safely. Bolts and deadlocks that work, neighbors you can trust, and windows that are adequately sealed from breakins and prying eyes are the basics. Additional precautions are simple touches like yelling good-bye when you leave the house (even if there's no one home), not leaving an overly detailed answering machine message ("Hi, I'll be away until . . ."), never reciting your personal details (phone number and address) over the counter at a bank or post office, never revealing your address over the Net, and being extra careful about anyone who knocks on your door, whether it's the pizza delivery boy or friendly Mormons.

✿ Respect yourself. Just because you can bring anyone home (no roommates, parents, or offspring listening in) doesn't mean you should. Once you get over the first flush of freedom, be selective (and safety minded) about who you fly home to your nest.

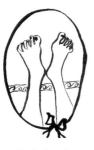     

Indulge in a bathtub pedicure. *Cruise the Pyramids.* *Dance naked in Ugg boots.* *Read into the wee hours.* *Be a total romantic slob.* *Bake, gab, and write long letters.*

Do the crazy stuff that privacy permits:

✿ Watch four pretaped episodes of *The Nanny* back to back.

✿ Do your housework in a crochet bikini, an apron, and a raspberry beret.

✿ Teach yourself to two-step with a broom.

✿ Floss with the bathroom door wide open.

✿ Memorize three Cole Porter songs word and pitch perfect.

✿ Read Proust *and Peanuts*.

✿ Sort through eight years' worth of black lace bras, love letters, and lipsticks.

✿ Speak Italian to your plants.

✿ Take Polaroids of your breasts for future generations to admire.

✿ Leap out of bed in the middle of the night with a brilliant idea, forget it on the way to the fridge, and build an even more brilliant sandwich.

✿ Do really icky beauty experiments that involve henna, raw foods, and clay mud.

✿ Play the sort of music guys hate at any hour.

✿ Allow yourself one soft toy or several.

THE MEAN REDS: LONELY TIMES

To celebrate all of the great things one can do alone is not to ignore the fact that being alone can, at times, feel difficult and empty, no matter how constructively you plan your time. Sometimes solitude can be thrust upon you when you least need or expect it. A few years back I woke up alone on Christmas Day. My relationship was dead in the water, I was the solo amiga in a big empty house, and my parents called to tell me about the snow, the champagne, and the crackling fire over in France. My nephew gurgled down the line and I burst into tears.

No tree, no caresses, no Santa Claus. After about ten minutes of unadulterated wallowing and self-pity, I leapt out of bed and threw myself into action. Why dwell?

To put my own misery in perspective I decided to spend Christmas giving instead of waiting for something to fly down the chimney. By 10:30 A.M. I reached Our Lady of the Snows soup kitchen and the kitchen in back was packed. Society ladies, solitary travelers, kids, eccentric locals, and all sorts of handsome forty-something divorcés were elbow-deep in fruit and salad and traditional holiday fixings. With carols playing on a tinny transistor radio, two kooky souls out front reciting psalms, and a gathering crowd of enthusiastic diners, the mood was somewhere between Tom Waits and Frank Capra. Christmas spirit was dripping off the walls. It was corny, it was crazy, I wanted to cry all over again. But for the right reasons. After three hours, twenty more volunteers turned up to help out. Everyone was immersed in their jobs—decorating salad plates, drizzling custard over puddings, waitressing to the appreciative guests— and no one was spending Christmas alone.

Later in the afternoon I visited my grandmother's house. I hadn't been there in some years. My uncle had scorched the turkey and was playing his opera albums full blast, another uncle had a lot to say about Jesus and the apostles, one auntie was awash in French perfume and another in patchouli, my fifteen-year-old cousin wore black lipstick, and my grandma wore a quiet smile as she watched TV throughout it all. Leaning against the fridge was a skinny oak branch that served as a tree. What began as a simple lunch unraveled into an uproarious reunion, plastic cups, fruit cake, milky tea, burnt turkey, and all. My grandmother's advice to me that day was "marry someone glamorous." Two weeks later she passed away.

The point of this story is that no Christmas (or Thanksgiving or Passover) has to be spent alone. There are people who need you even if you don't know them, and there are family members and friends who haven't seen you in years and miss you dearly. Loneliness and sorrow dissolve when you warm the hearts of others. In turn, they warm yours.

SPIRITUAL LIFE

Light Your Fire

The sun is love.
The lover, a speck circling the sun.
A spring wind moves to dance any
branch that isn't dead.

—**RUMI**

Few people sit down to contemplate their own spiritual path. We view it as a luxury, the indulgence of old age, or the vocation of nuns and priests. Sometimes we need a crisis to make us think about God, death, and the meaning of life, but why wait? If you want your life to be full, deep, and truly generous, then taking time for the spirit is a vital responsibility rather than a caprice.

To put your spiritual needs in perspective, just look at the way we put the needs of the physical body before everything else. We spend a lifetime trying to shape it, tame it, feed it, clothe it, feel and understand its workings. The body brings us great pleasure and great pain. That same body also houses a spirit and through our flesh we feel the movement of energies, both obvious and subtle. A spiritual life seeks to balance our attention between those two states: the physical and the immaterial, the concrete and the intangible, the empirical and the psychic, the obvious and the abstract. To cultivate a spiritual life takes time, energy, and love. Most of all it takes patience. It's about everyday application rather than singular flashes of inspiration. You don't have to drop out and go on a pilgrimage or join a cloister to light that precious inner spark. Spiritual people are actually all around us; they are the ones who love, forgive, and face suffering with deep understanding and compassion. The teacher who constantly forgives her rowdy class, the cashier at the local deli who always has a smile and a story for you, the old woman who spends her life fighting to save a patch of wilderness and smiles at her adversity are all role models for a generous spiritual life. Simple people doing simple things, but doing them every day without fail. History teaches us that.

A century or more ago the church, tribal ritual, local festivals, and family prayer provided a public forum for the spirit. In the modern age there is less shared tradition of

belief. Instead we seek meaning in romantic love, career, home, and family. All of these things can be deeply fulfilling but there is also something beyond them. Some call it a higher power, some call it Buddha nature, some call it God, and others call it divine grace. The pathway to that energy is fraught with uncertainty and fear. You may say, "Oh no, I'm not the religious type," or you may find the idea of organized religions or cults off-putting. You'd have a point; there are many distorted creeds and TV preachers out there. But by not exploring the spiritual you may be cutting yourself off from a whole other dimension of life—a rich, conscious life that makes room for everyday miracles and helps build a strong compassionate heart.

To live a spiritual life needn't imply joining a group or even espousing a credo. What it mainly asks is that you take the time and make the space in your life to look within—to build a soul space that is as strong as your outer physical body and to balance the two. Imagine having an inner sanctuary to retreat to after a really hard day, a voice to calm you when you are hurt or angry, and the tools to manage in a terrible crisis.

The stronger your commitment to a spiritual life, the greater your inner sanctuary becomes. When what you believe inside and what you do outside begin to converge, you are living your personal values and reshaping your world in a very profound way. Personally, I struggle with this goal. A lot. Quite often my despair, thoughtless words, and selfish actions don't match up at all with spiritual ideals. It is disappointing but it is part of the struggle. Slowly, there is a chance that the spiritual side of my nature, the patient, diligent, compassionate side, might grow to mirror my behavior day to day. Selfishness, doubt, anxiety, and old habits often block the way. It is a very long haul.

My personal spiritual ideal is to get out of my own way enough to be useful (to the people I love, to the people I work for, to people I haven't met yet, to the planet); yours may be to find peace or to understand death or just to love and accept yourself. All of these aims find their voice when you give them time and work at them without embarrassment. Building a spiritual life takes courage. People around you may question your motives and wonder why you aren't content with the here and now; they may accuse you of being lofty or escapist. But life is too brief to worry about the naysayers. Give yourself the privacy, the time, and the faith to find your own answers. Here are some simple activities that might open up your spiritual path.

ART

In his painting of *Venus*, somehow Botticelli has transmuted spiritual energy onto canvas, asking us to suspend our belief that we are merely gazing at a flat image. The quattrocento painters of Italy's early Renaissance believed they could infuse their art with the light of God. Looking at Piero della Francesca's angels or Giotto's Christ makes us feel the intensity of their faith these many centuries later. Sculpted images of the Buddha often unlock a secret that cannot be put into words. Traced across the cold surface of stone is a gentle, barely perceptible smile and a face suffused with love and compassion.

Human life and wisdom dwell within great art as well as something more. What was the spark that roused Van Gogh to wedge lime green against flesh pink or the subtle force that led Tina Modotti to find night shadows inside a desert flower? A bolt from the blue, a whisper from the muse, and a slash of divine madness. Nothing too rational. Galleries and museums on quiet days reveal those mysteries. Use art as a source of contemplation and rebellion against a logical life. Let it move you.

COMMUNING WITH NATURE

Now and then we are subsumed by something much vaster than we are. A big velvety night sky studded with stars, an ocean that crashes and swerves like the silver skin of a dancing fish, the outline of a mountain that nudges its massive haunches up against the clouds. These spectacles make us feel like a squidge in the mighty scheme of things, putting our petty worries into perspective. They also make us whole—completing that part of the soul that thirsts for solidity, elemental wisdom, and connection.

Nature is pulsing under everything. The city sidewalk bends to the curve of an old cow trail, and grass pushes its way up through the cracked cement to refresh our memory of the earth beneath cities. For the spirit to blossom, the earth needs to be listened to. Go somewhere silent enough to hear the birds, the wind in the grass, the fall of rain, and the swaying of tall trees. Find your place within that beauty.

LOVE

The love that humans share is made sacred by the smallest amount of reverence. In the East people bow in greeting to recognize the divinity that dwells in each of us. Imagine taking that attitude to bed with your lover; using your lovemaking to honor and celebrate the higher spirit within the other.

If you're lucky enough to have a lover who understands and values this part of you, the fragile, secret soul that searches for meaning, then perhaps your relationship can support your spiritual growth.

Love plays a central role in your spiritual life. All religions acknowledge love as the animating force that governs right action, compassion, and transcendence from earthbound pain. Contrary to the brutality we see all around us, the universe is held together with love; to tap into that takes faith. And application. Living in love means being forgiving and kind when you are ready to snap. Making a sacrifice as small as giving up your seat on the bus or as big as nursing your best friend through breast cancer. Being full of love makes you ready for anything. It is spiritual armor.

MEDITATION

Meditation is central to Buddhist practice, but you needn't be a Buddhist to make meditation part of your life. Learning to sit in tranquil repose, concentrating on your breathing and letting thoughts rise and fall away is a discipline that is also taught in yoga and meditation courses. In his book *Wherever You Go, There You Are* Jon Kabat-Zinn points out, "The incessant stream of thoughts flowing through our minds leaves us very little respite for inner quiet." This constant flow of thoughts is like a waterfall that sweeps us along and submerges our lives. Meditation, Kabat-Zinn suggests, "gets us out of this current [to] sit by its bank and listen to it, learn from it and use its energies to guide us rather than tyrannize us." It sounds really cool when he describes it, a quiet place to go inside your head, anytime, anywhere. But of course meditation is difficult. When you sit down to try it's easy to feel like a big fat failure. You get distracted, you want to itch the tip of your nose, you want to pee or phone your Mom or do anything except face the silence. Instead of chiding yourself for being the antiguru just smile and feel happy with your first effort. Any attempt at mindful relaxation is a start and, over time, your efforts will yield results.

I learned meditation at a Buddhist retreat in Hawaii, and the initial teaching was very basic. Sit upright on a zafu (meditation cushion) with your legs crossed comfortably and your back as straight as possible, half-close your eyes but don't close them (you can't doze off), rest your hands in your lap, count your breaths from one to ten, and when you reach ten, start again! Breathe gently through your nose (not stiffly or self-consciously). When your mind wanders (and it will), watch the thoughts rise like soap bubbles but don't follow them; just return your thought to your breathing. Twenty minutes is an effective amount of

time, but you can start with as little as five to get a taste for sitting. Now, I have been carrying this recipe around in my head for about six years and I *still* haven't summoned the discipline to sit every day, but I do know how to switch off. On a bus, or walking, or at the precipice of a raging argument I can retreat into my breathing and calm my mind.

Meditation is an amazing gift, and the more time you put into it (ideally twenty minutes before breakfast and twenty minutes before going to sleep), the greater your concentration and repose will become. Being able to sit down, compose yourself, relax, and just *stop* has tremendous advantages. On the most basic level it helps you relax, and on a loftier plane it enables you (over time) to live in the present moment, observing your thoughts without being captive to them. Buddhists call this state mindful awareness. I call it being a whole lot less obsessed with boys, shoes, and the future.

Once you have learned to meditate, it may be hard to maintain it within your daily routine. Something more pressing to do always conflicts with your little slice of "nothing" time. To strengthen your resolve, try attending a regular group meditation or a yoga class where breathing, concentration, and mindful awareness are central to the practice.

MUSIC

Van Morrison is forever raving on about walking through gardens wet with rain. Emmylou Harris sings "I hear a voice, how shall I answer?" Nick Cave bellows, "There is a kingdom, there is a king!" Etta James wants a Sunday kind of love. All of them are expressing their own brand of gospel, and it gets me every time. You don't have to listen to Gregorian chants and Zen flutes to lift your consciousness to a higher plane. In the right frame of mind even Barry White is holy music. Music is the most accessible reminder to come back to the bright flame inside your heart and to ease your soul. Your car can be a full choir loft, your bathtub a temple of sacred chanting, your kitchen a full-scale revival meeting. Whether it is Chopin's nocturnes or a love ballad by M'shell Ngdecello, give yourself music that goes deep and soars high.

READING
AND CHILLING

To make time for the spiritual dimension in your life, you may physically have to construct a space where you can go—a corner in your house or bedroom where treasured objects, uplifting reading, and soothing colors create a space for you to retreat and reconnect. Keep a cherished book close to you and refer to it as a friend in times of crisis or desolation. Let yourself read and reread the passages that resonate for you. Form a spirituality book club

to explore the authors, poets, and prophets you love. The books I always keep near me are by Rumi, Rainer Maria Rilke, Thich Nhat Hanh, Aitkin Roshi, and Dr. Seuss. See the bibliography for more ideas.

RETREATS

Retreats for yoga, meditation, inspirational learning, and spiritual teachings are available throughout the country. The advantage of a retreat is that all practical needs are taken care of and there are no external distractions: Someone else cooks, someone wakes you at dawn, birds sing, and everyone around you is united by curiosity and a common aim. The disadvantage of a retreat is that you have to come down from your cloud afterward and take up mundane responsibilities with grace. Whatever you take back to "real life," will last longer than a tan. Retreats are a truly creative and restorative way to use your vacation time. The ten days I spent at the Diamond Sangha Buddhist Zendo in Hawaii have stayed with me. A yoga school in the Berkshires is where my girlfriend is gradually training to teach yoga to children. Just a few weeks carved out of her year is changing her life path. If you don't wish to commit a large chunk of time to a long retreat, consider weekend forums and daylong seminars as an investment in your inner life. America has a tremendous range of both homegrown and international speakers from Tibet, India, and beyond who regularly tour, explaining their philosophies and practice. You don't have to get hooked on the wisdom circuit, traipsing after every New Age circus that pulls into town, but one great speaker *can* change your worldview. Be curious, be open, take a notebook.

SELFLESS SERVICE

Put yourself in a place you rarely visit. Helping the ill, the elderly, the homeless, the lost, or the troubled is one of the most useful things you can do. And it feels good. Selfless service makes you happy in a very simple way: The more immersed you become in someone else's problems, the less you focus on your own; the more you contribute socially, the better the world looks. People like to make fun of "do-gooders," but until you reach out you never know how deeply you are needed. For more information about giving hands-on help, see Political Responsibility, page 231.

YOGA

The basic philosophy of yoga unites the body, the mind, and the spirit and aims to bring them into harmony. Over time

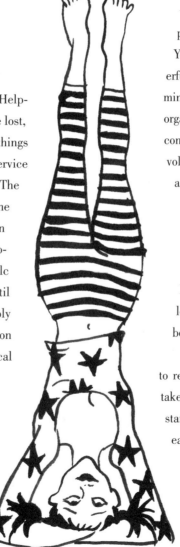

yoga strengthens the body and calms the central nervous system, purifying the vessel to receive higher inspiration and tranquility. Yoga is said to have evolved in the eleventh century as a way to make novices strong and balanced in preparation for long stretches of meditation. Yoga in America today is accepted as a powerful, relaxing, low-impact workout for the mind as well as for every muscle and internal organ in the body. As a form of exercise yoga consists of asanas (physical postures) that involve controlled movement, concentration, and conscious breathing all designed to invigorate and purify the body. Yoga as a spiritual practice invites you to cultivate an open heart, a focused mind, and a selfless love for the divinity inherent in every living thing. Doing yoga means putting that love into motion, restoring strength to your body to give you greater strength in life.

A beginner's yoga class will teach you to rethink and refine routine actions that you take totally for granted—simple stuff like standing on two flat feet and feeling the earth beneath you, breathing in and out, and touching your toes. When you learn a few of the asanas and master the moves, you start to create a flow. Not surprisingly, different thoughts, emotions, and feelings may surface. The yoga teacher you choose should support your level of flexibility and energy and never force a position. Despite the fact that Madonna can wrap her legs around her ponytail, superadvanced flexibility is not the point of going to class. Nothing in yoga should hurt or stretch you like a pretzel, and if a class is too aggressive or fast moving it's fine to quit and move down a notch. Finding the right yoga teacher for you is an important aspect of the practice.

Because yoga is a holistic exercise it is also deeply healing, not just attending to muscle, joint, and spine strength but also directing blood and oxygen to glands, nerves, and internal organs. Yoga is great for fertility problems, hormonal imbalances, spotty skin, and even the strength of your pelvic floor. Because it's noncompetitive and deeply meditative, it's a lovely way to integrate the mind's need to rest with the body's need to move. Yoga lifts your spirits as it lifts your self-esteem, learning how to stand on your head confers a magical pride of carriage, learning how to use your breath calms the mind, and learning how to cherish your body helps your heart blossom. The more you can enjoy your physical self as a strong, dignified, centered entity, the closer you get to the spirit that animates it all.

Giving Back

ECO GIRL

Green Ideas

NO
TREES
NO
FUTURE
SAVE
THE
AMAZON
CONSUME
LESS
GIVE MORE
THANK
YOU
FOR READING
THIS DRESS

We need the tonic of wildness . . .
We can never have enough of nature.
—Henry David Thoreau

Imagine that you kept every plastic bag you acquired in a month. It is possible that at the end of that brief period of time you could accumulate hundreds—a ball large enough to stuff a big beanbag chair or to strangle a school of fish. Everything you toss in the trash, wash down the sink, or flush into the sewer system goes back into the sea and back into the earth. Inside a clean, beautiful house it's easy to forget the mountains of rubbish that daily living generates and the chemical waste created by the technological production and constant consumption of luxury products. To redress the imbalance, you have to learn to be less wasteful and more thoughtful in your daily routines. Little things like cutting down on vacuum-packed take-out meals, refusing the dreaded plastic bags, and recycling the ones you have at home help the environment. As the Buddhist poet, monk, and teacher Thich Nhat Hanh puts it: Nature is not something outside ourselves, it is us. Even a big city has an ecosystem—it's up to you to decide how to live in it.

FOURTEEN WAYS TO LIVE GREEN

1. Be ozone smart

Avoid aerosols and, if possible, buy major appliances that do not use fluorocarbons.

2. Build well

❀ Material choices become moral choices when you are building with timber. Try to use plantation woods or secondhand timber instead of rain forest timber. Check out sources on www.ecotimber.com.

❀ Find out the lead content of most domestic conventional paint; milk- and water-based paints are much less toxic, and recycled latex paint is an option. See www.ecopaint.com

❀ Use recycled materials whenever possible—salvage yards are great sources for reusable wood, glass, and scrap steel. And used material usually has a richer, more beautiful patina than the new stuff.

3. Drive less or form a car pool

Lonely commuters who could be singing with friends, coworkers who rely on the bus while you luxuriate alone on the expressway, plump thighs that could do with a walk: All are reasons for rethinking when and how you choose to use that toxic convenience known as a car.

4. Cleanse with plants

Most people spend a majority of their time indoors. The six hundred liters or so of oxygen we breathe every day are consumed in a sealed environment (usually an office). Often, this environment is poisoned, containing toxic, volatile compounds that emanate from carpets, carbon monoxide, particleboard, paint, copy machines, cleaning solutions, and computers. Placing plants around the office actually improves the quality of the air we breathe—certain plants are capable of soaking up air pollutants and toxins. To help your plants survive, place them in good light and learn their individual needs for watering, fertilizing, and pest protection. If you place a

Toxin-Absorbing Plants

TOXIN	PLANT ABSORBER
BENZENE: Found in ink, gas, paint, plastic, rubber, dyes, detergents. Irritates mucous membrane of eyes, nose, and throat. Affects nerves and skin.	✿ *Dracaena deremensis* (recognizable by their pretty green and gray striped leaves) ✿ *D. marginata* (thin coppery leaves) ✿ English ivy ✿ Weeping fig ✿ Peace lily
TRICHLOROETHYLENE: Used as degreaser and dry-cleaning fluid; found in varnishes, adhesives, paint, ink, and lacquer. Potentially damaging as liver carcinogen.	✿ Chrysanthemum ✿ Peace lily
ELECTROMAGNETIC FIELDS: Generated by electrical equipment, power sockets, cables, and electricity meters. Web addicts beware. Can create headaches, menstrual and reproductive disorders, miscarriage, infertility, skin rashes, depression.	✿ Column cactus (place a large cactus near your terminal)
FORMALDEHYDE: Found in carpets, foam insulation, modern sofas, floor coverings, tissues, cleaning agents, cigarette smoke.	✿ Chrysanthemum ✿ Philodendron ✿ Poinsettia ✿ Spider plant
CARBON MONOXIDE	✿ Spider plant

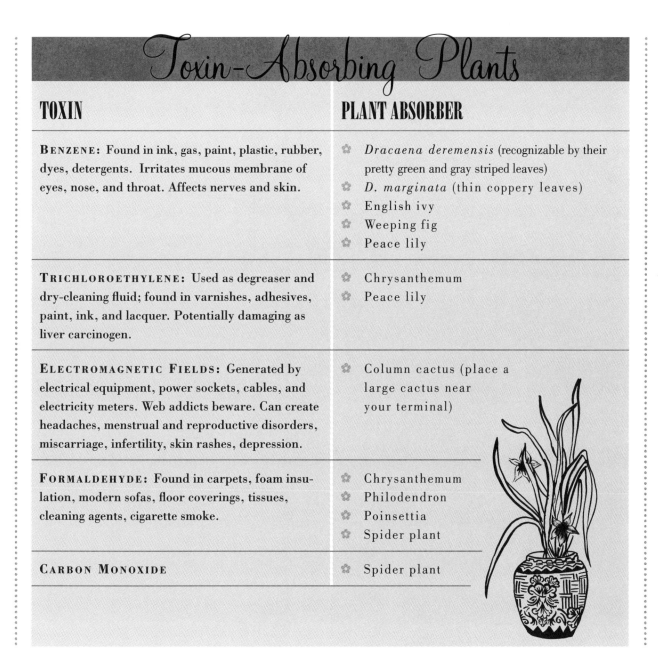

bunch of office plants near your desk, beware of wear and tear from passing human traffic and absentminded fondling. Don't let people fidget with your plants! They're working hard for you and they need tender care.

5. Get into the garden

Composting on a small scale with a plastic bin for scraps or on a large scale with a wooden slatted compost box helps you sort your rubbish while you feed the garden. For simple instructions on how to build a compost bin, consult *How to Do Just About Anything*, published by Reader's Digest. (If you live in an urban area, see Community Gardens, page 234.)

6. Recycle

✿ Use refillable bottles for your kitchen, cleaning, and beauty products. It's economical and it cuts down on waste.

✿ Encourage your coworkers to use recycled copy paper. Keep a recycling bin near the copy machine or anywhere else bulk paper accumulates.

✿ Reuse envelopes for mailing bills and other impersonal documents.

✿ Recycle all cans, bottles, and newspapers both at work and at home. If recycling is not mandatory in your community, start small with a neighborhood initiative.

✿ Make your NO JUNK MAIL sign huge and scary.

7. Invest ethically

Why buy stock in a company that is involved in destructive mining operations, the arms trade, or third-world child labor? It doesn't take a paranoiac nursing a conspiracy theory to deduce that some large companies have less-than-spotless affiliations. Investigating your options and seeking out companies that provide a safe and ethical investment means that your money works toward good, for your bank balance *and* for the planet.

The useful Web site www.ethicalinvesting.com lays out the basic tenets of ethical investing very clearly. To find out if companies you are considering buying stock in comply, check out the magazines *Mother Jones* and *Multinational Monitor*. If you have hired a stockbroker to handle your investments, make it very clear that your first priority is your conscience.

8. Make your own cleaning products

Making your own household cleaning products—from dishwashing liquid to furniture polish—not only saves you pennies, it saves your health. When you throw out bottles of bleach, liquid cleanser, drain cleaner, and air freshener, their chemical compound ingredients do not break down. Instead, they create hazardous waste—the kind that creates highly toxic and potentially carcinogenic landfills. Municipal councils are left with the problem of disposing of contaminated matter that threatens our soil, air, and water.

If you have products under your sink right now that are poisonous enough to kill a child, it's time to rethink the way you clean. If you are using naphthalene mothballs in large quantities, they could cause breathing problems, vomiting, and urinary irritation. Lye made from sodium hydroxide (found in toilet, oven, tile, and drain cleaners) is corrosive enough to eat through your esophagus, skin, and face if swallowed. The list goes on—and it gets worse.

Make your own natural cleaners with these trustworthy recipes, store them in thoroughly washed glass bottles and containers, and label. Don't use plastic containers recycled from commercial cleaning products, because any trace of the original will affect your mix. The basics you'll need are:

- ✿ Baking soda
- ✿ Lemon juice
- ✿ Purified water
- ✿ Essential oils
- ✿ Salt
- ✿ Vegetable oil or glycerin-based liquid soap
- ✿ White distilled vinegar

With these materials you can clean your house from top to bottom. You may have to put more elbow grease into it than when you use a chemical cleaner, but consider it healthy exercise! Here are two recipes to get started.

GENERAL KITCHEN CLEANSER

Fill a stainless steel or plastic shaker (the kind used for powdered sugar or Parmesan cheese) halfway with baking soda, sprinkle in ten to twenty drops of lemon essential oil, then add more baking soda to fill the shaker to the top. Cover and shake vigorously until the whole mixture is scented.

A light shake on the base of pots, counters, stainless steel sinks or tubs, sponged off with a damp cloth, cuts grease. Baking-soda based cleansers are slightly abrasive and good for removing floor scuffs. Keep this cleanser away from aluminum pots or surfaces as it tends to discolor them.

WOOD POLISH

- ✿ 1 cup raw linseed oil
- ✿ ½ cup strained lemon juice
- ✿ 10 drops lemon essential oil

Blend this mix thoroughly and store in a clean glass or plastic pump pack. Shake well before use. A great dust magnet, this polish is suitable for all types of wood and smells as tart and fresh as a citrus orchard. Apply to wood surfaces with a soft rag.

For further recipes, safety instructions, and ideas on eco-cleaning, consult *Clean House, Clean Planet* by Karen Logan.

9. Replant

A lot of women living on the land, no matter how small the property, have started to replant with native trees and shrubs. If you are worried about the loss of trees and old-growth forests, it feels good to plant seedlings for your children to enjoy. The imperative is the same in cities. A fast-growing tree outside your apartment will work better than an air conditioner in summer once those glossy, oxygenating leaves reach your window ledge.

10. Conserve water and electricity

Really basic stuff like owning fewer appliances, turning off lights in rooms that aren't in use, drying your hair in the sunshine, using low-wattage lightbulbs, taking shallow baths, installing water-saving devices in your shower and toilet, and turning the tap off while you wash dishes or brush your teeth all help conserve resources.

11. Shop smart

Take your ethics to the supermarket. Some earth-friendly products cost more (dolphin-friendly tuna, organic produce, some green cleaning products), but others cost next to nothing. Plan well and the cost of shopping with a conscience need not be a luxury.

The money you spend supporting responsible, smaller brands shows your power as a consumer. If enough people shopped green, larger companies would have to respond to the market demand and reduce their use of toxic ingredients.

- ✿ Recycled, unbleached toilet tissue may be a bit rough, but it's a simple way to protect the environment from the toxic PCBs involved in bleached-paper production and the loss of trees for paper products. Do you really need perfumed, flowery tissue to wipe your bottom?

- ✿ Products from companies like Ecover and the Vermont-based Seventh Generation are made with gentle, nontoxic recycled materials. To request a Seventh Generation catalog, call (888) 59-EARTH, or check out the company's Web site at www.seventhgen.com.

- ✿ Carry your own sturdy cotton or hemp shopping bag or basket. You'll cut down on plastic, and you could be mistaken for a fascinating European eccentric.

✿ Join or form a food co-op with your friends or neighbors to buy in bulk. To find out if there is a co-op near you, check out www.foodcoop.net.

✿ Make up your own shampoos, cleaning agents, and herbal oils and vinegars.

✿ Support organic farming. Including organic produce in your diet cuts down on the pesticides, hormones, chemicals, and additives common in supermarket fruit and veggies, processed foods, and mass-raised meat, poultry, and dairy products. Foods grown with the help of pesticides regularly have chemical residue on them, and imported tropical fruits may have been plunged into a postharvest dip to guard against pests. Washing the skin of your avocado or apple won't be enough. For more information on pesticides and other possible toxins found in fresh food, contact the Food and Drug Administration's Center for Food Safety at (800) FDA-4010 or the Environmental Protection Agency's National Pesticide Hotline at (800) 858-7378.

✿ Resist glamour packaging. Today's divine luxury eye shadow sold in a glossy box, encased in a velvet pouch, wrapped up in an acre of product info typed small on fine tissue and sealed with vacuum-packed plastic is tomorrow's trash. The same goes for individually wrapped sanitary napkins. When one of those plastic panty liner pouches covered in daisies falls out of your handbag, just who are you trying to kid? Women bleed—

and advertising companies and the rest of the world should get over it!

✿ The manufacture of clothing consumes energy and generates chemical waste, from the bleaching of cotton through the dyeing and finishing. Balance your consumption of new clothing by making your own (if you can), recycling from friends, and buying secondhand. Certain fabrics, like hemp, are earth-friendly alternatives to cotton. These clothes are often the color of damp muesli, but don't despair. Dunk them in a vat of natural dye.

12. Support environmental organizations

There are numerous organizations—including Greenpeace, the Nature Conservancy, the Rainforest Action Network, the Wilderness Society, and the World Wildlife Fund—devoted to the preservation of nature and the protection of the environment. Help them out with donations of cash and spare time. See Political Responsibility, page 236.

13. Stop dry cleaning

Dry cleaning exposes you to perchloroethylene, a toxic chemical that can damage the central nervous system and the reproductive system, according to studies by the Environmental Protection Agency. "Perc" has been designated a hazardous air pollutant by the government.

Some safe alternatives to dry cleaning are handwashing, steam-cleaning, and professional ironing. A more recent development is wet cleaning, a perc-free process that can be used on most articles of clothing labeled "dry-clean only." For more information (and to find a wet cleaner near you), contact:

Center for Neighborhood Technology Alternative
Clothes Cleaning Project
2125 West North Avenue
Chicago, IL 60647
Wet-cleaning hotline: (773) 278-4800, ext. 299
www.cnt.org/wetcleaning

14. Teach your children well

Kids love to feel useful and after a while they form good habits. I know one nine-year-old who follows her parents around the house switching lights off and checking dripping taps! You don't need to raise baby green avengers, just children who care. Flipping the switch away from cartoons to the Discovery Channel and renting nature documentaries is a start. So is making recycling a fun activity (a plastic bottle makes a great base for a papier-mâché doll or cut in half becomes a garden planter for seedlings), planning an adventure out to the local park, or a family vacation to a place where you can see the

stars, hear the crickets or the coyotes, and hug some grand old trees.

Get your child interested in the natural world by borrowing these books from the library:

❀   *1 Day in the Tropical Rainforest,* by Jean Craighead George (Ty Crowell, 1990).

❀   *Recycle! A Handbook for Kids,* by Gail Gibbons (Little, Brown, 1996).

❀   *A River Ran Wild,* by Lynne Cherry (Harcourt Brace, 1992).

❀   *Roots, Shoots, Buckets and Boots,* by Sharon Lovejoy (Workman Publishing, 1999).

❀   Or play Tom Chapin's CD *This Pretty Planet*—featuring songs about Mother Earth, recycling, Earth Day—around the house.

POLITICAL RESPONSIBILITY

Change the World

Everybody wants to do something to help but nobody wants to be first.

—Pearl Bailey

Viewed en masse, social and environmental problems just seem too vast to address: The forests are burning, children are starving, whales are being slaughtered, orangutans are endangered, the ice caps are melting. It's all enough to make you want to put a pillow over your head and sob, "How can a few cents in a can save a life or a tree? How can I make a difference?" The answer, of course, is in hundreds of ways.

Saving the world (or just a neighborhood garden) starts with being active and feeling confident that one small action contributes to something way bigger. Think like a worker ant! When you find an issue you really care about, there are plenty of ways to make a difference. Giving according to your abilities is the most sensible and constructive way to take political and social action. If you're not a confrontational person but have great administrative skills, you might want to help out in the office of a cause you respect a couple of days a month. If you can't handle groups but love kids, you might take on a mentoring project and hang out with one child for a few hours each week. You may choose to work quietly or to spread the word about your cause or project through the Net and small publishing ventures; you may give money or you may give time. The time you give could be a major sacrifice (like spending two years tree sitting like Julia Butterfly Hill or working for very low pay at a nonprofit organization), or it could be just one small spontaneous action. The urge to do something good out of the blue, just once, can be accommodated by your local hospital or nursing home, especially at times like Christmas or Thanksgiving.

The best way to give back is to remain as faithful as you can to your character and beliefs. Less a case of feeling guilty for not doing enough and more a matter of pride in doing just one thing well. When I see my friends glowing after a rally they organized themselves, or giving a big bag of clothes to the Salvation Army, or know my best friend has just volunteered an afternoon at a women's refuge, that free-floating anxiety about the state of the world eases a little. The selfish short-term benefit of taking the time to give back is obvious—it makes you happy. The long-term effect is more subtle but no less powerful. Positive action creates an immediate example to everyone you know; if you inspire others to give back,

the network of socially active, politically aware, and compassionate women starts growing. Every really great action and the movement that follows that action begins with a single idea. Some of the most influential conservation, women's liberation, and civil rights activists began in unspectacular circumstances: one woman, Rachel Carson, looking at the pesticides used in modern farming and asking, "Why?" Another woman, Rosa Parks, taking her seat on a segregated bus. Two women like Elizabeth Cady Stanton and Susan B. Anthony sitting in a parlor talking about the right to vote. You might make your contribution by licking stamps at Greenpeace, but it still makes you an agent for change.

It's impossible to list all the great organizations that set out to make a difference. Those listed here are all nonprofit, nationally accessible, and nonextremist. Use the Net, the newspaper, and even your community bulletin board to find out what's going on locally and globally, and then become a part of it. The Web site www.idealist.org is a great resource for matching your interests with a volunteer opportunity. Every little bit counts.

ACTING LOCALLY

Right now, in your own town, there's a soup kitchen getting ready to serve a few hundred hungry people—and it's probably understaffed. There's a nursing home looking for volunteers to spend time with its residents. There are kids in need of mentors. There's a homeless shelter that needs blankets and clothing, and an English-as-a-second-language course is looking for an enthusiastic tutor. There's a local Habitat for Humanity project in the works. And there is you—two hands, a heart, and a little free time.

Good starting places are schools, hospitals, and nursing homes. Pick up the phone book and make a few calls. Local churches and temples are also great resources: Whether you belong to a congregation or not, pastors and rabbis will be happy to direct you to a nearby soup kitchen or shelter where your help would be welcome. (Franciscans, Quakers, and Unitarians—all with strong traditions of charity and community service—are especially knowledgeable in this area.) Here are some other possibilities.

MENTORING

If you're a natural with kids, mentoring is a cool way to share your time and skills—you get to hear CDs you can't even spell, eat pizza without guilt, and bring positive change into a young person's life. Mentored teens are 46 percent less likely to use drugs and 59 percent more likely to get better grades than their unmentored peers. They have the advantage of constructive input at one of the most fragile times of their lives. Mentoring is a commitment and responsibility not to be undertaken lightly. You need to be realistic about the amount of time you're able to give: Continuity is crucial here, and mentors usually commit to at least six months. This commitment is less about being a "good influence" and more about being there. You provide trust and, hopefully, inspiration. Whether you and your mentee spend time together playing basketball or piano, filling out college applications, or going to museums, it can be a challenging and illuminating experience. To learn more about mentoring, contact any of the following organizations:

The National Mentoring Partnership
1400 I Street NW
Suite 850
Washington, DC 20005
(202) 729-4345
www.mentoring.org

Big Brothers/Big Sisters of America
230 North 13th Street
Philadelphia, PA 19107-1538
(215) 567-7000
www.bbbsa.org

Boys and Girls Clubs of America
1230 West Peachtree Street NW
Atlanta, GA 30309
(404) 815-5700
www.bgca.org

COMMUNITY GARDENS

"To create a little flower," wrote William Blake, "is the labor of ages." If you live in an urban area, the place to learn this sweet lesson is your local community garden—and it definitely needs your help. Of all public spaces, these are often the most threatened by development. To learn more about community gardens—and to find one near you—contact the American Community Gardening Association at (215) 988-8785. The Urban Community Gardens Web site (http://alexia.lis.uiuc.edu/~sewells/communitygardens.htm) is an excellent informational resource, as is the community gardens forum at www.gardenweb.com/forums/commgard.

BUILDING SHELTER

 Since 1976, Habitat for Humanity has brought volunteers of all ages together to help build homes for families in need. So far Habitat has built more than seventy-five thousand houses around the world, providing some 375,000 people with safe, simple, affordable shelter. Using volunteer labor and tax-deductible donations of money and materials, Habitat builds and renovates homes with the help of the homeowner (partner) families. Habitat houses are sold to partner families at no profit and financed with no-interest loans. The homeowners' monthly mortgage payments go into a revolving fund that is used to build more houses. This is as close as America gets to socialism and there should be more of it.

Nationally, almost 50 percent of Habitat volunteers are women—but they account for less than 15 percent of the volunteers who actually swing hammers and put up drywall. In 1998 Habitat launched a new department, Women Build, to teach women construction skills in a nonthreatening, supportive environment. Now more women are ready to strap on their tool belts and join the building crew. If there is no project in your community, the people at Habitat's headquarters can direct you to a site elsewhere, or help you initiate a local Habitat project. Tax-deductible donations are also welcome.

Habitat for Humanity International
Women Build
121 Habitat Street
Americus, GA 31709-3498
(912) 924-6935
www.habitat.org

ACTING GLOBALLY

Just as you can contribute to the life of your own community, you can also take on causes that engage with the world outside it. You can play a part in protecting the environment, fighting racism, supporting human and civil rights, and helping strangers in need. Here are some organizations that can help you make a global difference.

AMNESTY INTERNATIONAL

Founded in 1961, Amnesty International is a Nobel Peace Prize–winning organization with over one million members worldwide. Amnesty works "to free all prisoners of conscience" imprisoned for their beliefs or because of the their race, sex, ethnic origin, language, or religion—provided they have never used or advocated violence. AI campaigns to ensure fair and prompt trials for all political prisoners; to end torture, "disappearances," political killings, and executions; and to promote human rights. It attempts to change government policy and unjust laws by feeding information to the media, to our government, and to the United Nations, and urging them to take action. It sends representatives to observe political trials, to monitor the treatment of prisoners, and to speak personally with the victims and their families.

Amnesty accepts no funding from governments or political organizations and relies instead on the contributions of individuals, through memberships, donations, bequests, and the sale of merchandise.

What You Can Do

✿   Join Amnesty by paying an annual fee. As a member, you'll receive regular campaign updates, a quarterly newspaper, and information about how to participate in AI's letter-writing campaigns and other actions.

✿   Work for AI through one of its many volunteer and internship programs—open to people of all ages. These programs are all outlined on AI's Web site.

✿   Make a tax-deductible donation—of any amount you can afford. The funds will be put to use in AI's operation and campaigns.

Amnesty International USA
322 8th Avenue
New York, NY 10001
(800) AMNESTY
www.amnestyusa.org

DOCTORS WITHOUT BORDERS

In 1971 a group of French doctors founded Doctors Without Borders (Médecins Sans Frontières), the world's largest private, nonprofit emergency medical relief agency. The people who work for Doctors Without Borders are all highly trained professionals committed to giving impartial medical and humanitarian aid to the victims of conflict and disaster in places such as Chechnya, Mozambique, and Sri Lanka. Most Americans are exposed to the work of Doctors Without Borders through the media coverage of its workers in the field. In war- and disease-stricken regions all over the world, hundreds of American doctors, nurses, and support staff have courageously helped those in need, often working in extremely dangerous, volatile environments.

An important aspect of DWB's worldwide policy is that administration costs (including fund-raising) are kept to an absolute minimum. Currently, around 83 percent of all funds raised reach the field. These funds send workers to trouble spots and pay for the supplies they need, sanitation, high-protein food, and educational programs to deal with infectious diseases and land mines.

What You Can Do

❀ Make a tax-deductible donation. Twenty dollars is enough to provide antibiotics for ten seriously wounded people, and $100 will vaccinate one hundred people against meningitis, measles, or polio. If you opt to participate in DWB's monthly giving plan, you save the organization administration costs.

❀ If you are a medical professional with extensive experience, courage, and a commitment to helping others, you can apply to volunteer in the field; keep in mind that the minimum time commitment is six months, and a year is more typical. If you are not a medical professional and live in or near New York City or Los Angeles, you can volunteer to help out in DWB's national offices. To find out more, visit DWB's excellent Web site (it has great links, too!).

Doctors Without Borders USA
P.O. Box 2247
New York, NY 10116-2247
(888) 392-0392
www.dwb.org

GREENPEACE

Greenpeace, which began in 1971 with a protest against nuclear testing, is now an international environmental organization with two and a half million members whose purpose is the protection of the planet. Using the tactics of nonviolent civil disobedience—an approach taken by Mahatma Gandhi and Martin Luther King Jr.—Greenpeace activists "bear witness" to crimes against the environment and try to prevent these devastating activities from taking place—often by putting their lives on the line.

Because of its presence in 158 countries, Greenpeace is able to target environmental trouble spots globally and respond quickly to changing circumstances. Today its chief campaigns are to stop global warming, to protect the oceans, to save ancient forests, to control genetic engineering and to put an end to nuclear power.

What You Can Do

❀ Join Greenpeace. An annual membership of $30 includes a subscription to *Greenpeace Magazine*.

❀ Volunteer some time to work on Greenpeace campaigns.

Greenpeace USA
1436 U Street NW
Washington, DC 20009
(800) 326-0959
www.greenpeaceusa.org

THE SOUTHERN POVERTY LAW CENTER

Growing out of the civil rights struggles and victories of the 1950s and 1960s, the Southern Poverty Law Center was established by two southern lawyers, Morris Dees and Joseph Levin, who shared a commitment to racial and economic justice and equality. By handling pro bono cases that few others were willing to take on, Dees and Levin helped implement the Civil Rights Act of 1964 and the Voting Rights Act of 1965—often in the face of violent opposition. In 1971 the SPLC was formally incorporated, and civil rights activist Julian Bond signed on as president.

With the resurgence of the Ku Klux Klan in 1979, the center created a new division, Klanwatch, to monitor the activities of organized hate groups across the country. Within a few years SPLC attorneys developed strategies to hold white supremacist leaders accountable for violence committed by their followers. In 1991 the center expanded its educational efforts by launching Teaching Tolerance, a program to provide teachers with free, top-quality classroom materials on tolerance and diversity.

What You Can Do

❀ Become a tolerance activist. If your community is experiencing hate or bias problems, get the SPLC'S free publication *Ten Ways to Fight Hate*—available on its Web site—and share its strategies with concerned neighbors.

❀ Monitor hate in your community. Send clippings about hate crimes from your local newspaper to the SPLC's Intelligence Project, and be sure to include the newspaper's name and the date when the story ran. These clippings help the SPLC maintain a comprehensive record of hate-based violence in the United States.

❀ Make a tax-deductible contribution to the SPLC. The donations of individuals are what make the center's work possible.

The Southern Poverty Law Center
400 Washington Avenue
Montgomery, AL 36104
(334) 264-0268
www.splcenter.org

THE LONG HAUL

If you've made up your mind to quit your day job and get out there and change the world—even if it's only for a year or two—that can be arranged. In some cases a year of service can even help you pay back college loans, or earn money toward graduate school. Through AmeriCorps, you can get involved with any of approximately one thousand domestic programs like AmeriCorps*VISTA (usually entailing a one year, full-time assignment to a nonprofit, community organization) or Teach for America (a two-year, full-time assignment to a public school in need of teachers). AmeriCorps workers are given a modest living allowance, health insurance, loan deferment, and training.

Since the Peace Corps was established in 1961 by President John F. Kennedy, 155,000 Americans have taken up its mission "to help the people of interested countries in meeting their need for trained men and women." When you join the Peace Corps, you make a two-year commitment to working for free in any of seventy-eight participating countries, using your exper-

tise and specific skills to help others acquire their own. The majority of current Peace Corps volunteers are working in the fields of education, environment, and health.

AmeriCorps
Corporation for National Service
1201 New York Avenue NW
Washington, DC 20525
(202) 606-5000
www.americorps.org/joining

Peace Corps
1111 20th Street NW
Washington D.C. 20526
(800) 424-8580
www.peacecorps.gov/home

Teach for America
www.teachforamerica.org/main

BIBLIOGRAPHY

Adams, Jessica. *Astrology for Women* (HarperCollins Australia, 1998).

Angelou, Maya. *I Know Why the Caged Bird Sings* (Bantam, 1983).

Applewhite, Ashton. *Cutting Loose* (Harper-Collins, 1998).

Aucoin, Kevin. *The Art of Makeup* (Harper-Collins, 1995).

Bank, Melissa. *The Girls' Guide to Hunting and Fishing* (Penguin, 2000).

de Beauvoir, Simone. *The Second Sex* (Vintage, 1989).

Berry, Carmen Renee, and Tamara Traeder. *Girlfriends: Invisible Bonds, Enduring Ties* (Wildcat Canyon Press, 1995).

Buscaglia, Leo. *Born for Love* (Fawcett, 1994).

Calasso, Roberto. *Ka: Stories of the Mind and Gods of India* (Vintage, 1999).

Carrigan, Catherine. *Healing Depression* (Heartsfire, 1997).

Colette. *Flowers and Fruit* (Farrar, Straus & Giroux, 1986).

Conran, Shirley. *Superwoman* (Crown, 1978).

Dustman, Karen Dale. *The Woman's Fix-It Book* (Chandler House Press, 1998).

Domar, Alice D., and Henry Dreher. *Healing Mind, Healthy Woman* (Delta, 1997).

Dowrick, Stephanie. *Forgiveness and Other Acts of Love* (W.W. Norton & Company, 1997).

———. *Intimacy and Solitude* (W.W. Norton & Company, 1996).

Eason, Cassandra. *The Handbook of Ancient Wisdom* (Sterling, 1998).

Flannery, Tim. *The Future Eaters* (George Brazilier, 1995).

Goodman, Susannah. *Girls Just Want to Have Funds* (Hyperion, 2000).

Graves, Robert. *The Greek Myths* (Penguin, 1993).

Hall, Jerry. *Tall Tales* (Pocket Books, 1985).

Hayes, Alan. *The Essential It's So Natural* (Consortium, 1999).

Herrick, Lyn. *The Woman's Hands-On Home Repair Guide* (Storey Books, 1997).

His Holiness the Dalai Lama. *Awakening the Mind, Lightening the Heart* (Harper San Francisco, 1995).

Homer. *The Iliad*. Translated by Richmond Lattimore (University of Chicago, 1987).

How to Do Just About Anything (Reader's Digest, 1997).

Hughes, Ted. *Tales from Ovid* (Farrar, Straus & Giroux, 1999).

Hutton, Julia. *Good Sex: Real Stories from Real People* (Cleis Press, 1995).

Iyengar, B. K. S. *Light on Yoga* (Schocken, 1995).

Johnson, Robert A. *We: Understanding the Psychology of Romantic Love* (Harper San Francisco, 1985).

Juvenal. *The Sixteen Satires* (Penguin, 1999).

Jansson, Tove. *Moominpappa at Sea* (Sunburst, 1993).

———. *Moominland Midwinter* (Farrar, Straus & Giroux, 1992).

Kabat-Zinn, Jon. *Wherever You Go, There You Are* (Hyperion, 1995).

Kalman, Maira. *Max Makes a Million* (Viking, 1990).

Kaplan, "Motorman" Leon, *Keep This Book in Your Glove Compartment* (Berkley, 1997).

Kama Sutra. Translated by Sir Richard Burton and F. Arbuthnot (Berkley, 1995).

Kama Sutra (illustrated) (Lustre Press, 1996).

Logan, Karen. *Clean House, Clean Planet* (Pocket Books, 1997).

Lovelock, J. E. *The Ages of Gaia: A Biography of Our Living Earth* (W. W. Norton, 1995).

Manheim, Camryn. *Wake Up, I'm Fat!* (Broadway Books, 2000).

Marquis, Don. *Archy and Mehitabel* (Anchor, 1970).

Mindell, Earl. *Food as Medicine* (Fireside, 1998).

Mumford, John. *Ecstasy Through Tantra* (Llewellyn, 1988).

Neruda, Pablo. *100 Love Sonnets* (University of Texas Press, 1986).

Neihardt, John G. *Black Elk Speaks* (University of Nebraska Press, 1988).

Nhat Hanh, Thich. *Peace Is Every Step* (Bantam, 1992).

———. *Teachings on Love* (Parallax Press, 1998).

———. *Touching Peace* (Parallax Press, 1992).

Ondaatje, Michael. *In the Skin of a Lion* (Vintage Books, 1997).

Orman, Suze. *The 9 Steps to Financial Freedom* (Crown Publishers, 1997).

Ovid. *Metamorphoses.* Translated by Rolfe Humphries (Indiana University Press, 1955).

Polunin, Miriam. *Healing Foods* (DK, 1999).

Ragan, Kathleen. *Fearless Girls, Wise Women and Beloved Sisters: Heroines in Folktales from Around the World* (W. W. Norton, 1998).

Rilke, Rainer Maria. *The Book of Images* (North Point Press, 1994).

———. *Letters to a Young Poet* (W.W. Norton, 1994).

Rinpoche, Sogyal. *The Tibetan Book of Living and Dying* (Harper San Francisco, 1999).

Rose, Phyllis, ed. *The Norton Book of Women's Lives* (W.W. Norton, 1995).

Rothenberg, Jerome. *Technicians of the Sacred* (University of California, 1985).

Rumi. *The Essential Rumi* (Harper San Francisco, 1997).

RuPaul. *Lettin' It All Hang Out* (Hyperion, 1995).

Saint-Exupéry, Antoine de. *The Little Prince* (Harcourt Brace, 1968).

Shaughnessy, Susan. *Walking on Alligators: A Book of Meditations for Writers* (Harper San Francisco, 1993).

Shonagon, Sei. *The Pillow Book* (Columbia University Press, 1991).

Stanway, Dr. Penny. *Healing Foods for Common Ailments* (Firefly Books, 1995).

Tausend, Marilyn. *Cocina de la Familia* (Fireside, 1999).

Thompson, Kay. *Eloise* (Simon & Schuster, 1969).

Tourles, Stephanie. *The Herbal Body Book* (Storey Books, 1994).

Thoreau, Henry David. *Walden* (Dover, 1995).

Sendak, Maurice. *Where the Wild Things Are* (Harper-Collins, 1988).

Dr. Seuss. *My Many Colored Days* (Alfred A. Knopf, 1996).

———. *Horton Hatches the Egg* (Random House, 1966).

Storr, Anthony. *Solitude: A Return to the Self* (Ballantine Books, 1989).

Toklas, Alice B. *The Alice B. Toklas Cookbook* (The Lyons Press, 1998).

Toohey, Bill and Mary. *The Average Family's Guide to Financial Freedom* (John Wiley & Sons, 2000).

Vreeland, Diana. *DV* (Da Capo Press, 1997).

Waits, Tom. *Tom Waits Anthology* (Music Sales, 1990).

Wishik Englander, Debra. *Money 101* (Prima, 1997).

Whiteley, Opal. *The Singing Creek Where the Willows Grow: The Mystical Nature Diary of Opal Whiteley* (with a biography and an afterword by Benjamin Hoff) (Penguin, 1995).

Yoshimoto, Banana. *Kitchen* (Washington Square Press, 1994).

INDEX

Shopping, 109–10
  green concerns and, 228–29
Silk, caring for, 47
Skin care, 57–61
Skirts, 43, 44
  hemlines of, 37–38
  three black, 43–44
Sleep, 4, 10, 58
Smoking, 58, 106
Social Security, 101
Solitude, 204–12
"Sorry," when to say, 170
Soups, 19
Southern Poverty Law Center,
  237–38
Spending. *See* Expenditures
Spinning your wheels, 6
Spiritual life, 203–20
  art and, 215
  meditation and, 216–17
  solitude and, 204–12
Stereo systems, 71
Stopgap jobs, 130
Storage, 68, 69–70, 71, 73
Stories, writing, 29
Stretching, 9
Studs, in walls, 88
Style, 31–78
  chic and, 33–41
  decor and, 67–78
  wardrobe taming and, 43–48
Success, friendships and, 178
Sun exposure, 58–59, 61

Superhealing foods, 23–24
Swaps, 110

Taxes, 97, 101
Teens, looking good in, 50
Television, 70–71, 136
Thirties, looking good in, 51
Time management, 133–36
Tithing, 108–9
To-do lists, 10
Toilets, repairing, 85–86
Tools, 81, 82, 83
Training, for career, 126
Travel, with friend, 179
Trees, planting, 228
Tweezers, 55
Twenties, looking good in, 50–51

Unemployment, 129–30
Unreliability, friendship and, 177
Utility shutoffs, 82–84

Vacations, 137
Veggie Curry, 114
Vitamins, 22, 58
Volunteering, 187, 212, 219, 232–33

Wall hangings, 72
Wallpaper, 77–78
Wardrobe, 43–48. *See also* Clothing;
  Shoes
Washing machines, vibrating, 86
Water, conserving, 228

Water intake, 4, 58
Water shutoff, 82
Waxing, 65
Well-being, 1–30
  balance and, 3–10
  bare bones basics for, 4–5
  body image and, 11–16
  exercise and, 4, 8–9, 14, 58
  nutrition and, 4, 7, 17–24
  sex energy and, 25–30
Whining, 177
Whiteley, Opal, 159
Window treatments, 71
Wine, 119, 120
Winter, depression in, 150
Wood polish, 228
Work, 121–44
  communication and, 168, 169
  discipline at, 136–38
  in home, 141–42
  job hunting and, 126, 127–30,
    169
  keeping a job and, 131–38
  making a change and, 126
  motherhood and, 139–44
  rivalry with friend at, 178
  stopgap jobs and, 130
  time management at, 133–36
  vocational quiz and, 125
Workaholics, 133–34
Worry, 4, 5

Yoga, 219–20

Autobiographical Note

Anna Johnson was born in London one year after Jean Shrimpton bared her knees at Flemington Racetrack, and her professional life has been up and down more often than a Fifth Avenue hemline ever since. Starting her journalistic career with *Stiletto* magazine in Sydney at the age of nineteen, she went on to serve as fine arts editor at *Interior Design* magazine; an art critic for the *Sydney Morning Herald*, Radio National, and ABC-TV; and a freelance writer for publications including *Vogue Australia*, *Vogue UK*, *Condé Nast Traveler*, *Vanity Fair*, *ELLE*, *Australian Style*, *Marie Claire Lifestyle*, *The Good Weekend*, and the *Australian*. There were arty glamour gigs working for BBC Scotland, and being a TV presenter on SBS-TV and, most recently, on Foxtel's *By Design*. And then there were less glamorous jobs: coat-check girl at Raoul's and waitress for one shift only at a burger joint called Stingy Lulu's, both of Manhattan. Currently Anna divides her time between New York City and Sydney.